The CHARACTER of
AMERICAN HIGHER EDUCATION
and INTERCOLLEGIATE SPORTS

SUNY Series
FRONTIERS IN EDUCATION
Philip G. Altbach, Editor

The Frontiers in Education Series features and draws
upon a range of disciplines and approaches in the
analysis of educational issues and concerns, helping to
reinterpret established fields of scholarship in education
by encouraging the latest synthesis and research.

Other books in the series include:

The CHARACTER of AMERICAN HIGHER EDUCATION and INTERCOLLEGIATE SPORT

DONALD CHU

State University of New York Press

Published by
State University of New York Press, Albany

For information, address State University of New York Press,
State University Plaza, Albany, N.Y., 12246

Library of Congress Cataloging-in-Publication Data

Chu, Donald.
    The character of American higher education and intercollegiate
sport / Donald Chu.
        p.   cm. — (SUNY series in frontiers in education)
    Bibliography: p.
    Includes index.
    ISBN 0-88706-791-3.   ISBN 0-88706-793-X (pbk.)
    1. College sports — United States.   2. College sports — United
States — Organization and administration.   3. Education, Higher —
United States.   I. Title.   II. Series: SUNY series, frontiers in
education.
GV351.C484   1989
796'.07'1173 — dc19   87-34015
                                                                          CIP

10 9 8 7 6 5 4 3 2 1

A dedication:

To my parents, who made everything possible, and to my children, who make everything meaningful.

Contents

Figures

Tables

Acknowledgments

A book requires the writer to play both skeptic and egotist. Authors must be uncertain enough of their understanding that they remain open to alternative formulations, yet writers must be egotistical enough to believe that they have some insight that others need to know. Like most games, the intellectual play of writing is most fruitfully carried on in the company of those who support the game. But invariably a book takes so long to put together that its production entails a certain intrusion upon the good graces of friends, family, and colleagues. It is my good fortune to have had in my professional and personal life others who have helped me through both the writer's skepticism and self-centeredness. Some have forced me to rethink smug assumptions, by feeding me new, at times discomforting, but important ideas. Others have helped soothe anxieties and self-doubts. To all who have helped me I am thankful.

To my professors at Oberlin College who first showed me the questions, to my teachers at the University of Massachusetts and Stanford who taught me both how to find answers to those questions and also the legitimacy of questioning the questions themselves I will forever be indebted. To Skidmore College I owe a great deal. It is a liberal arts institution that recognizes the many forms that significant questions may take, and it is a school which allows its faculty and students to address those concerns. Very practically, Skidmore's Faculty Research Grants have eased the financial burdens of my writing.

Finally to my wife Christine I am grateful. Through her principles, good humor, and commitment she gives me the confidence to express my feelings and the courage to say what needs to be said.

Introduction

The American university has become unique in the world. One aspect of that uniqueness is the existence, to say nothing of the character and effects, of our Big Game. These are facts: they are among the 'givens' of our situation and can neither be wished away nor ignored with impunity. They demand to be understood more explicitly and broadly than we have managed hitherto. (Cady 1978:6)

Where did you get all those enormous players?
Your majesty, that's a very embarrassing question.

> — Queen Elizabeth and the Governor of
> Maryland at a 1957 football game
> (Will 1986)

To academics in the United States, the relationship between institutions of higher education and intercollegiate sport may be simultaneously a source of pleasure and of embarrassment. For them, it may be a curious question requiring study, of they may see matters athletic as of little significance, only meriting attention occasionally because of some extraordinary event such as a bowl appearance or a "Big Game." I believe it is fair to say, however, that most in the academic world are affected in some way by the tradition of sport that has developed at American colleges and universities since the late nineteenth century. In the public mind, college populations may be less scholars and professors than Buckeyes, Trojans, Sooners, or Hoyas. To students, the concerns of the game, the pep rally, or practice may take easy precedence over classes, laboratories, or papers.

Certainly, the U.S. judiciary has taken note of the curious relationship between higher education and sport. Although courts have a troublesome way of reversing themselves, federal Judge Miles W. Lord in January 1982 recognized a distinctive difference between education

1

at the University of Minnesota and its intercollegiate athletics. Although declared academically ineligible for further competition, a Gopher basketball player sought nevertheless to remain on the basketball team. It was Judge Lord's ruling that the "student-athlete" as a single status is a fiction. Although enrolled at the University of Minnesota, an avowedly educational institution, it was the court's judgement that the raison d'etre for that student athlete's campus presence was primarily to earn money for the University of Minnesota and to gain the player entry into the professional basketball leagues. Although the court recognized that the student would probably never attain a degree, that student

> was recruited to come to the University of Minnesota to be a basketball player and not a scholar. It may well be true that a good academic program for the athlete is made virtually impossible by the demands of their sport at the college level. If this situation causes harm to the university, it is because they have fostered it. . . . The court is not saying that athletes are incapable of scholarship; however, they are given little incentive to be scholars and few persons care how the student athlete performs academically. . . . (Wehrwein 1982:5)

We apparently have, then, a situation where the courts have declared that the most rational of all social institutions, the university, is acting hypocritically in maintaining the myth of the "student-athlete."

It has become apparent that the closeness and formality of the connection between higher education — an institution traditionally concerned with the mind — and the vigorous physical exertions of organized sport is a peculiar characteristic of American colleges and universities. While journalists have exposed the seemingly endless varieties of intercollegiate sport abuses, and while academics have studied various aspects of campus sport's purposes and problems, few studies have focused their attentions on perhaps the most interesting point concerning intercollegiate athletics — the very fact that they exist. To those concerned with college sport, the requisite questions are historical, sociological, psychological, economic, and philosophical. How did intercollegiate athletics come to be? What are the benefits claimed for such sport on participants — individual and institutional? If athletics does not have these benefits or has other, negative effects, how can college sport continue to thrive in the face of such criticism? Should there be intercollegiate sport? What should be done? It is with such questions that this book is concerned.

From the student-controlled games of the nineteenth century, campus sport has become a formal part of the governance and economic structure of U.S. institutions of higher education. Budgets for elite sport usually exceed $3 million dollars at schools with big-time sports, and can cost at least $200,000 at small colleges with modest athletic programs. Teams and coaches acting as symbolic representatives of their school continue to draw public visibility and prestige with their victories, but also criticism, scandal, and cynicism.

In my view, almost all of higher education is affected by inter-collegiate sport. Particularly at the "big-time" level, which provides the focus for this analysis, the fanfare and furor which has been historically associated with athletics both benefits and detracts from the purposes of higher education. After a historical account of the rise of intercollegiate athletics, this book will look at the rationale for sport's existence at our colleges and universities, the effects of sport on individual participants, and the economic benefits and costs of a campus sport.

By taking a sociological look at higher education, we will see that the American variation on the early European models is a form both burdened and blessed by insecurities in resource flow and a lack of clear, firm definition of the purposes of post-secondary education and institutions. This immature "charter" has led to a flexibility in programming that has been exploited by college and university leaders in response to their precarious institutional position. By studying the forces which facilitated the growth of intercollegiate sport, we shall see the institutional autonomy and openness of institutional definitions which have earmarked U.S. versions of the college and university. The American school has been given and has gladly accepted responsibilities beyond the more purely cognitive goals of the European schools. Because of program flexibility and the openness of institutional purposes in the United States, college and university leadership has employed intercollegiate sport as a response to school resource uncertainties and for the spiritual and character development responsibilities that mark the North American form of higher education.

In a way, the story of intercollegiate athletics is the story of American higher education itself — an institution historically charged with the mission of uncovering and perpetuating truth and knowledge, but an institution planted in a soil not particularly receptive to its traditional European mission. How was the college and then the university idea adapted to a country where financial support of education was anything but guaranteed, where the dominant beliefs concerning mobility posited that anyone could get ahead as long as he or she was blessed with talent and worked hard enough — even without a university education?

The story of campus sport also reflects upon the characteristics of the U.S. society which have shaped its institutions. Government and religion, as well as education, have been redefined from the original European models to suit the particular native climate. The very same American drive which has led to productivity and achievement has recast our social institutions. Colleges and universities must show results, they must demonstrate their value relative to competitors in the education marketplace, their teams must win, just as their professors must publish and their departments must rank high. American pluralism has been mirrored by the diversity of power groups affecting higher education. With so many groups to please, it appears understandable that organizational tools such as myth and sport have been employed to balance the often-conflicting demands of different groups upon the organization. Sport which appeals to multiple constituencies and myths about the efficient workings of an organization both serve to engender the support needed for organizational survival.

While much has been said about college sport since its controversial birth and official adoption by American higher education, until recently much of this criticism and support has been nonacademic or not based upon verifiable research. Although they are insightful, works like *The Big Game* (1978), by Cady, and *Sports in America* (1976), by Michener, have not chosen to take advantage of the research literature. While certain questions are beyond scientific answers (example: Should sport be a part of the college or university?), others would greatly benefit from empirical and theoretical analysis: Do sports build character? Do sports make money for their educational institution? Are athletes socially mobile? By employing the developing literature in the field of sport studies (the psychology, sociology, history, and philosophy of sport) many of the questions concerning sport's effects on athletes and schools can be fruitfully examined.

In the preparation of this manuscript, I have seldom lost my sense of wonder at the utter peculiarity of this official connection between the university and athletics. I make the assumption that an inspection of this relationship will tell us something about both of these institutions. In this way, I share Cady's view when he writes of college sports that,

"They express organically the character and ethos of those communities" (Cady 1978:5–6). Sports tell us something important about Collegetown, USA, and they do so in an authentic way, developing a picture of higher education devoid of the befogging rhetoric of which academics are all too capable. To capture the character of the American college and university, we must go beyond rigid and traditional intellectual visions of the institution, and look at the spirit of the American dream as manifested in campus athletics.

I hope that this book will help faculty, administrators, and others concerned with sport to better understand the many problems confronting both American higher education and its intercollegiate athletics. In writing this book, I have certainly come to appreciate better the systemic nature of many of these matters. Questions concerning the enforcement of athletic rules, the continuation of sport despite its great cost, and the reasons for continued unethical behavior in connection with intercollegiate athletics are not questions whose answers can be confined merely to the athletic arena itself. The rise of American colleges, their continuing resource insecurities, the sensitivity of their leadership to curricular and program changes that might attract money and students from so many groups on which they are dependent, and the malleability of the mission claimed for colleges and universities have demonstrated to this writer that the reason for sport's original inclusion in higher education, for its perpetuation in the face of rampant costs and improprieties, lies ultimately in what those in American society want from the social institution of higher education.

CHAPTER 1

Intercollegiate Sport: An Overview

From its humble student-controlled beginnings, college sports in the United States has grown into a central place in higher education. Of 3,282 two- and four-year colleges in the United States in the fall of 1983, approximately eight hundred belonged to the National Collegiate Athletic Association (NCAA),[1] 520 were members of the National Association for Intercollegiate Athletics, and 580 were members of the National Junior College Athletic Association (excluding California, which has its own regulating board for junior college sport) (Atwell 1979:370). In addition to NCAA membership, 63 of the biggest football playing institutions are members of the College Football Association, and, typically, most schools (with the notable exceptions of Pennsylvania State University and Notre Dame University) belong to regional athletic associations such as the Ivy League, the Big Ten, and the Southeastern Athletic Conference. In all, well over two thousand American institutions of higher education field intercollegiate teams, with budgets ranging from $10,000 to over $15 million per year.

And what of the possible return on this investment in big-time sport? The size of the market is indicated by the $71 million four-year contract signed by the sixty-three big-time members of the College Football Association with CBS and ESPN television, the $50 million four-year contract signed by institutions in the Pacific Ten and Big Ten football conferences with ABC television (*Chronicle of Higher Education*, October 1, 1986:40) and by the $55.3 million per year contract signed by the NCAA with CBS for television rights to the next three basketball championship tournaments — a sum 73% greater than previous fees of $32 million per year for the period 1985-1987 (*NCAA News*, January 14, 1987:2), which was itself twice that paid for rights

7

in the previous three years. In 1986, despite fears of an oversaturated football market with the ending of NCAA monopoly control over television rights, overall attendance was up by 75,000, to 36,387,905, over spectator figures from 1985 (*Chronicle of Higher Education*, February 11, 1987:35). At the Division IA level alone, attendance at games was up approximately 10%.

While only 187 institutions belong to Division I football, the tremendous media visibility given to these schools, and the fact that nearly 80% of all athletic attendance is generated by them, guarantees that institutions such as the University of Southern California, Ohio State University, and the University of Michigan will play the dominant role in the development of the public's image of what athletics mean to American higher education (Atwell 1979:369). Schools such as the University of Akron have sought to become first-rank institutions through NCAA Division IA membership. As President William Muse asserts, the hiring of former Notre Dame coach Gerry Faust has increased public exposure. Such exposure is thought to improve student as well as faculty recruitment, enhance alumni donations, and increase student pride (Lederman, October 15, 1986). Similarly, the State University of New York at Buffalo has sought to enhance its reputation with a gradual upgrading of its competitive stature to the Division I level (*Chronicle of Higher Education*, February 11, 1987). Apparently, for the University of Akron and the State University of New York at Buffalo, enhanced institutional standing requires athletic competition at the highest levels. The leadership of these schools seems to expect academic reputation alone to be insufficient for raising their rank among other colleges and universities. Although less than 5% of all students play intercollegiate sport, television, magazine, and newspaper coverage gives "big-time" schools a disproportionate share of the public's conception of the programs, values, and goals of higher education in general.

And what has the public seen? A study conducted by George Hanford for the American Council on Education (1974) cited the following illegal practices usually performed by overzealous coaches, alumni or boosters of athletics:

Altering high school transcripts

threatening to bomb the home of a high school principal who refused to alter transcripts changing admission test scores

offering jobs to parents or other relatives of a prospect

firing from a state job the father of a prospect who enrolled elsewhere than the state's university

promising one package of financial aid and delivering another

tipping or otherwise paying athletes who perform particularly well on a given occasion.

More recently, exposes in popular magazines (Underwood 1980; *Sports Illustrated* 1982:10, 12) and local and national newspapers have continued the saga. Recruiting rules have been violated, admissions and eligibility standards have been ignored, players have been slapped by coaches, and presidents have resigned or been fired amid the scandals for which they have been held responsible or which they have not been permitted to clean up. We see this happening at all types of schools — public universities, private institutions, technical colleges, and religiously affiliated universities. Regardless of the hand wringing of faculty and administrators over athletic improprieties, however, the popularity and stability of football and basketball programs remain high; so popular are they, in fact, that Jackie Sherrill, formerly the football coach at Texas A & M University earned approximately $267,000 per year for his athletic duties (Looney 1982:26–29), which was a great deal more than the $90,000 salary of the president of the university but still a great deal less than the reported $450,000 earned by Paul "Bear" Bryant when he was head coach at the University of Alabama (*Chronicle of Higher Education*, June 2, 1982:13).

The question, then, is how, in spite of the historically verified problems and abuses in big-time athletics, has intercollegiate sport gained and retained its significance? Perhaps intercollegiate sport maintains its importance because it fulfills important functions for the constituencies it affects.

Some of the explanation for the robust condition of college sport may lie in the perceived need to draw from it resources necessary for institutional survival. Tangible resources such as money and students are institutional necessities in education. Some say that sports participation build athletes' character. Others contend that sports help athletes gain jobs and money after college. More significant, however, may be the intangibles. Perhaps sports serve the masses in a manner consistent with the role that has historically emerged for American education in general: perhaps people holding divergent beliefs may be unified; or perhaps through sports we may find Becker's (1971) self-esteem, or, as Fromm (1965:131–132) relates, a sense of "breaking through the surface of routine and getting in touch with the ultimate realities of life." The college athlete becomes a vessel for our hopes. He or she symbolizes in bold relief our struggles, and models the qualities of greatness that are part of the American dream — a dream which requires periodic reaffirmation in a cynical world.

The American college, although a direct descendent of European models, has been given a number of additional objectives — objectives that have adapted ancient definitions of an intellectual higher education to the American economic and value environment. They are responsibilities that today help the college maintain its validity as well as fulfill its overall mission. In the next section, the development of the institution of higher education in the United States will be evaluated. As we shall see, in addition to the traditional cognitive objectives of higher education, the American variant has been charged with a variety of other roles.

CHAPTER 2

The Development of American Higher Education and Intercollegiate Sport

From the martial and spiritual conflict of the American Revolution, there emerged a United States concerned with both the maintenance of its cultural roots and the cultivation of its unique national character. While they had inherited government, educational, religious, and other social institutions that shaped their lives, Americans were not content to leave these institutions as they had been. These institutions were not perfect. They required change and were considered changeable for the better. The purposes and structure of economic, political, religious, and educational institutions for the infant nation were open to new definition — definitions that, although based upon European models, required modification to suit the American condition.

The very newness of the nation meant that there were no feudal traditions, no encrustations of conservative institutions, no corrupt and gothic history to live down (Tyack 1966). There were few well-established definitions of how things should be done, or assumptions concerning the proper goals and the structure of such social institutions as the government or the new schools. With the safety of the Atlantic moat, with the vast tracts of land yet to be exploited, with primitive systems of communication and transportation, the America of the 1800s was more provincial than tightly knit. Federalism was the rule, not centralized authority. Diversity of opinion was encouraged by these conditions — diversity in educational, as well as political and religious beliefs.

Early American educational leaders such as Rush and Webster openly pondered the appropriate directions for educational institutions.

While they recognized the need for the free-thinking American, they also recognized the necessity for some uniformity of thought (Cremin 1980:103–128, 251; Tyack 1966). Individual freedom of thought should be encouraged, but there was the recurring dilemma of how to cultivate that freedom while transmitting the common belief systems that would bind all Americans together. In a society pluralistic in beliefs and in norms of behavior, questions concerning the means toward necessary homogeneity were and continue to be vexing problems.

With few established assumptions and commonly held understandings of the purposes and means through which Americans should be educated, it is not surprising to find that there was controversy concerning the best forms of higher education for America. As the German observer Friedrich Schonemann (1930:115) noted, there was little in the way of a single American theory of education.

According to Shils (1981:37) "no generation creates most of what it uses, believes and practices." The eighteenth- and early nineteenth-century American vision of higher education was a result of various conceptions of goals and processes. There was not so much a single collective memory of higher education as there were a number of remembered and reconstructed images of what higher education should be. Different conceptions of purposes and goals, each conception the result of its own cultural milieu, were to have an impact on American colleges and universities, reflecting and encouraging openness and flexibility in the definition of America's social institutions. Composed of bits and pieces of first English and then German conceptions of higher education, there was just enough of each to lead to "a certain confusion." While the English emphasis on cultural transmission and generalizable mental discipline through classical study provided some of the fabric of nineteenth-century American college study, there was woven into the cloth threads of German devotion to scholarship and the discovery of knowledge. The result, according to Schonemann and other observers (Knoles 1930:64), was a cloth with no discernible pattern.[1]

Cambridge and Oxford provided the first models for higher education in America. The goal of the first college leaders was clear. According to Williams

the early Puritans in New England conceived of themselves as helping to bring about a "translatio studii," i.e., a transfer of the higher learning from its ancient seats in the Old World to the wilderness of America. The founders of Harvard took for granted the essential continuity of Western learning. . . . The precious "veritas" for which the world was indebted to the Hebrews and the Hellenes had been handed down from generation to generation, and now the settlers of the "Holy Commonwealth" must take up this torch of learning and carry it along. (1954:298–299)

Practical education was considered inappropriate. Electives were unheard of. Study of classical works in Latin, Greek, mathematics, philosophy, rhetoric, and logic was the core of the young man's college study (Warfield 1901). Through rigorous attention to these enduring works, it was presumed that students would not only acquire the discipline to be able to competently study any problem, but, in addition, would learn to appreciate the value of these works and in turn pass them on to future generations. Study of impractical and abstract works was considered the core of the Yale education of 1828 (Brubacher and Rudy 1958:16). This was a view of higher education confirmed by Brown President Francis Wayland (1842:81), and then by Princeton President James McCosh in 1868 (Veysey 1965:23).

Diversity of opinion, however, concerning the appropriate curriculum for American higher education increased with the growing influence of the German model of higher education in the mid-nineteenth century. The German "scientific school" did not presume the eternal importance of one set of books or one body of knowledge. According to this view, the proper responsibility of higher education should be the discovery of knowledge. Through the scientific method, myths could be exposed, assumptions questioned, and truth verified. Truth was not inherently tied to one culture, to one social group, to one set of coursework or subject matter. Instead, truth could be — *should be* — uncovered through rational and, if possible, empirical techniques at the university. Pure research and the development of scholars able to discover knowledge were the goals of the German curriculum. Only mature and highly skilled students should work with outstanding scholar-professors. Through their long years of tutelage, students would acquire the philosophy and techniques of scholarship (Burn et al. 1971).

A view of scholarship through the scientific method as the primary mission of higher education became increasingly important with the support of American college presidents like Henry Tappan of the

University of Michigan and James Morgan Hart of the University of Cincinnatti (Veysey 1965:10; Hofstadter and Smith 1961:408). Without entrenched assumptions and publicly held understandings of what our colleges and universities should teach and how they should teach, American institutions demonstrated great flexibility in their avowed purposes and methods. There was an openness of "mission" as exciting, unhallowed, and disconcerting as its means. With no broadly accepted road map for the route American colleges should take, there was both freedom and fear in newly defined objectives and alternate paths toward undefined overall goals.

Also contending for curricular dominance in American education was a model for colleges and universities that stressed utility and application. Forester (1937) has suggested that the European enlightenment and the American and French Revolutions contributed to a utilitarian view of the appropriate functions of social institutions. The government, the church, and the educational institution should all concern themselves with the direct improvement of the human condition. The quality of life should be improved through the application of knowledge and resources.

The mission of higher education, as voiced by Benjamin Franklin in 1749, Samuel Johnson, President of King's College in 1754, and William Smith, President of the College of Philadelphia in 1756, must be more utilitarian than the impractical European schools. With the growing importance of the urban merchant classes there rose the call for practical education to fulfill the needs of the newly important business classes (Brubacher and Rudy 1958:19; Cremin 1980:270–272; Nevins 1962:35; Wayland 1850). American higher education, according to the Amherst College faculty of the 1820s, had not kept pace with the new social and economic realities transforming America. Unless curricular reforms were incorporated, it was their fear that the American college "would soon be deserted by potential benefactors in the community as well as by the students themselves" (Cremin 1980:271).

The Civil War provided a boost for practical education by spurring the industrialization that facilitated growth of the business classes and by the passage of the Morrill Act in 1862. With 150,000 acres of land granted to each institution specifically chartered for agricultural and mechanical purposes, the "state college" was born.

These land grant schools stood for two purposes. As a "service station," any educational need of any enrolled student ideally should be answered. The classics were offered side-by-side with agricultural engineering, law, and medicine. German scientific inquiry could be promoted along with mechanical engineering and accounting.

Secondly, the land grant school was designed to directly contribute to the community. Soil could be tested for farmers. Consultants were provided for public school districts. Engineers could design bridges, meteorologists predict the weather, and the drama club provide entertainment for the state's citizens. The state university idea affected all of American higher education. In the view of Harry Gideonse, President of Brooklyn College, higher education must never return to the "Ivory Tower of absolutist metaphysics" (Gideonse 1937).

In the course of this brief history of the curriculum of American higher education from the post-Revolutionary period until the early 1900s, we have seen a great deal of diversity. Research by Burke (1982) demonstrates the flexibility and willingness of colleges in the period 1800–1860 to modify their curricula and programs to meet the demands of their sponsors and the needs of their students. While there may have been one model of higher education more popular than others at any one time, there was certainly not one conception of what higher education should be in this country. Whatever the model employed, whether it emphasized the classics or science, whatever it was that the faculty developed, whether the intellect or spirit, there was not one vision of American higher learning toward which all institutions progressed.

According to Burke, pre-Civil War colleges were far from all being the heavily classics oriented, educationally, politically, and ideologically conservative schools pictured in the traditionalist view of institutions in that era. Instead, Burke has found substantial evidence that these early colleges (at least 20 in 1800 and 217 in the 1850s) were indeed differentiated on the basis of the preparation and social background of their students and in the curriculum offered to meet their various objectives. Oberlin College in Ohio, for example, responded to the wishes of its sponsors by offering a range of instruction in its primary, normal schools, regular, and theological colleges (Burke 1982:38). For most of these schools, the lack of uniform regulation and state or national government aid made possible and necessary rapid change in educational policy and philosophy to suit the requirements of supporting constituencies. The American college has been more market oriented, diversified within and between the institutions, and subject to less state control (Jarausch 1983). The continued responsiveness of the nation's colleges to their social environment has been noted by Burke (1982:262), who sees the "advances" of many leading institutions as but attention to changing market conditions.

Cremin has similarly noted that the two middle quarters of the nineteenth century were periods of relentless diversification in curriculum (1980:405-406). There was little if any widely accepted understanding of what rightly belonged and what did not belong in American institutions of higher education. Originally modeled after the abstract classical English mode American higher education was greatly affected by German scientism and then what some would call the American predilection for the practical and applied (Veblen 1918). Lacking constant threats from any nearby warring neighbors, with great bodies of insulating water and land, there was little pressure to centralize authority. Relative to its European ancestors, the American school leader had no central ministry of education in government or church to dictate a unified set of beliefs, theories of education, or curriculum. Willingness and ability to respond to the demands of the environment, signaled by constant changes in curriculum and programs, has marked American colleges at least since the 1800s. By the twentieth century, American higher education was larger and more diversified than any European educational system.

The diversity of American higher education was recognized early by Robert Hutchins, President of the University of Chicago, when he observed that

> the most striking fact about the higher learning in America is the confusion that besets it. The college of liberal arts is partly high school, partly university, partly general, partly special. Frequently it looks like nothing at all. The degree it offers seems to certify that the student has passed an uneventful period without violating any local, state or federal law, and that he has a fair, if temporary recollection of what his teachers have said to him. (Hofstadter and Smith 1961:924-925)

The very "openness" of the *process of definition* concerning the appropriate programs and structures for governance of those programs in American higher education provided an opportunity for colleges and universities to incorporate programs radically different from those up to then accepted in European institutions. We have already seen how community service came to be embraced and justified as a legitimate function of American higher education. Without a priori assumptions held by a central body of leaders in education as to what programs did not belong, a new business-minded leadership in American colleges and universities could, in the late nineteenth and early twentieth centuries look for programs capable of fulfilling the emerging responsibilities being given to higher education in America; programs which might in important ways enhance the often shaky finances and prestige of their institutions.

In the next section, the unique control and financial structures of American higher education will be examined. While European curricular models were brought to these shores more or less intact, centralized governance and support were not transferred as completely. With neither consistent funding nor oversight from any single outside source, the viability of individual colleges could and had to be enhanced through the idiosyncratic programs and objectives of these relatively autonomous institutions.

Control and Finance in American Higher Education

> Everybody is running hard and not quite staying even. . . . That's the gut problem in the economics of higher education. President Donald Kennedy of Stanford University on embarking on a $1.1 billion fund-raising campaign (Desruisseaux 1987:23).

In cross-cultural comparison, it is apparent that American colleges and universities are generally governed and financed quite differently from their European models. Fulton (1984:196) has characterized as a "free market" system the means by which resources are directed to higher education in the United States. In this model, government plays little part in the financing and regulating of education. Correspondingly, however, resources must usually come from tuition, bequests, and other nongovernmental sources. By way of comparison, in the centralized bureaucratic Swedish educational system, the government clearly spells out national goals and translates them into educational programs. In the contrasting British "guild model," institutions are appropriated substantial government resources which supplement endowments and fees. In addition, the English institutional goal-setting process is relatively autonomous.

While the American college has inherited the tradition of institutional autonomy, it has not similarly benefited from consistent financial support. Because of historical instabilities in the supply of students and money powerful American colleges and university presidents, themselves only theoretically answerable to business-minded boards of trustees and relatively weak faculties, have searched for ways to maintain their institutional viability.

The Search for Money and Students

While the universities at Oxford and Cambridge were the earliest models for British colonial higher education, the financial conditions and internal governance of the English institutions were not literally transferred to their American counterparts.

Organized initially as guilds for the protection and nurturing of scholars in the twelfth and thirteenth centuries, Oxford and Cambridge enjoyed financial support first from the aristocracy and then from the church, business interests, English royalty, and, eventually, Parliament. By the sixteenth century Cambridge had sufficient property and money to maintain its economic stability (Curtis 1959:39).[2] Support from the central government in 1948-1949, for example, accounted for 50% of Cambridge's and 56% of Oxford's income. In comparison, the U.S. federal government contributed only 17% of the income of American higher education in 1949-1950 (Harris 1978:590-591). In 1980, federal appropriations contributed but 2.8% of public, 1.1% of private, and 0.5% of church-related college and university funds (*Academe* 1981:388). For the fiscal year 1984-1985, American public colleges and universities received only 2.3% of their revenues from federal appropriations, while private schools obtained only 0.7% of their incomes from this source.[3] Even state institutions received only 43.6% of their revenues from state legislative appropriations, while private colleges and universities gained only 0.9% of their monies from state allocations. Tuition and fees accounted for 23% of the revenues for all public and private institutions in 1987 (*Chronicle of Higher Education*, April 1, 1987).[4]

Recently, publicly supported institutions have felt the financial pinch of budget reductions because of falling revenues. In twenty states dependent upon agriculture, oil, or energy-related industries, tax revenues have dropped from $7.1 billion to $6.4 in the twelve months ending in June 1987. Declining revenues forced midyear budget cuts of 17.5% in Arkansas, 10.5% in Texas, and 8.8% in Louisiana for their institutions of higher education in 1987 (Mooney 1987). Due to declining federal support for scholarships, fellowships, and facilities, even as well-endowed and secure an institution as Stanford University has felt the need to raise $1.1 billion in its new campaign merely to maintain the quality of its programs (Desruisseaux 1987).

Economic security due to endowment and yearly appropriations have permitted Oxford and Cambridge to pursue their own scholarly interests, paying relatively little heed to the wishes of public interest groups.[5] Without the worry over resource for operation, these English universities have been relatively free to pursue their own definition of "higher education" and to transmit that orientation to the elite minority chosen as students. As early as the sixteenth century, Oxbridge universities were sufficiently endowed with properties to lease that these academies possessed the freedom to study and teach as the faculty saw fit.[6]

In the British colonies, however, control and funding of higher education were largely the responsibility of nonfaculty boards. While nominal public subsidies were accepted, policy formation and program selection were zealously retained by this group, distinct from both faculty and government (Brubacher and Rudy 1958:142-143).[7]

Without consistent sources of appropriations, however, American institutions of higher education were constantly forced to attend to the problem of making ends meet. American higher education has a history of ingenious fund-raising methods. Lotteries, ferry tolls, and the bartering of agricultural produce all provided urgently needed resources. Some schools more directly appealed to wealthy donors by offering immortalization through the school's name. In 1825, Colonel Henry Rutgers donated $5,000 to the school that rewarded this generosity by taking his name. James Bowdoin, William Denison, and William Carleton gave their fortunes to the institutions that bear their family names (Rudolph 1968). Other wealthy benefactors supported their namesake institutions: Ezra Cornell ($500,00), Cornelius Vanderbilt ($1 million), Johns Hopkins ($3.5 million), Leland Stanford ($20 million). John D. Rockefeller donated $30 million to the University of Chicago.[8] Other American institutions gained large tracts of land through the Morrill Act of 1862. Largely owing to the beneficence of individuals and the federal government there was approximately a 300% increase in the properties and endowments held by American higher education between 1892 and 1914.

Despite growing enrollments and resources available to higher education at the turn of the twentieth century, however, uneven distribution of monies and fluctuations in enrollments made resource acquisition an ever-pressing concern for the bulk of college and university leadership (Chu 1979). By 1914, 60% of all post-secondary schools controlled only 6% of their combined annual working incomes, only 10% of school property and endowments, and only 12% of all students (Claxton 1915:188–189). Insufficient funding in the years before and after World War I, and during the Depression worsened the already tenuous situation of many institutions (Ross 1976). The uncertainties of World War I and the economic decline of the Great Depression reinforced their commitment to boldly experiment with means to attract needed resources (Henry 1975:8). The weak financial position of American higher education was chronicled by Savage in 1933. In his report, *Economy in Higher Education*, prepared under the auspices of the Carnegie Foundation for the Advancement of Teaching, the financial stability of American higher education was severely questioned: funding for faculty salaries was a point of particular concern. In 1940, the pattern of resource concentration in a minority of American colleges and universities continued, with only 20 institutions receiving 75% of all foundation grants. The remaining 25% was distributed among 310 schools. Seven hundred institutions received no foundation subsidies at all (Brubacher and Rudy 1958:61). More recently, the growth of corporate and individual philanthropy indicates enhanced support of education from the private sector. Yet the continued uneven distribution of these resources signals financial anxiety for major areas of higher education. A sampling of 71 colleges and universities indicates 46% overall growth in corporate support, a 17.5% rise in foundation grants, and an 0.8% upturn in private gifts in 1984–1985 from the previous year. But while larger institutions received an increase of 16%, women's colleges experienced a decrease of 13% (Desruisseaux 1986:35).

Early colleges were not well supported by the American gentry, who were more apt to send their children to England for schooling than to risk an American education (Handlin and Handlin 1970:271). Unstable enrollments and financial difficulties were the rule for American colleges 1968:6).

Historically, enrollments have mirrored inconsistency of financial support. The mission of American higher education was not well established nor accepted in the nineteenth century. America was a land of opportunity that seemingly did not require a college degree for a grip on the ladder of mobility. There was no assumption on the part of Americans that it was their responsibility to support scholarship and higher learning. As Benjamin Rush explained, in this land of resources and opportunities for enterprise, "to spend two or more years learning two dead languages is to turn our backs on a gold mine" (Boorstin 1977:53).

The family contemplating college for their child had to consider not only the cost of tuition, room, and board but also "income foregone" (money not earned while studying) and the relative cost-benefit of the alternative of apprenticeship to a trade. For families with limited incomes in this nation of possibilities, and in an occupational environment where formal schooling had not yet become essential, college attendance was even less attractive.

While it is true that by the 1860s total enrollment in American colleges and universities had begun to rise dramatically, careful inspection of the pace of this growth demonstrates reason for administrative insecurity. Although absolute enrollment seemed to double every fifteen years beginning in 1870 (Ross 1976:43–42), fluctuations in yearly patterns of growth indicated to college leadership the need for continued alertness and openness to new programs that could enhance institutional support.

Despite a general broadening of the curriculum, a relative reduction in average college costs,[9] and more lenient admissions standards, after the Civil War American colleges and universities only minimally increased the proportion of young men enrolled. Whereas in 1870 1.28% of white males age 20 to 24 were enrolled in undergraduate colleges and universities in the United States, by 1890 this figure had increased to only 1.49% (Burke 1982:218). The rate of increase in college attendance in the late nineteenth century was not keeping pace with the rise in number and proportion of students attending high school. College leadership was quite understandably responsive to fluctuations in student enrollment.

Without the sophisticated statistical projection techniques available today, college leadership was continually concerned with ways to increase the survival prospects of higher education in America. According to Veysey, the economic deprivation of the late nineteenth and early twentieth centuries dictated economically oriented behavior by American college leadership.

> Trustees of existing institutions . . . sometimes preferred to risk experimentation rather than continue in the unpromising ways of the past. . . .
> Once one respectable institution moved in a new direction, others found

themselves under a powerful compulsion to follow suit. The changes,
if they meant anything, were bound to attract students. Colleges which
lagged behind for any reason had to face the threat of eventual starva-
tion. (Veysey 1965:10–11)

Without guarantees of steady monies, faced with public indif-
ference to the value of higher education and uncertain of short-term
enrollment trends, college leadership constantly searched for means to
attract the funds, prestige, and enrollments that meant survival for their
schools. Therefore, nineteenth-century American college presidents
were forced to be constantly in search of any program or policy that
might attract students, money, and other resources to their institutions
(Pritchett 1905). According to Charles Eliot, President of Harvard, it
was the responsibility of the college president to make himself constantly aware of the "business" of higher education. In his inaugural
address, he declared that

> the Corporation should always be filled with the spirit of enterprise. An
> institution like this College is getting decrepit when it sits contentedly
> on its mortgage. On its invested funds the Corporation should be always
> seeking how safely to make a quarter of a per cent more. A quarter of
> one per cent means a new professorship. (Eliot 1869)

Without the security of adequate endowment and steady supplies
of appropriations and students, the American college president then
was forced to be ever aware of public forces, needs, and desires that
could bring improvement in support and a greater consensus on purpose and future directions (Henry 1975:3). It was a time when financial solvency for the vast bulk of colleges was so precarious that these
schools had to be always sensitive to the smallest external pressure
(Jencks and Riesman 1968:6).

The Governance of Higher Education in the United States

Whereas the original leadership structure of American higher
education had been dominated by the clergy and professional
educators, the new leadership that evolved during the 1800s became
increasingly business-minded. The new business-oriented presidents
often administered the college or university more as a corporation than
did the religiously oriented leaders of the previous era (Pritchett 1905;
Veysey 1965:10–11). With the Constitution's lack of provisions for the
centralized control of education in this country and with the Dartmouth
College case of 1819 undermining the extent of state control over

American colleges and universities, the basis for institutional autonomy was established. Relative to their English and German administrative counterparts, American presidents came to assume greater power over the direction of their institutions.

The British universities have been traditionally dominated by their faculty. The most powerful ruling bodies, the Hebdomadal Council of Oxford and the Council of the Senate at Cambridge, for example, have been largely directed by the wishes of the faculty. German administrative heads, the rector and pro-rector, have been traditionally elected to one- or two-year terms by the professors of each institution (Burns et al. 1971). In comparison, however, the American college or university presidency by the mid-nineteenth century remained a relatively strong centralized office.

At most early institutions, the transient tutors that originally staffed American colleges did not develop a tradition of faculty control. Judicial precedent for relatively great presidential power was established by the failure of Nicholas Sever and William Welsted in 1721–1723 to establish faculty control of Harvard (Hofstadter and Smith 1961:3–4). Later, the isolation of faculty into disciplinary cells, another peculiarly American innovation, further diminished faculty power relative to central administration (Bok 1982:118). While husbanding their authority to hire their colleagues and to determine curriculum, American faculty demonstrated relatively little power to define institutional direction. Instead, faculty too often concerned with the particular interests of their departments exerted relatively less influence over the direction of the school as a whole. Faculty from other departments were more often looked upon as rivals for funds and students than as colleagues with whom the educational interests of the institution and the faculty could be defended. While departmentalization might have engendered expert specialization, it also split the faculty into competing camps, thus rendering the faculty an unorganized counterweight to the power of the president.

Without a strong tradition of control by faculty or by central or local government, while only theoretically answerable to nonresident trustees, the long-term American president became a central figure in directing higher education toward money and students. The powerful American college president at the turn of the twentieth century could order the establishment of programs that were perceived to draw the resources necessary for survival.

As early as 1779 it became apparent to the Harvard Corporation that the college should be led by more than mere academicians. Instead they should be versed in business and practical affairs (Lowell 1934). Lacking a strong public presumption of the importance of American higher education, and without healthy endowments and guaranteed yearly incomes, a practical business-minded individual was deemed necessary to guide the academic institution through the troubled financial and political waters. Survival exigencies required an authority structure different from the faculty-dominated governing boards of the English and German universities.

Contributing to the legitimation of business-minded presidential leadership in the nineteenth-century American post-secondary school was the composition of the boards to which the president was theoretically answerable. According to Nearing (1917), 80% of all American college trustees in the approximate period 1910–1917 were merchants, manufacturers, capitalists, corporate officials, bankers, doctors, lawyers, and religious leaders. These findings were later corroborated by Leighton (1920), who concluded that professional educators indeed were grossly underrepresented on these theoretically supreme governing bodies for American colleges. Beck (1947) similarly found the following class composition among college and university trustees during the period 1934–1935: businessmen, 41.5%; lawyers, 25%; independent professionals, 11.8%; clergy, 6.6%; politicians, 4.9%; others, 5.6%; and educators, 4.6%.

The policy matters that required trustee approval were brought before boards with minimal professional faculty representation. If we may assume that professional orientation has a strong effect on the individuals' judgements and evaluations, then we may conclude that the ultimate governing bodies controlling higher education in the early twentieth century were dominated by business and other noneducation interests. These were individuals not steeped in the traditions of education nor firmly socialized into the mores and norms of the classical university. Given this board composition, it is not surprising that business-minded presidents were chosen to run American academic corporations in the nineteenth and early twentieth centuries. As Shils (1981:273) has indicated, the traditions of the dominant sphere of society may very well expand into other areas of the society. Certainly the processes and goals originating from the business sector were extended to higher education. The academic tradition was, depending on one's view, either complemented or diluted, improved or corrupted by the modus operandi and world view of business. Organizational success became equated with dollar balances and student enrollments. Institutional efficiency demanded measurable criteria, such as ledger sheets, understandable by business-dominated boards, as opposed to educational criteria such as difficult-to-assess "degrees of learning." College programs could be constructed to promote institutional fiscal health with only a minimum of faculty on boards of trustees.

College Leadership's Use of Programs to Attract Students, Money and Prestige

The tenure of John Swain, who became President of Swarthmore College in 1902, illustrates the extent to which real-life concerns of the college demanded alteration of traditional conceptions of the curriculum and student life. Brought from the University of Indiana, Swain was convinced of the need to modify Swarthmore's "old ideals of a conservative sectarianism" to meet the needs of a more worldly environment. Overcoming the resistance of faculty and staff, Swain saw that a college so dependent on tuition revenues had to be made more attractive to students while maintaining the institution's connection with its Quaker social base. The diverse, competitive market demanded a strengthening of the applied fields of study such as engineering, an enlargement of the student body from 200 to 500, and, most important, the development of the "life of fun," that is, social activities and sports (Clark 1970). The extracurricular and big-time football were then married, comfortably or not, with Swarthmore's traditional liberal studies for the purpose of institutional survival in a market of institutions competing for students.

Similarly influential within their institution were presidents William Rainey Harper and Robert Hutchins of the University of Chicago. Review of their presidential terms clearly illustrate the power o these college leaders to initiate or terminate intercollegiate athletics. Lawson and Ingham (1980) provide examples of the power of the American college president to rapidly and radically alter institutional programs and orientations with respect to academics and sports. Harper, President of the University between the years 1890 and 1906, had before him the task of building a major university in the Midwest. With $600,000 from John D. Rockefeller, Harper embarked on his mission to develop the "university idea." Primary in his design for the University of Chicago was the need for prestige and money for the institution — money which was needed to recruit the most capable and well-paid scholars from the Northeast, and prestige that was required to lure them from major institutions. Harper's success is indicated by enrollments. Between 1896 and 1909, enrollments roughly tripled, from 1,815 to 5,500 students. By 1900, Chicago, along with Harvard, Columbia, Johns Hopkins, and California, accounted for 55% of all earned American doctorates.

An important component of Harper's plan to gain prestige for the University of Chicago was the drawing card of sport. Sport success would provide evidence of the kind of university being built in the Midwest — one that could compete with schools of the established Northeast or any in the Midwest that predated Chicago. By luring to Chicago former Yale colleague Amos Alonzo Stagg, Harper brought with him one of the premier football coaches of the era and went a long way toward his objective of providing symbolic representation of institutional quality. To President Harper, sport provided an important means of acquiring the resources necessary for institutional survival and growth. At half-time of a losing contest against Wisconsin, Harper exhorted the Maroon in their dressing room.

> Boys, Mr. Rockefeller has just announced a gift of $3,000,000 to the University. He believed that the University is to be great. The way you played in the first-half leads me to wonder whether we really have the spirit of greatness and ambition. I wish that you would make up your minds to win this game and show that we do have it. (Related by Stagg, in Lawson and Ingham 1980:45)

Harper consciously used athletics to recruit students and engender support for the University (Lawson and Ingham 1980:46). Under Harper's leadership, big-time sport played a central role in the resource recruitment efforts of the University. The height of the University of Chicago's athletic fortunes was marked by its Big Ten championship in 1924, eighteen years after Harper's death.

Upon his assumption of the presidency in 1929, however, Robert Maynard Hutchins saw little place for big-time college football at an institution that in his mind should be devoted to intellectual leadership. Overcoming the protests of Stagg and his allies, by 1932 Hutchins successfully led the move to rescind the University of Chicago's "physical culture" requirement, which had been used as a farm system to develop players for the football team. Faced with the prospects of ever-shrinking powers and influence, Stagg was forced to resign in 1932 as football coach and Director of Physical Culture and Athletics.

As might be expected, dismantling the once-potent University of Chicago football machine was met with vociferous opposition by alumni. According to a 1936 article in the University of Chicago alumni magazine, the intellectualistic "New Plan" was attacked as the root of the decline in Chicago's football success. Because entrance requirements were set too high, sport talent turned elsewhere and athletic recruitment efforts were curtailed. In a particularly revealing reply to a concerned alumni in 1936, Hutchins offered the view that,

> the future of intercollegiate athletics at Chicago depends partly on what the University does and partly on what other institutions do. . . . To the extent to which other institutions in this region adopt the principles of the University of Chicago — this university will be more and more successful in intercollegiate competition (Lawson and Ingham 1980:55).

Hutchins, supported by the financial generosity of John D. Rockefeller's $34.7 million, saw Chicago as a leader — let others follow. Big-time intercollegiate sport in Hutchin's conception of higher education had nothing to do with university leadership. After a long period of losing seasons, the Maroon eventually dropped intercollegiate football in 1939.

In the history of early American higher education, the college president possessed considerable power to initiate or terminate sports programs. Without strong faculty opposition, and only theoretically answerable to nonresident boards, the president was able to rapidly alter the orientation of his institution. Although the powers of the college president have been considerably reduced in the second half of the twentieth century, chief executive officers of an earlier day were less bureaucratically stifled than their modern counterparts. Without a strong faculty opposition, federal restrictions or meddling trustee boards individual presidents were able to alter school programs, depending on their vision of the college or university. While Harper supported intercollegiate sport as a means of institution building, President Hutchins, blessed with financial security, saw incongruence between big-time sport and the intellectual mission he planned for the University of Chicago, and was able to drop intercollegiate football from the formal responsibility of the university.

The Development of Intercollegiate Sport

As colonial education was religiously dominated, so were American attitudes toward sport, play, and games.[10] Although generally negative valuations of organized physical "frivolity" were laid down by church, state, and education leadership, regional differences and the attitudes and behavior of the common people somewhat softened anti-play restrictions.

In William Penn's Moral Commonwealth of 1682, the Quaker principles of piety and self-denial were embodied in the conscious restriction of "balls, . . . plays, cockfights, bull baits, cards, dice and other games . . . " and "rude and riotous sport" was prohibited by the Great Law (Jable 1974:108).

In stark contrast to the moral commonwealth of Pennsylvania stood the colony of New Amsterdam. Without restriction from the Dutch Reformed Church, Dutch fondness for play took the form of skating, sledding, and hockey in winter; during the summer, interest moved to golfing, bowling, racing, and shooting. Similarly, the play of Southern gentry was relatively unrestricted by the Anglican Church. Once pro-hibitive "blue laws," which cast a jaundiced eye towards frivolous recreation had diminished in significance, the gentry increasingly imitated the English landed nobility's passion for play. By the end of the seventeenth century, horse racing, cockfighting, hunting, and fishing were enjoyed by these Southern descendents of the English cavaliers (Lucas and Smith 1978:17–19, 21).

Of particular significance to the discussion of intercollegiate sport, however, was the attitude toward play held in Puritan New England. With both Harvard and Yale under the strong influence of the church, it was assured that these seats of American higher education would be greatly affected by the negative attitude toward play held by the Puritans.

To the ministerial oligarchy, playful activity was regarded as sinful. Magistrates of the Massachusetts Bay Colony attempted to legally prohibit physical diversions from the people's "rightful" lifelong concern with devotion to God. All works should be in His name and not for mere merriment.[11]

As Corwin (1975) has indicated, early American education was much more religious than it was either political or vocational. To education leaders in New England, schooling meant rigorous study of the classics and disciplined devotion to God. In such a work-oriented society, idleness was detested, frivolity and play abhorred, recreation and sport restricted (Barney 1979). The early history of American higher education reflected these dominant attitudes of New England —

attitudes which pervaded the early colleges at New Haven and Cambridge. Especially among these leading American institutions the Puritan ethic of hard work and asceticism had become part of the character of American colleges by the early nineteenth century.

A number of factors, however, were to contribute to the alteration of American higher education's generally negative attitude toward sport, play, and games. By the first third of the twentieth century, colleges and universities in this country would not only come to accept play and recreation, but they would actively embrace sport, even justifying it as part of the legitimate mission of higher education. How did all this happen? What was the process by which sport became part of the academic enterprise? To understand this process, the development of the institution of higher education in the United States must be examined.

A Theoretical Overview of Higher Education in the United States

As previously indicated, the leadership of American higher education about the turn of the century was faced with bleak financial and enrollment realities. Quite apart from philosophical concerns with the definition of educational purpose, there stood the constant worry about basic survival. Business-minded leadership of the era searched for new means to acquire the necessities for continued existence.

Blau and Scott (1962) have noted that formal organizations such as schools are dependent upon their "task environment" for resources. All organizations, whether church, government, factory, or college, must constantly be aware of the effects of the organization's programs and goals on the diminution or increase in resources. Rather than thinking of institutions of higher education as "closed systems," that is, as organizations that are essentially self-sufficient, it is more instructive to conceive of American colleges and universities as living in an "open system." Each college and university must continually negotiate with groups in the task environment — that is, with the parts of the environment outside of the organization which are potentially important to goal attainment and goal setting — in order to gain the support of those groups. Employing this logic, school decisions are not based entirely upon factors internal to the organization. Curriculum, personnel, and extracurricular program decisions are based on evaluating the effects of possible decisions on constituents of the task environment. What will be the effect of a core curriculum requirement, for example, on potential student enrollments? What will be the effect of a no-tenure decision for an immensely popular professor? How will trustees and potential donors feel about abolishing the nursing, home economics, football or basketball programs? While some decisions may be made strictly on educational grounds, based upon an evaluation of the options' impact on the school's philosophy and educational operations, it may be that few decisions in the university are made without an eye to their possible repercussions on important members of the task environment.

Given the historical lack of consistent financial and student support for American colleges and universities, the higher education "business" has had to make varied appeals to these constituencies. Financial support is sought from government, alumni, and other donors. Support must also come from students whom American higher education must attract to have the raw material on which to work.

An important means of acquiring requisite support is through prestige. Garvin (1980) argues that prestige, a reputation for excellence, is more important than actual institutional quality in the definition of the market to which an institution can appeal. The perceptions of outside observers determine the prestige of the institution, and these perceptions may be based on a variety of material and immaterial factors. The school with prestige is much more powerful than the organization without it. Institutions that are highly respected by groups in the task environment are more likely to attract quality students and money, and to graduate products (that is, students) who are assumed by the public to be superior. The importance of declared objectives (what a school says it will accomplish) and visible programs (how it says it will accomplish its objectives) for organizational attainment of environmental support is especially significant for organizations, such as schools, that have difficulty in measuring their products. How to evaluate objectives such as learning, thinking, and questioning is problematic, at best. Evaluation of the effects of any school on these student skills is highly subjective. The institution that is highly prestigious is less subject to questions concerning the effectiveness of its programs and the legitimacy of its objectives. The school with high status, therefore, may more easily attract resources necessary for survival.

In sum, American institutions of higher education may be viewed as dependent upon other groups in the task environment for the resources necessary for survival. Through its programs and stated objectives, the school seeks to attract money, students, and prestige from the general public, state and federal governments, alumni, "boosters," private donors, faculty, educational foundations, and other groups in the environment. This is quite a different view of organizations from one that sees school success or failure dependent upon the actual attainment of organizational objectives. Rather than viewing the school as an organization whose goal is "to educate" and whose success or failure in society is dependent upon how well it educates, it is useful to consider that the valuation of school performance may be more dependent upon the *statement* of its goals and programs — that is, by what it claims to be its objectives and how well it convinces its constituents of the quality of the job it is doing. Institutional prestige, whether actually deserved or not, acts to strengthen or weaken confidence in the efficiency of the school in attaining its objectives through its programs. In other words, a school's success may depend less on the actual job it is doing than on others' perceptions about the job it is doing. Schools may create that perception through their public statements, and the credibility of those statements are affected largely by the prestige of the school.

Without the consistent resources enjoyed by its English and German counterparts, American institutions of higher education have been forced to negotiate with their environment through the manipulation of their programs and stated goals. In return for stating its objectives and programs, the school seeks vital resources from the environment. (Figure 1 illustrates this process.)

Figure 1: The Formal Organization of Higher Education's Negotiation with Its Task Environment

number & quality of students		prestige and legitimacy from faculty, foundations, interest groups
foundation money	American colleges and universities	
alumni		corporations
government money		booster money & time

In a very real sense, the trading of programs and objectives for resources is a negotiation.[12] In this relationship, each group formulates a bargaining position from its perception of its own desires, needs, and expendable resources and its estimate of those of the groups with which it will negotiate. If the state legislature wishes to see a program of agricultural science, then the university may develop a program in that area with the hope that an acceptable agrarian science program will lead to increased state funding. Given the nonpractical and overly theoretical nature of a program originally proposed by the school and subsequently rejected for funding by the state, the university may produce a revised program for a more down-to-earth cooperative extension farm program to justify larger funding requests.

This view of American colleges and universities stresses their external relationships with potential donor groups. Programs and stated objectives are only partly the result of fine tuning of traditional educational programs. It may be that it is not objectives that result in a program for which resources are found (see Figure 2) so much as that organizations in search of resources devise programs and modify original institutional programs and objectives in order to attract these resources (see Figure 3).

Figure 2: Alternative Models of Objectives/Resources Relationship

Educational Objectives	Resources
Programs	Programs
Resources	Educational Objectives

Certainly, the history of intercollegiate sport argues for the validity of the latter model of American higher education's program and goals development. The development of an appreciation of the classics and a concomitant mental discipline, the ability to discover new knowledge, practical education, and the creation of a liberally educated well-rounded individual have in the past served as education objectives for American colleges and universities. From these objectives, which are of primary importance to the organization, programs of study or training, would be designed that would facilitate achievement by the organization's members (students, faculty, and administration), as well as by the entire organization itself, of the explicitly stated objectives.

In this model, resources have relatively low priority and are only significant in the sense that they contribute to achieving the educational objectives through facilitating programs designed to attain these goals.

In the second model (see Figure 2), however, we have a very different relationship between resources, programs, and educational objectives. Of primary significance to the organization are the resources and the institutional survival they serve. Money, students, and prestige are of utmost importance to educational institution leaders. In order to attract these survival necessities, the organization develops programs that serve to lure support from the task environment. Initial education objectives are modified to rationalize and legitimize new programs. Whatever movement there is toward the organization's original objectives is determined and limited by their compatibility with the extremely important resource-acquiring programs. In this model of higher education, resource acquisition and organizational survival are primary. Programs that attract resources, if they are in philosophical conflict with originally stated education goals, may dictate a modification of those original goals.

The American colleges and universities of the late nineteenth and early twentieth centuries were limited in both their current resources and their ability to acquire further resources. Without consistent government funding, faced with a population generally unconvinced of the need for higher education in this land of opportunity, having tried ferry tolls, produce bartering, and name-selling, as well as philosophical appeals, leaders of American higher education were faced with an unstable flow of dollars and students. While Robert Hutchins of Chicago and a few well-heeled institutions concentrated in the East could afford to design programs in order to directly achieve well-defined education objectives, the majority of institutions could not afford this luxury. Survival required addition of programs and modification of traditional mission to suit potential students and the public imagination.

The growing popularity of sports represented an opportunity for resource acquisition unknown before the late nineteenth century. While the need for resources has remained an ever-pressing imperative throughout the history of higher education in this country, it was only at the turn of the century, with the invention of mass sports in America and the complex of factors that affected the university's internal and external constituencies, that resource acquisition through athletics became a possibility. A sports-hungry populace consumed athletic entertainment with increasing gusto as the tempo of industrialization, urbanization, leisure time, and accumulation of expendable capital quickened. The large land-grant schools saw a means of acquiring increased support from the legislature and the people. Representing the community, each school's victory provided it with rights to boast to the people of its state. Through each victory, the often culturally diffuse and geographically disparate peoples of the region could be unified.

Private institutions, too, saw athletics as a powerful vehicle for resource acquisition. Faced with a somewhat different task environment from that of the state land-grant university dependent on the state legislature, the private schools could unify distant alumni and gain visibility difficult to achieve through purely academic means. This was particularly true for the religiously affiliated private institution. Whereas these schools had once dominated the American college scene, an outmoded classical curriculum, an inherent limitation in the size of the potential resource-awarding population (given their particular sectarian affiliations), and the growth of competing numbers of nonsectarian schools had stripped these institutions of much of their appeal. Through sport, however, the public could be once again made aware of these schools, and resources could be acquired. While the discipline and moral character assumed to be of such importance to sport was similar to religious concerns with these matters, sport more immediately and perhaps more importantly could attract wide non-religiously based recognition and support. While continuing to press for funds from traditional government, public, and private sources, a sports-hungry public could be given athletics in a college guise. This was particularly so with football, especially in those regions where there were no professional sports teams competing for spectators.

As has been noted, however, not all elements of the task environment supported big-time intercollegiate athletics. Apart from athletic brutalities, improprieties in recruiting, and difficulties with athletes' eligibility, the following questions remained: should programs whose primary purpose was attracting resources be formally incorporated into the structure of the colleges and universities and rationalized as a legitimate part of higher education? Was sport a real responsibility of American colleges and universities? Particularly to the college faculties of the late nineteenth and early twentieth centuries, the answer to these questions was a resounding "no." Intercollegiate sport, particularly in its big-time form, stood outside the purposed of higher education

(Slosson 1910:503; American Association of University Professors, 1926:228). These were sentiments echoed by Savage (1929, 1933) in reports written for the Carnegie Foundation. Intercollegiate sport was overemphasized, in his view, and distracted from the purposes of higher education.

Still, it remains to be asked how Savage and other education critics could claim that big-time sport was outside of the proper domain of higher education's institutional responsibilities. What criteria were used in this determination?

More generally, the question may be posed: How does any social institution come to accept and claim certain programs as within or outside of its responsibilities? Institutions like the federal government or the churches, for example, have come to see as their responsibility the achievement of defined goals through particular programs. These may be peculiar to our country, of course. Similarly, governmental and religious institutions in foreign countries may demonstrate their own particular objectives and programs. While the German government, for example, sees the direction and support of higher education as its responsibility, the American federal government has historically not accepted or claimed this responsibility. While American institutions of higher education have claimed intercollegiate athletics as within their responsibility and have formally incorporated its funding and governance within their formal structure, athletic responsibilities have not been similarly accepted as within the legitimate functions of the German or the English schools. Why? What is it about the American condition which has led to this very different view of program responsibilities in higher education? Why is it that the American school is often perceived by the public first as a sports team, football mascot, or athletic "fight song," and only secondarily as an academic institution?

Certainly, much of the reason for the claim of athletic responsibility by college leadership has been under pressure from the need for financial and student support. For the bulk of schools about the turn of the century, the need to attract money and students was vital. Most fundamental, however, was the openness of American conceptions of the "charter" of higher education, that is, its proper goals and functions. With no traditionally accepted understanding of the methods and objectives appropriate for American colleges and universities, there was an openness of "charter" definition that permitted the inclusion of radically different programs within American higher education.

In the next section, we will look more closely at the "charter" of American higher education. With an open, flexible charter, the very structure of the college was open to redefinition, a redefinition made necessary by the financial and enrollment realities of the era. For the most part, business-minded college presidents and trustees, after initial resistance or apathy, were to openly embrace intercollegiate sport during the twentieth century, adding it as a program and altering their educational philosophy in the wake of this addition.

The Charter of the American College

A "charter" is an understanding. In this sense of the term, a charter is not primarily a state-registered document. Instead, it is an assumption on the part of an institution's constituency of what the institution should do (that is, strive to achieve) and how it should go about gaining its objectives. It is this often unconscious definition of institutional purpose and process that determines what an institution is. Its charter is an understanding of the characteristic "identity" of the institution. As Lasch (1984) rightly points out, early, less-sophisticated notions of "identity" saw it as stable regardless of the circumstances. By the 1950s, however, social scientists began to see identity in a more fluid sense, as socially relative, dependent upon its reference group. Instead of one unchanging "person," for instance, new conceptions of identity saw this as multifaceted, a definition as dependent upon the perceiver as on the perceived, and on the circumstances that called forth a particular component of that identity.

By the 1970s, along with changed notions of institutional identity, no longer were organizations viewed unidimensionally as reflections primarily of the technical requirements of their work. Few institutions have but one essential inviolable essence. Instead, there has developed a more fluid view of institutional character, in the belief that organizations must copy from and adapt to the environment (Meyer and Scott 1983:13–14). The definition of "appropriate and legitimate" institutional characteristics is determined by those in the environment around the organization, as well as those working within the institution. Definitions of the institutional charter may change over time, and be dependent upon the persons or groups in the environment to which the institution is addressing itself with its charter.[13]

The charter may be used to address people or groups who are important to the institution. Since figures in the environment may have something to say about what an organization's goals and programs are, the organization may adjust its *stated* mission and programs depending on the particular group being addressed. And, of course, the real reasons for visible programs may be very different from the rationales presented to justify the real or apparent organizational charter and its modifications.

As John Meyer (1970) has conceived the term, all social institutions have charters. The charter for the American federal government, for example, is an understanding that this organization will regulate group and personal behavior to the extent that this regulation maximizes freedom in our social setting. It is assumed by the population that the government has the right to collect taxes in order to finance social programs as well as the national defense. The government should also help victims of disaster and negotiate with the world community. The charter is also an understanding in the population of what an institution *should not do*. In this theoretical conception of "the charter," the bulk of human goals and the means to reach those goals cannot be claimed as within the scope of one institution's purpose — the institution should claim only carefully specified objectives and technologies. It is, for example, an accepted understanding in the American population that the government should not be (although it has in the past been and may continue to be) engaged in the business of spying on average citizens. Similarly, a church as a social institution may have a charter which precludes it from claiming as an appropriate program the selling of massage service — for what has this to do with the matter of saving souls in the eyes of those legitimating such a church?

The charter usually works at the unconscious level. The state-registered charter of a college, like other formal and conspicuously available legal documents, is but a reflection of that unconscious understanding of its legitimate institutional purpose. The government, given a generally accepted right to collect taxes, for example, develops legislation to carry out that right. In other words, law is but a formal classification and legitimation of the more fundamentally important unconscious understanding in the population of legitimate purpose and programs for each societal institution.[14]

The charter for higher education is an understanding in the collective unconscious of the sorts of goals to be expected from colleges and universities and the sorts of programs expected of the schools to reach these goals. The charter arises from the society's historical and contemporary values and attitudes, traditions of the past, and expectations for the institutions' future role in achieving the society's goals. All schools of higher education will be affected by the society's perception of their charter. Thus no one school acting on its own may change the charter for all of higher education.

The charter for higher education varies in its strength. While Oxford and Cambridge enjoy strong charters, American institutions have not been held in similarly high regard by the society in which they are enmeshed. Differences in the strength of these charters are indicated by differences in resources — money, students, and prestige. Since the twelfth-century origins of Oxford and the thirteenth-century beginnings of Cambridge, these ancient schools have gained a status bordering on reverence. Originally formed to protect scholars and to facilitate their work, these academies gained both the respect and monetary support of the church, aristocracy, nobility, business, and government.

The work of these scholars was sacred. Knowledge belonged to all mankind and was not owned by any one person or group. In addition to their "strong" charter, the ancient English schools then possessed "clear" charters. Their specific objective was to perpetuate classical knowledge. Their clear means of doing this was through the tutorial system of instruction. Such was their responsibility to the Hebrews, Greeks, and Romans and handed to them through the medieval scholasticism of the church (Chu, Seagrave and Becker 1985).

Matters of finance should theoretically not impinge upon the scholar. With large endowments provided from both religious and secular sources, and with consistent financial support by the central government, support historically unfettered by Parliamentary demands, Oxford and Cambridge remain today far less hampered by the need to develop programs to attract funds than their American counterparts.

With their strong, clear charters, the ancient English schools were highly respected by their society. Consequently, enrollments were of relatively little concern. Student flow was further guaranteed by a society that consciously kept the number of university seats available far below the number of applicants. With societal acceptance and approval of its mission, programs and stated goals did not proliferate. There was little need to appease resource-bearing groups in British society. Endowment incomes and yearly stipends contributed to stability in programs and objectives. With relative clarity of mission and the resulting stability of programs, Oxbridge's leaders had before them a well-defined vision of appropriate and inappropriate additions to the curriculum.

For a number of reasons, however, the vast bulk of American schools have charters neither as well defined nor as strong as those enjoyed by Oxford and Cambridge. Part of the reason for this difference must surely rest with time itself.

Post-revolutionary America felt the need to redefine its political, economic, and educational institutions. According to Tyack (1966:29), "America had no feudal tradition, no encrustation of illiberal institutions, no corrupt and gothic history to live down." Accompanying the infancy of nationhood was a disposition to redefine institutions without the weight of tradition and inertia. The people did not have a generally accepted understanding of what higher education should do. This openness to redefinition was bolstered by the relative lack of legal instruments that justified and concretized one simple conception of higher education. Compared to the almost nine-hundred-year-old histories of the English universities, American schools — with their history roughly one-third as long, at their oldest — have not had the generations to develop a clear conception of purpose. American colleges and universities have not had as long to develop a conception of higher education that will sufficiently satisfy the environment to the point where resources in the way of prestige, money, and students will be consistently available.

The pluralistic American society made clarity in higher education's charter highly problematic. The college that served the Brahmin class might be very different from that intended for the children of the Midwest. Catholics, Protestants, Jews, merchants, and missionaries, women and men all had their own view of the education best for them or their children. And in a society without legally prescribed ruling class, where the American creed pronounced acceptance of diversity, varying definitions of higher education's purpose and content were to be respected.

As Tyack (1966), Cremin (1980), and more recently Boyer (1986) have noted, there was in American education considerable diversity of opinion concerning the proper goals of education and the appropriate programs and courses that should be established in order to achieve those goals. It should come as no surprise, then, that lack of societal consensus as to values leads to a somewhat confused and inconsistent educational services (Martin 1982:38). Without a long tradition of accepted purpose and programs, the entire issue of the charter of American higher education was open to question. On the other hand, without a clear-cut understanding of what colleges and universities should try to do, there was available to American college leadership the opportunity to experiment with programs and goals that might attract the resources necessary for survival. Without a clearly defined and well-accepted charter, decisions concerning the appropriateness or inappropriateness of the curriculum or the extracurriculum could be made on more pragmatic grounds.

Brubacher and Rudy (1958), in their history of American higher education, describe the early nineteenth century as an unstable period in which to plant colleges and universities with clearly defined purpose. In the diversity of American culture, there were few widely accepted purposes and programs deemed universally appropriate for higher education. For example, there was certainly a need for the perpetuation of classical knowledge, but at the same time there arose an antithetical need to define and promote a distinctively American culture. Building on an English inheritance that based higher education upon the classics, college leadership was able to try out the scientific and applied models for the American post-secondary school.

As previously indicated, the initial American college curriculum stressed classical study. The humanities as developed over the ages was passed from the ancient English seats of learning to developing schools in the American wilderness (Williams 1954:298–299). A conception of higher education's purpose as the transmission of culture through means of classical study was embodied in the Yale Report of 1828 (Wayland 1842). Intellectual culture, concomitant mental skills, and a core of fundamentally important knowledge would be acquired through abstract, nonpractical study. The object of higher education, according to Brown University President Frances Wayland, was to "communicate knowledge and to confer discipline" (1842:81). Teachers of the nineteenth century were in addition responsible for the social and moral as well as the intellectual behavior of students (Finkelstein 1978:34; Bok 1982:2–3). The English tradition of education held that transmission of traditional attitudes, patterns of behavior, and even manners were essential for the cultivation of proper character.

As Veysey has noted however (1965:vii),

those who participated in the academic life of the late nineteenth century displayed sharply dissonant attitudes. Their outlook offered no smooth consensus, despite the eventual efforts of an official leadership to create one. Instead, theirs was an arena of continual dispute, of spirited conflicts over deeply held issues, of partisan alignments and sharp individual thrusts, which gentlemanly loyalties might soften but could never wilily subdue.

Without a clearly defined American charter for higher education, developing colleges and universities in the latter half of the nineteenth century were able to entertain and adopt other models of purpose and method. Without definite or agreed-on assumptions by influential elements in the task environment about what a college should and should not do, these educational organizations were able to try new programs and espouse different objectives. By the 1840s, the English "cultural school" of higher education was challenged by the German "scientific school."

Supported by a new generation of college presidents, the purpose of higher education was seen as less the perpetuation of the values of traditional culture. According to the German view, there was no *veritas*. The key to truth was not classical culture. Instead, the key was a method — the scientific method with all its safeguards for discovering objective truth. Without a widely accepted understanding of the purpose and process of higher education, American colleges and universities could alter their curricular structure and stated objectives. Schools in a pluralistic society respectful of diversity were able to incorporate German scientism and teach it in place of or alongside the classical curriculum.

The openness of charter, that is, the lack of one single established definition of legitimate institutional goal and method, also permitted the "applied mode." To borrow a term from Sir Eric Ashby (1967:4) "to dismantle the walls around the campus" was the great American contribution to higher education. American higher education should not be divorced from reality. All social institutions should serve the interests of the people. Pain and suffering should be diminished. Knowledge and resources should be applied toward this end — the betterment of the human condition (Foerster 1937). As previously indicated, the applied school of higher education found its primary embodiment in the land-grant institution. Service to all was the key. Whereas knowledge may have been enough by itself according to proponents of the "cultural school," and objective truth sufficient for supporters of the German "scientific school," in the unclearly charted waters of American education President Welch of Iowa State Agricultural College could declare in 1871 that, "knowledge should be taught for its own uses; that culture is an incidental result" (Welch 1871).

This utilitarian view of higher education's purpose was taken by Andrew Carnegie. A strong opponent of impractical abstract education, Carnegie called for an education that would serve the practical needs of the emerging business class (Nevins 1962:35). As Wayland notes (1850) Daniel Gilman observed that while the first American colleges saw professional training in areas such as law and medicine as outside of their responsibilities, the American college of the late nineteenth century sometimes saw practical training in the more worldly professions as within its purview. Private as well as public education felt this call. The prospectus of Leland Stanford Junior University announced that "provision would be made for the instruction of anyone in any subject matter demanded" (Warfield 1901) — a far cry from the narrow rigor of the English core curriculum of classics.

Without a clear charter, American institutions and their strong presidential leadership were able to entertain a variety of notions concerning the appropriate purpose of these social institutions. The English, German, and applied models of education were each tried, and all retain influence today. But without a strong charter — an understanding of the importance of higher education by resource-granting elements of the task environment, financial and student support of American colleges and universities could not be assumed. Developing institutions found it necessary to use their curricular freedom to adjust program and stated objectives in order to attract vital resources. Bok (1982:3) notes that by 1910 competing visions of the purpose of the American university had somehow joined in an uneasy coexistence to the benefit of the university's public acceptance.

Higher education as a glorification of the intellect was, according to W.H.P. Faunce, President of Brown in 1928, in itself not valued as much as it was valued as a means of material gain:

> I am inclined to think most Americans do value education as a business asset, but not as the entrance into the joy of intellectual experience or acquaintance with the best that has been said and done in the past. They value it not as an experience but as a tool (quoted in Hofstadter and Smith 1961:915).

In much the same way as the general public may have finally come to appreciate higher education as a means to an end, American college leadership was forced to look upon their programs and objectives — that is, their charter — as means to acquire the end of institutional survival. Theirs was a recognition of the consumer-oriented nature of the higher education "business." Embodied most specifically in the service station view of the American university, the organization would, through its plethora of programs, gain the support of as many constituencies as possible. Through its myriad offerings, practical and nonpractical, "thinking" as well as "doing" course, night as well as day classes on campus as well as extramural, the college sought students, money, and the recognition that could bring both.

The quid pro quo of college programs for resources was not, however, legitimized by all college leadership. Robert Hutchins, in 1936, stated that:

> According to this conception a university must make itself felt in the community: it must be constantly, currently felt. A state university must help the farmers look after the cows. An endowed university must help adults get better jobs by giving them courses in the afternoons and evenings. Yet it is apparent that the kinds of professors that are interested in those objects may not be the kind of professors that are interested in developing education or advancing knowledge. (Quoted in Hofstadter and Smith 1961:26–27)

In a very real sense, the business of higher education, through "diversification" into the athletic marketplace, sought to draw the resources necessary for continued existence. Thompson (1967) has defined diversification as a means of opportunistic growth. If the organization is constrained by its task environment and unable to confidently secure resources necessary for survival from that environment, then it may seek to enlarge its task environment in areas of opportunity. American institutions of higher education, generally unable to be confident of adequate levels of federal and state aid, students, and prestige from the general public, diversified into the sports area — an environment which in the late nineteenth century provided new opportunities for the university. Here there was great public interest. Legislators took note of athletic achievement. While academic matters did little to stir the public fancy, publicity was freely available for team exploits. Through sports developing schools could compete with the well established. The power of public respect could be acquired through athletics and not only through decades of academic toil.

With the diversification of growing numbers of schools into sports American colleges and universities found it necessary to swim with the tide. When a manufacturer develops a new product, competing firms feel compelled to develop like products for fear of being left behind in the contest for consumer fancy. Similarly, American higher education became increasingly involved with athletics at the end of the nineteenth and the beginning of the twentieth centuries. Faced with a consumer-oriented society with many schools vying for limited numbers of quality students and essential dollars, intercollegiate sports apparently provided a tangible indicator of institutional worth.

Such behavior is quite understandable if higher educational organizations are viewed sociologically as "organized anarchies" (Cohen and March 1984). Because of vague goals and conflicting, unclear methods (how is the work of the university — its teaching, research, and service — best done?), fluid participation (its temporally and geographically transient population of students, faculty, administrators, staff, community, government), and ambiguous organizational environment (what groups are most important in the constituency?), the college as an organized anarchy is faced with "explicit" (that is, visible) control problems and "implicit" (examples are authority and acceptance) control difficulties. Without clearly established organizational purpose nor power to achieve any purposes through demonstrable means, the college must rely on "unobtrusive levels of control" (as opposed to the obtrusive mechanisms found in many manufacturing industries). As Swindler (1979) also points out, highly bureaucratic, rigidly controlled structures do not develop successfully in unpredictable environments and where tasks involve great uncertainty. In groups with specialized skill, with a need for creativity and professional autonomy, and with unpredictable tasks, there is the need to find alternatives to hierarchal authority.

According to Cohen and March (1974), and Meyer and Scott (1983), it is myth, on the one hand, and uniformity in institutional rules, on the other hand, that provide unobtrusive control. Control of internal populations and groups in the environment is afforded to the institution by its demonstration of institutional quality. With quality comes the assumption of organizational efficiency and rationality. While institutional quality is usually assessed by how well the school conforms to "institutional rules" — credentials of the faculty, library holdings, and laboratory facilities, for example — research by Astin (1968) has demonstrated that conformity to these institutional rules almost never have anything to do with the actual effects of the institution on their students. Still, schools conform to these institutional rules, to these generally accepted measures of institutional quality, because they give the school some control over its constituent and participant groups. Impressive libraries, faculty credentials, and teacher-student ratios all serve to engender an assumption of university quality. Cultivation of this assumption is absolutely necessary to the institution that seeks resources necessary for survival.

Ritual and myth provide unobtrusive control over the organized anarchy of higher education. With commonly found myths of institutional distinctiveness and excellence there often follows public assumption of the appropriateness of existing institutional practices and leadership. Carefully cultivated legends of the superiority of the Harvard Man serve to back up assumptions concerning the legitimacy of the university and its way of doing things.

Myth, ritual, and adherence to institutional rules are controls employed by colleges and universities which work on the unconscious level. With the expansion of the university into a multifaceted curriculum, with the incorporation of diverse groups onto the campus, with the need to satisfy benefactors external to the campus as well as suspicious faculty split into their own disciplinary allegiances, the university at the turn of the twentieth century required such measures of unobtrusive control. Without means of rationally demonstrating the value of its product (the educated man or woman) or the efficiency of its mode of production (teaching), the university was understandably ready to grasp at a means of gaining greater control over its fate.

As Veysey (1965:340) has noted, by 1910 the structure of American institutions of higher education had assumed some stable form. To build a major university, certain structures were necessary — a board of trustees, faculty of various rank, a president, departments organized by discipline, department heads, and an athletic stadium. Thus, by the first decade of the twentieth century a sports program became both the institutional rule and a means of engendering an institutional myth. As the Harvard Man came to symbolize the distinctiveness of that institution, so too did Frank Merriwell of Yale and the Fightin' Irish of Notre Dame, come to represent the qualities of all from those schools.

In the next section the "garbage can model" of higher education will be examined. We see that a number of factors entered independently into the decision at the turn of the twentieth century to promote the formal incorporation of big-time athletics as an official responsibility of the heretofore intellectual colleges and universities. Continued pressure for funds and students made the search for resources a constant problem for administrators. The lack of government regulation, the newness of the educational system, the consequent lack of established traditions in the pluralistic American society, and the flexibility of understandings concerning the charter of higher education provided freedom to diversify into new resource markets. Nonresident business-minded trustee boards dependent upon central administration for information, and faculty newly fractured into disciplines that decreased their power, similarly provided room for business-minded presidents to maneuver the institution through troubled waters. Opportunities were provided by industrialization which led to increased leisure and excess capital to be captured through the burgeoning sports market. A ready rationale was provided for the college's entry into the arena through Hall's developmental psychology and the invention of the "adolescent," its legitimation of play, and a return to notions of the importance of character training in education. Observations of the power of the British Empire and the good that sport participation could apparently do for the individual as well as the campus community provided further justification for this new college program. The media was ready to extol the virtues of these new heroes to a public newly constrained by bureaucratization. Furthermore, university leaders searching for means to control both institutional participants and constituents found sports programs a means of engendering institutional myths and public assumptions of institutional quality.

These were the elements in the decision makers' environment. Given freedom to act and with the pressing need to do so, college presidents followed the example of their peers who had elevated previously minor schools to national prominence. Especially for the institutions with more ambitious presidents, who spent large sums on stadiums, national sports schedules, and heavily recruited athletes, the decision to enter big-time athletics irreparably directed these institutions toward the satisfaction of the needs of external constituencies — a decision with potentially negative implications for the internal constituencies of the institution.

The College Sport Decision

Whereas the conventional wisdom suggests that incorporating sport within the official responsibilities of American higher education must have been the result of studied calculation, one must be wary of such explanation. Some have claimed that intercollegiate sport was seen as the answer to the newly created problems of adolescence (Kett 1977), or as an antidote to the boring and overly classical curriculum of the late nineteenth century (Cremin 1980), or as a response to financial and student needs (Lawson and Ingham 1980; Chu 1979), in fact, such specification of potential factors in the calculation of university decisions may contribute toward unwarranted assumptions about the process through which decisions are made in educational bureaucracies.

The Garbage-Can Model for American Higher Education. The conventional model of rational decision making holds that organizational leaders coolly calculate options for organizational behavior. Objective information is rationally considered in an open forum of administrative peers. Deliberation based upon the best interests of the whole institution leads to decisions concerning the most appropriate behavior for the college or university. While such a model may seem to make exquisite sense for higher education organizations — the reality of the decision-making process may be far from this model. Too often in the analysis of education organizations, singular cause and particular decision makers are spotlighted as *the* cause and *the* agent for the school's decision to alter a curriculum, or, for example, to incorporate athletics.

Cohen and March (1974:2-3) have described contemporary American colleges as "organized anarchies." Modern higher education institutions are often characterized by uncertain or multiple goals (for example, should colleges focus on "liberal education" or "specialized training," on "moral development" or vocational training?") unclear teaching methods, fluid participation by internal members of the organization (faculty, students, administrators), and outside constituencies (such as federal and state agencies, trustees, and government officials entering and leaving the organization), and an ambiguous organizational environment (unlike the manufacturing of nails, for the college or university there is little clarity as far as which outside

elements are most important to the work and survival of the school —
is it the government? business? private agencies? the public?)

The contemporary American university differs markedly from the
small religiously directed institution of the eighteenth and nineteenth
centuries. Colleges are no longer small groups of insulated students
and scholars whose missions are clear and whose teaching and learning
techniques are unquestioned. Decision making became much more
problematic for the colleges and universities at the turn of the twentieth
century, as they grew in size and complexity. With more constituencies
among students from highly diverse backgrounds, from the faculty
splintering along disciplinary lines, and from alumni, trustees, the
government, and private agencies, each with their own particular
vested interests, the process of decision making became all the more
difficult. Add to this a lack of consensus concerning the proper curriculum for the newly discovered or invented or generated category
called adolescents, and we have a most complicated set of factors for
college leadership to consider. Presidents, ever concerned with potential diminution of resources required for institutional survival, had to
be most cautious for fear of alienating any one group important to the
institution.

Organized anarchies are unable to function efficiently by using the
same decision mechanisms as the manufacturer of a material good such
as nails. In the latter organization, bureaucratic hierarchy is well
established, and hence lines of authority are clear. The market is well
established and the quality of the product is easily assessed by both
producer, distributor, and consumer. Obviously, decisions concerning
material procurement, cost, salaries, and the like must be made at
specified periods. All this is not the case with higher education.

Whereas the rational model of decision making by hierarchy of
functions may fit the manufacturer of hard goods, to expect the
discovery of the single most important reason for such decisions as
incorporating sport with the formal functions of the college may be
fruitless. School program and curricular decisions may be made, not
in the rational linear context of "problem definition," "information
collection," "option analysis," "decision," and "implementation," but
according to the "garbage-can model." Cohen and March (1974:81)
propose that

> an organization is a collection of choices looking for problems, issues
> and feelings looking for decision situations in which they might be

aired, solutions looking for issues to which they might be an answer, and decision makers looking for work.

Applying this model to decision making in higher education, we see that at any one time in the organization several relatively independent streams of problems (personal problems of school personnel, and college, regional, and world problems), solutions (some product or plan developed by school or external personnel looking for an appropriate problem or concern), participants (school or nonschool), and "choice opportunities" (occasions calling for decisions) are dumped into the "garbage can," shaken about (in committees, reports, task forces, discussions, open letters, protests, responses and nonresponses), and then followed by some decision. Decisions made from this procedure are largely dependent upon "timing" (:Has a controversial report just been issued backing some cause? Did all committee members attend important meetings? Were there illnesses or other crises which affected decision makers?), as well as the particular components of the garbage can at any one "choice opportunity." "Choices are made only when the shifting combination of problems, solutions, and decision makers happen to make action possible" (Cohen and March 1974:90).

Although sport had been popular in America well before the 1890s, it did not become an official function of most post-secondary schools until that period. A number of factors taken in combination and then shaken about in the "garbage can" led to the decision to formally incorporate athletics: the lack of a clear, accepted definition of the purposes and programs of the American college; unabated pressure on administrators to secure students and funds for their institutions; the relative weakness of the faculty vis-a-vis the administration; industrialization, which had promoted urbanization, leisure, and expendable capital; technological advances in transportation and communications that promoted the possibilities of extraregional student recruiting; the development of a psychology that legitimized adolescence and supervised play; the business orientation of a new breed of college presidents and trustees who replaced the religiously and academically grounded administrators of an earlier time; and the effects of the newly rediscovered Olympic Games and the English sporting tradition. These and other factors entered into the decision-making process at that time. While some of the factors were educationally based and focused on the student, others were centered on the college's survival requirements and its response to the world outside the campus — an American scene fanatical about sport.

Sport and Changing American Values.   Although Puritan America officially frowned upon vigorous play — labeling it frivolous, at best, and sinful temptation, at worst — in Puritan rejection of Roman Catholic ritualism and Anglican "sorcery," divine grace was recognized as the only source of salvation, according to Mrozek (1983). Human action was seen as a reflection of the state of the soul. Eventually, this view was amended to assert that action was not only a sign of one's possibility for salvation but that conduct possibly even shaped moral character. In other words, salvation was perhaps possible in the secular realm and achievable by humans themselves on this earth.

This was a view of humanity most appropriate for America — a land that saw itself as distinctly superior to the corrupted European visions of society. As children of the Enlightenment, we Americans could benefit from the mistakes of the unfortunate. Through reason and will, we could create from the abundant resources that were our inheritance a more wonderful kingdom. Without generations of kings, peasants, and Popes, and with open land before us and the energy that comes with hope, a religious philosophy that valued the here and now fit America and provided the justification for human action. While Europe's princes might squabble and its peasants struggle to survive, America sought a spirit that accepted the perfectability of man and society.

Whereas earlier generations had sought supernatural explanations for life and death, an America unencumbered by a state church sought answers in science and reason. The question of death became secularized, and individuals were thereby given responsibility for their own renewal. "Late nineteenth-century Americans came to the profound conviction that the visible world exists" (Jones, quoted in Mrozek 1983:xviii) and that attention to the material world was legitimate and valid. We could act to shape ourselves and our world. We should try to perfect the kingdom of God and His creations. On the other hand, as children of Darwin, we could understand the world in a secular way without the ethereal mysticism of traditional religious explanations with which many Americans were uncomfortable. It was our birthright to seek excellence of thought and action befitting our place atop the evolutionary ladder.

This was a culture of active dynamism rather than passive contemplation. By incorporating athleticism into the academy, college and university leadership responded not only to the financial and enrollment needs of their institutions but also to the needs of the populace which had historically been met by churches. Action through sport apparently demonstrated by behavior the goodness of man. Sport answered a thirst in secular America for human perfectability. Athletics provided, in its asceticism, its discipline, its requirement of courage and grace, answers to questions about the reasons for our existence, the relationship between civilization and nature, our need to know how good we are, the need to adhere to eternal values greater than ourselves. Sport provided a means for active consideration of these religious questions — an active consideration more suited for Americans. In Mrozek's words, "sport assumed a role in linking contemplation and action" (1983:23). By watching as well as playing, students and the other spectators could see actively demonstrated the symbolic questions that had come within the domain of American higher education, and see played out the various scenarios that life has given us in response to these eternal questions.

The new business-oriented college presidents and trustees also operated in an intellectual environment in which the interpretation of stages of individual development were feeling the pervasive effects of Darwinian theory. Whereas earlier conceptions of human development viewed play and games as the stuff of children — perhaps to be tolerated, but certainly not the substance of maturity — evolutionary theory suggested that this period before the full assumption of adulthood, with all its roughhouse and symbolic play activity, might be of real value in itself. According Joseph Kett (1977), the key contribution of the early twentieth century was the "invention of adolescence." Critical to the establishment of adolescence and its play as a legitimate respectable period of development was the psychology of G. Stanley Hall.

Hall viewed adolescence as a period where youths are torn between dualisms — hyperactivity as opposed to inertia, social sensibility versus self-absorption, lofty intuition as opposed to childish folly. In Hall's view, for the young adult to fully mature, adultlike pressures must not be added to the strains already inherent in the age. Instead, this period and its characteristic behaviors should be respected. Owing in part to this view of adolescence, play and the newly burgeoning interest in sports gained respectability as a natural part of individual human development.

Indeed, American school administrators, pressed by financial and enrollment considerations, could hardly fail to see the precedents that had been established in the English "public schools," the great private preparatory schools of the upper classes. Charles Vaughan of Harrow, G. E. L. Cotton of Marlborough, and Edward Thring of Uppingham, as well as Thomas Arnold of Eton, were instrumental in legitimizing the educational value of developing "the whole boy." The "cult of athleticism," with its rituals, garb, ceremony, and discipline, was purportedly able to turn a rowdy and rebellious mob of boys into good citizens respectful of authority and promoters of England's preeminent position in the world of the 1850s and 1860s (Mangan 1981). American authorities, always mindful of the legitimating capabilities of anything English, were better able to justify sports within their own institutions given this precedent. College administration faced with students avid for athletics and a "choice opportunity" for sport on campus, could point to an English school system that highly valued athleticism.

American philosophers John Dewey and Charles Sanders Pierce preached the inseparability of thought and action. Through our secular efforts we might perfect the human organism and the social system. William James further validated the importance of the material world. We could understand the universe and our place in it according to this new science of psychology, through consideration of the visible world — no need for blind faith in that which could not be seen. Our new American heroes were heroes of action — those who shaped God-given nature to suit our worldly requirements.

Henry Cabot Lodge was one such hero. In his mind, sport served as a means for personal and societal renewal.

> The time given to athletic contests . . . and the injuries incurred on the playing field are part of the price which the English-speaking world has paid for being world conquerors (Mrozek 1983, 28).

High ideals were inseparable from concerted action. To Lodge, sport provided a means for actualizing the destiny of the white race. American nationalist support for growing American imperial power fed off the conviction that this nation was the chosen one. Action through sport provided both the training ground for leadership and evidence of moral goodness. As a substitute for religion, sport through its vitality gave Americans an antidote to death. It gave Americans a reason for being and a direction for behavior. Through sport it appeared we could promote not only our own health but our nation's as well; we could fulfill God's will as well as fulfilling a scientific imperative.

College Sports. According to Kett (1977), by the late nineteenth century it was intangible benefits of a college education that were valued most highly by American educators. The spirit of competition, high ideals, and ambition instilled through college life would serve well the graduate and the nation. President Hyde (1906) of Bowdoin typified the colleges' new view of college students. No longer was the extracurriculum viewed as an "addictive vice" that must be suppressed. Instead, college life outside of the formal curriculum should be viewed with tolerance and with the understanding that some student excesses were part of maturation. The play and sport demanded by students did have an intellectually justifiable rationale. Given the excesses of student-run athletics, however, institutionally regulated sport became the rule. It was argued that, while play and sport were avenues of maturation, supervision by education authorities would ensure the development of proper values.[15]

Although the first intercollegiate contest was held between crew teams of Harvard and Yale in 1852, this and other physically vigorous campus recreation had occurred either over the opposition of faculty and college leadership or, at best, without their support (Lucas and Smith 1978:191). The student-run "extracurriculum" developed in reaction to a classically oriented program that stressed the asceticism of the study of the classics. Campus athletics mirrored American society's increasing enthusiasm for sport and recreation. Intercollegiate baseball was first played in a contest between Amherst and Williams in 1859, and intercollegiate football was contested for the first time by teams from Rutgers and Princeton in 1869. By 1900, intercollegiate sport was commonplace (Sage 1975:399).

Despite its growing popularity, however, the dominant control and financial responsibility for campus sport still rested primarily with the students. The athletic association, a student-run organization to oversee travel, finances, fields, equipment, and other athletic necessities, was the common form of organization between the years 1870 and 1900. While athletic expenses might be covered from regular college funds for special purposes, such as to defray costs of the victorious Cornell crew in the early 1870s (Smith 1976), primary responsibility for sport remained outside of the formal role requirements of the faculty, administration, or other education staff. Football, according to the discouraged presidents of Wisconsin and Princeton at the beginning of the twentieth century, was a diversion from the important concerns of higher education (Lucas and Smith 1978:202–207). But there was a growing acceptance among college administrators of the part which big-time intercollegiate sport could play in the enhancement of the institution's survival. It was an acceptance that would catalyze institutional commitment to sport far surpassing that of the English schools to their primarily student-run sport. It was an acceptance that would turn into enthusiasm as college leadership threw institutional resources and prestige into the construction of stadiums and arenas to house the spectators who would form the new focus of college sport.

As Betts (1974) has documented, industrialization spurred by the Civil War made the United States the leading industrial producer in the world by the 1880s. The technological advances of industrialization, readily transported the population to recreational sites and sporting arenas. College and professional sports teams could now compete against heretofore too-distant schools. Intercollegiate and interstate rivalries were born: Texas versus Oklahoma became inevitable, Ohio State against Michigan almost a necessity. The development of the telegraph and mass newspapers facilitated the growth of national exposure for colleges. No longer were the exploits of a famous eleven known only to the college town. National reputation, a place among the elite institutions of the country, was seductively available to the school with high-quality athletic programs. The sports pages promoted hero worship and Red Grange thrust the "Fightin' Illini" into the national consciousness.

Sporting goods and apparel could be produced in quantity and made available to the growing leisure classes. The nouveau riche, only lately plucked from the drudgery of labor for survival, now had the time to consume sport as both spectators and participants. Indeed, for this group the demonstration of sports interests became a means of exhibiting newly acquired status. To take part in sport, which previously had been an activity limited to the wealthy, demonstrated higher social and economic position.

Accompanying industrialization, urbanization removed the population from the small-town recreations of the past. Whereas in 1860 only 6 million Americans lived in towns larger than 2,500, by

1890 22 million lived in cities (Betts 1974:174). With conglomerations of heretofore geographically diverse peoples there came anonymity and unfamiliarity. No longer was everyone known, as in the small town. No longer did extended family groups provide the link of kinship. Sport for the urban masses provided familiarity among strangers. An interest in sports was a shared interest between Catholics and Protestants, between Irish and Germans. Dialogue and play could bring them together, whereas before strangers had merely existed side-by-side. As both Boyle (1963) and Betts (1974) have noted, sport was both partly the result of and the cure for the ills of urbanization.

The anonymity of conglomerations of new neighbors could be remedied through sport. It is Rader's (1978) thesis that sport provided new means of association for the masses. Sports clubs became one of the basic means by which subcommunities were established within the larger society.

Extending Rader's thesis on the function of public sport, one might suggest that the new intercollegiate sports of the late nineteenth and early twentieth century served the important function of tying together an increasingly complex society. Especially for the large land grant schools, a diverse student body drawn from a geographically and often culturally diverse population could find common identity through sport. Students spread across different disciplines, and taught different values, norms, and goals could be integrated through their common allegiance to their school athletic teams.[16] Scientists taught to doubt subjectivity, humanists taught the limits of empiricism, artists given an appreciation of the esthetic, and business students schooled in the importance of hard management could join on a Saturday to root in common for some mascot beast, some totemic human caricature, or even a school color - crimson, maroon, garnet. Beyond their major's particular learning they were symbolically reminded of the characteristic discipline, perserverance, and teamwork of sports valued across the university and society. In this way the contradictions within the school were integrated and solidarity engendered throughout the university. With society's increasing concern for sport, American higher education came under mounting pressure to accommodate student interests in sport and also found support among the general populace for school-related athletic activities.

By the beginning of the twentieth century, American society had become increasingly complicated and bureaucratized (Rader

1983:176–177). Dreams of rugged individual success and idealized images of dynamic action had to be reconciled with the realities of life dominated by corporate organizations. The public, hungry for heroes that embodied traditional dreams, cultivated sport figures such as the Four Horsemen of Notre Dame. The growth of college football, according to Veysey (1965:276), can be traced to its combination of "romanticism" and "realistic effort"; while the sport was "immediate, physical and real," it provided at the same time the stuff of "dreams, legend and hero worship."

College sports became an integral component of that mix of urban milieu and cultural style called the "New Sobriety." As part of the trio of jazz, movies, and sports, college athletics played an important part in the determination of popular culture until 1933. According to Hoberman (1984), sport's association with crowds, mass media, machines, and dynamism made it a stylistic expression of the times. And it was the same rationalization, organization, technology, and sensitivity to the market in American business that affected sports in the 1920s and 1930s. Rule changes to enhance scoring, the use of time clocks to speed up play, and the wide-open offensive game appealed to the growing American population, themselves possessed of more real income and leisure time — a people in the midst of dispensing with Victorian values and of legitimating "fun." By 1930, "the age of the spectator" was realized. Big-time sport became increasingly valued for its instrumental value — a fact attested to by the construction of large stadiums to house the public throngs (Rader 1983). Public craving for sport, the cultivation of heroes and their teams, and the dynamism of the 1920s and 1930s, all spoke for a less-insulated campus and one more responsive to the public's desires.

Although sport had been on the American scene before the 1890s, intercollegiate athletics had not been recognized as a "solution" as much as it had been defined as a "problem." Thereafter, however, the perennial collegiate concerns of money and student recruitment could be combined with these new possibilities. These included a new concerns for supervised adolescent educational activities, the unification of students splintered by disciplines, the English "whole boy" rationale, and a burgeoning sport spectator market. The latter was itself a product of industrialization, urbanization, and the transmutation of the American conception of the "rugged individual" through the advances in national transportation and communications. These were all combined to create a type of institution in American higher education vastly different from that of any other country and time.

It should be little wonder that American institutions of higher education so firmly embraced sport at the beginning of the century. "In a society impatient with metaphysics, rationality and social control were the substitute for contemplation, . . . " (Mrozek 1983:230). The American styles of higher learning that were first modeled on the classical English humanities and then German scientific education had failed to capture the American imagination. Instead, by the late nineteenth and early twentieth centuries, it was often felt by college leadership that the exploits of their athletic teams attracted monies from the state, alumni, and other donors. In addition, winning teams were seen as maintaining institutional visibility among potential college students.

College leadership could hardly fail to notice the national exposure afforded heretofore minor schools such as Notre Dame and Swarthmore, as well as the attention paid to the major institutions like the Ivy League schools and the military academies. College presidents, themselves hungry for evidence of their effective leadership, felt they had in sports success a symbolic representation of the value of their institutions. Whether or not these beliefs were true, athletics was formally embraced as part of the college and university program around the turn of the twentieth century. Student-managed athletic teams gave way to college and university assumption of responsibilities for hiring and paying coaches, arranging and financing games and travel to games, the building of stadiums, and the promotion of college athletics in general (Savage 1933).

Support and Criticism for Intercollegiate Sports. By 1931, the once-lamented existence of college athletics had been so eagerly embraced by college administration that the Carnegie Foundation reported

> The avidity of the colleges themselves for publicity has in the past been partly to blame for the unsatisfactory relation between newspapers and college sports. Comparatively few institutions have attempted to give newspaper writers the opportunity to learn that athletics are only one of the activities of a college or university. (Carnegie Foundation. 1931:52)

As with other businesses, the "recognition factor" was important.[17] Sports Information Directors sprang into being on the campus as professionals in the area of public relations. The weight of sport news releases more than drowned whatever academic publicity there was under a sea of scores, records, and athlete–coach biographies sent to local, state, national, and hometown wire services. The growing popularity of the "service station model" for higher education provided justification for college sport. The public certainly wanted athletics. Why should not local youth represent the community in sport? By the 1930s it was well established in the minds of the public and most college leadership that American institutions of higher By serving the desires of the people, learning could gain the support of this constituency. But then, not all were convinced of the appropriateness of this quid pro quo.

Questions were raised concerning the legitimacy of programs of this sort within the mission of higher education. Often, these sentiments were expressed by the faculty:

> University presidents, with few exceptions, express approval of intercollegiate contests, alumni give enthusiastic support, students vent their displeasure upon any who presumes to question their value and the outside world encourages and applauds, but in every university there is considerable, and I believe, an increasing number of instructory staff who are profoundly dissatisfied with the athletic condition today (Slosson 1910:503).

Although with relatively less power than their European counterparts, American faculty were a major source of opposition to the formal incorporation of athletics into the structure of American higher education. In the view of many faculty, college football, although a recreation and a unifying vehicle for the campus community, had overall an adverse effect on higher education. Values were distorted and student concerns diverted from the more central educational and moral purposes of American colleges and universities. Football was condemned by faculty for the spectators' betting, drinking, and general hysteria, and the players' non-amateur professionalism. Big-time coaches were sometimes paid more than faculty — a symbolic institutional seal of approval upon the diminution of the faculty's importance vis-a-vis athletics (*American Association of University Professors*, April 1926:228).

In 1936, Robert Hutchins, President of the University of Chicago, commented, that, "It is sad but true that when an institution determines to do something in order to get money, it must lose its soul and frequently does not get the money" (Hofstadter and Smith 1961:26–27). Hutchins feared that altering the mission of higher education (understood by him as intellectual leadership) in order to attract resources would adversely affect American colleges and universities. In his mind, the mission of the University of Chicago to extend scholarship could not be tied to money. Knowledge must not be tied to popularity and the whims of the nonacademic. The institution that alters its mission in order to gain money invariably slants its programs away from academic concerns and detracts from the efficient pursuit of knowledge.

As reported previously, however, few American institutions were as financially secure as Chicago. The vast bulk of schools were poorly endowed, received little if any foundation grants, and had little confidence in their ability to consistently attract needed income (Claxton 1915:188–189; Brubacher and Rudy 1958:361). By 1930 the presidents of Michigan, City College of New York, Iowa, Columbia, Middlebury, Bates, and Princeton had all publicly defended the propriety of college sport (Betts 1974:347). In response to faculty critics of intercollegiate athletics, Dean S. V. Sanford, President of the University of Georgia, remarked that there was little cause for alarm. Minor adjustments to athletic programs would assure intercollegiate sport of an important place in "the hearts and mind, of the American people." (American Association of University Professors, April 1931)

Notre Dame's football, consciously developed in the 1890s as a means of promoting the institution, had by the 1930s established the school as a major institution in the eyes of the public. The sports successes of the Massachusetts Agricultural College brought the institution increased state appropriations and praise as a "real college" (Rudolph 1968:154). The benefits of winning athletic teams did not escape the notice of college trustees and presidents. Publicity, enrollments, and monies were the perceived rewards of victorious sport teams (Savage 1929:21; Betts 1974:347). In sum, sport provided good public relations for the business of higher education.

By the 1930s, American institutions of higher education had formally incorporated intercollegiate sport within their governance and economic responsibilities on a scale far surpassing the English public school sport system. Coaches often were hired as faculty and paid more than their academic "colleagues." Athletic transportation, facilities, and equipment were arranged and paid for by the college or university.

Sports Information Directors trumpeted the successes of athletic teams, and college presidents defended athletics as within the legitimate functions of higher education in America.

As the German observer of American culture, Freiderich Schonemann noted, however, the athletic condition of the 1930s was worrisome.

> The big financial returns derived from the ticket sales have caused the authorities to close their eyes to the evils of the whole situation, even corruptive practices. The buying and selling of college athletes may be a sport necessary for the semi-youthful enjoyment of certain aged alumni with ample means, but it tends to cheapen both the college and its sports. (Schonemann 1930:126–127).

Conclusion.   Unlike its early English and German models, the American college and university struggled for legitimate definition. What should our schools try to accomplish? What programs were appropriate and which were not? As we have seen, often it was the powerful American college president who wrestled with the problem of definition of purpose and program. Without secure and consistently bountiful sources of monies and students, the problem of definition became even more complex. Definition itself was extremely troublesome in the diversity of multicultural American society. With the vagaries of student and financial resources, however, the problem of defining institutional mission was exacerbated.

It has been suggested that intercollegiate sport was used as a vehicle for attracting students and money. College presidents, eversensitive to new means of resource acquisition, altered previous criticism or apathy toward college sport to assume an enthusiastic stance and rationalize the intercollegiate sport program. Without the financial and enrollment securities of their English and German models, the American college and university were forced to pursue their missions while cultivating the support of potential students and those controlling the flow of funds into the academic purse. With these resource uncertainties, however, lack of a traditionally well-accepted "charter" defining legitimate institutional goals and means to attain those goals permitted a flexibility in institutional structure and objectives. Institutional purpose and programs designed to uncover or disseminate knowledge could be altered if that redefinition of college offerings and mission might attract the necessities for institutional survival.

Intercollegiate Sport: The Search for Rationalization

If I don't know I don't know.
 I think I know.
If I don't know I know.
 I think I don't know (Laing 1970, 55).

According to Edward Shils (1981), a legacy of the Enlightenment has been the need for rationalization. Standing directly opposed to the force of tradition, the skeptical and critical attitudes emergent from the Enlightenment have often forced social institutions to justify their existence and present condition according to defensible explanations. It has been necessary to justify the legitimacy of institutions like the school and its programs, and in terms that are measurable by objective criteria.

Smith (1981:434) refers to the modern Western mind set as "naturalism" — the view that "nothing that lacks a material component exists, and in what does exist the physical component has the final say." If it may be true that a college education is of value for character and deportment, then that is well and good; but evaluation of the demonstrable, physically measurable effects of the institution on the student are most important in the final assessment of the value of higher education.

With the growing acceptance of the bureaucratic model for organizational management during the nineteenth and twentieth centuries, there has been an accompanying need to rationally explain the purpose of organizational programs, and to justify them as contributing to the primary goals of the organization. To the degree that programs

61

can be shown to sufficiently contribute to the socially important objectives of the organization, those programs acquire legitimacy as appropriate components of that organization.

The organization which, for example, claims to fulfill the society's need for hammers, must demonstrate the rationality of its programs for constructing the implement. Plainly, the acquisition of wood and metal for handle and head are important, as is the shaping of both, and their joining. Because of the obvious rationality of these processes and the direct manner in which they contribute to the fulfillment of society's demand for hammers, that organization may be accepted by society as legitimate. All organizations require this acceptance. They seek a strong charter from society, which is acquired largely by statements of organizational purpose (how does the organization fulfill societal needs?) and by demonstration of rationality in its processes and programs. The hammer manufacturer able to produce symbols of rationality — for example, bureaucratic management charts, logical policies regarding personnel and manufacturing programs — and appropriate machinery is more likely to acquire the societally granted strong charter than the manufacturer who seems to make decisions base on subjective whim and who seemingly has no rationality in its programs. If, for example, our hammer manufacturer sought to incorporate voodoo, witchcraft, and incantations in the hammer fabrication process, then the rationality and legitimacy of that corporation would be open for question in modern society, which does not accept such once-popular processes. Society and, in particular, the task environment that brings resources must be convinced of the rationality of the organization's programs and processes that are claimed to be necessary for the attainment of the group's goals. The organization will be granted a strong charter only if the goals of that organization are deemed important for the society, and if the programs developed to acquire these goals are judged as rational.

What is true for our fictitious hammer manufacturer is also true for formal organizations involved in the American business of higher education. Colleges and universities must convince society of both the importance of their product and the rationality of means used in production. Without societal acceptance of the importance of higher education and the rationality of the educational process, these organizations stand the chance of losing material and nonmaterial support from the society.

As Marshall Meyer (1975) has noted, organizations, whether they be in hammer manufacturing or college teaching, use "claims of domain" in order to compete in the environment. With limited funds and potential student enrollments, college organizations seek to acquire these resources through claims for the "specific goals it wishes to pursue and the functions it seeks to undertake in order to achieve these goals" (Brinkerhoff and Kunz 1972:177). By claiming responsibility in the area of sport, and by fielding teams — responsibilities not claimed as late as the mid-nineteenth century by college leadership — the American college or university at the turn of the twentieth century clearly sought to acquire necessary resources in the way of money, students, and support.

Organizations cannot, however, make claims for responsibility over any need and realistically expect acceptance of these enormous claims by society. The poorest school cannot realistically hope to make money and gain students through claims that its new program in astrology is consistent with the mission of the institution and that the program fulfills the need of society. For a domain claim to be functional for an institution, that is, in order to attract resources, there must be agreement on the part of significant groups in the task environment that the organization's claimed domain of responsibility is legitimate (Thompson 1967:28). There remains the need to rationally and, ideally, empirically justify institutional purposes and all programs as necessary and efficient. Organizations cannot merely at their own discretion make claims concerning programs for that organization and then hope to acquire resources from a supportive environment. The organization that seeks to diversify must symbolically or materially convince important groups in the environment that the newly claimed program will be efficiently operated and will conform and contribute to the charter of the organization. The college that took up sports had to rationalize it as a program well run and contributing to the educational purpose of the organization.

Because of the number and variety of constituencies important to American higher education, the problems of program rationalization was made still more difficult. Separate groups such as students, legislators, alumni, educational foundations, critics, and faculty in their disciplines all bore resources essential for the survival of the school. Each desired specific and sometimes conflicting objectives and programs from the institution. All had to be convinced of the rationality of programs and the necessity for these programs in order to acquire the primary goals of higher education. Without consensus concerning appropriateness of program or the organization's goals, monies might be withheld, students might not enroll, and faculties might be resistant.

With little assumption on the part of students concerning the inherent worth of higher education, American colleges and universities of the late nineteenth and early twentieth centuries often felt the need to justify student attendance as a means of practical preparation for later life. In a similar manner, American schools had to justify their worth to state and federal government. To advance knowledge was enough for some but not all who controlled the government purse. Helping the farmers as well as the scholars was a broader purpose. Because of the lack of a powerful central ministry of higher education, individual donors and private foundations also assumed great importance. American colleges and universities felt it necessary to please the alumni as well as Rockefeller and Carnegie, Danforth and Kettering. The school's primary labor force, namely, the faculty, despite its departmental splintering, was also a potentially powerful element in the task environment. This was so, not because of faculty control of material resources, but because of its ability to influence internal consensus and efficiency. The college administration that blatantly defied the sentiments of faculty ran the risk eventually of developing an image of an inefficient organization. The school that developed a public image of disarray and conflict ran the risk of a possible decrease in material resource flow from other elements of the task environment. Donor groups and potential students whose attention was diverted from a chaotic school could easily channel their resources to any number of schools with better public image.

The diversity of task environment presented particular difficulties for American colleges and universities. The alumni and legislators that idolized winning athletic teams, and the public that equated sport successes with the quality of the institution, presented an appeasement problem very different from that presented by the Carnegie Foundation, a Teddy Roosevelt concerned with overzealous football play, and the faculty concerned with the educational content (however defined) of college programs. Despite diversity in wishes and expectations, American school organizations, if they were to draw resources from all these groups, were faced with the requirement of achieving "domain consensus." Without agreement from all these groups that the newly claimed sport enterprise was both well run and a contributor to the purposes of educational organizations in America, colleges and universities risked the loss of resources from any unconvinced group.

Response to this need to rationalize the newly claimed athletic enterprise centered around claims that intercollegiate sport not only aided the economic prosperity of the college but that it also had educational benefits for the individual athletes. If athletics could be demonstrated to be a learning enterprise, or at least one which provided the capital necessary for the work of the college, then domain consensus might be achieved. If alumni, legislators, and the public could be given winning sport teams, while educational critics and the faculty accepted that athletics aided the brick and mortar as well as the character-building concerns of education, then acquisition of the resources of money, students, and internal support might be possible.

But then, just how valid are claims concerning the benefits of intercollegiate athletics? Just how much do they contribute to the achievement of the goals of higher education? It will be suggested here that intercollegiate sport may indeed have an impact on the efficiency with which higher education's mission is realized, although both the effect and the manner through which it has this impact may be quite different from the process and result originally predicted by the supporters of collegiate sport.

In order to evaluate the validity of the claims for intercollegiate athletics, the *cui bono* criteria will be employed — who are the primary recipients of benefits? Justifications for intercollegiate sport have been based upon claims that there are benefits both for students and for the college. Let us look at each set of claims in turn.

Benefits for Students: The Question of Character

> Sport is a vital character builder. It molds the youth of our country for their roles as custodians of the republic. It teaches them to be strong enough to know they are weak, and brave enough to face themselves when they are afraid. It teaches them to be proud and unbending in honest defeat, but humble and gentle in victory. . . . It gives them a predominance of courage over timidity, of appetite for adventure over loss of ease. (General Douglas MacArthur 1971:75)

What is "character?" Like many words in common parlance, the term has multiple meanings. As most often used in discussions of education, the term "character" refers to a set of personality attributes or well-established values possessed by individuals. Some of these qualities are confidence, aggressiveness, discipline, poise, cooperativeness, responsibility, dominance, tolerance, flexibility, independence, and perserverence. These qualities are highly prized in our society and are commonly assumed to be important for individual behavior. Character is not fully described by cognitive faculties, however, nor is its meaning fully embraced by the psychologist's definitions. Instead, its richer meaning has to do with the qualities of heart and soul and the human spirit. While one may invisibly possess character, it finds its greatest expression in the face of adversity. The adversity may be mental — say, a scientific problem that seems to defy solution; or it may be physical — the pain of the marathon; or it may be combinations of mental, physical, and spiritual — the physically exhausting competitive effort in the face of rationally obvious futility.

Historically, the development of character has to some degree been seen as a responsibility of American higher education. The English model, with its stress on the transmission of culture, had some concern for character. Mental rigor was valued and the ability to study the classics was thought to engender overall personal discipline. Appropriate behavior was expected to accompany traditional attitudes and values. Although originally intellectual in its origins, the English concern for character was later to provide a ready atmosphere for the schoolboy athleticism which supposedly worked toward the same ends of character development. The German conception of higher education was more cerebral. Knowledge was the key. Even here, however, character necessary for scientific enterprise was marked by the discipline required to discover knowledge.

American concern for character in its mental, physical, and spiritual forms found expression in the liberal arts conception of the well-rounded individual. Emotional, spiritual, and physical qualities should be developed along with traditional cognitive concerns. This was a view of education that paralleled the philosophy of Olympianism, the full development of mind, body, and spirit as epitomized in the ideal Olympic champion and which was brought to the attention of the world with the revival of the Olympic Games by Baron Pierre de Coubertin in 1896.

A life-long Anglophile, Coubertin saw in the sport tradition of Rugby, Eton, and other English preparatory schools a means of developing the spirit that had made the small island an empire. Through participation in sports, by the preparation required for it and its tests of competition, Coubertin thought the human character could be tempered out of the rawness of youth.

With the increasing acceptance of the importance of the well-rounded individual, which paralleled growth in public sport enthusiasm and American Olympic successes, notions that sport participation built character were reinforced. With the need to rationalize college sports as an educational enterprise, these notions were generally advanced by college leadership and the athletic governing bodies.[1] Today, the primary governing body for intercollegiate sport, the NCAA, maintains this view, that sport participation is educational in and of itself (Koch and Leonard 1978).

In the face of such support for the educative value of sports participation, questions remain concerning the notion's validity. Can it be proven that sport participation causes positive changes in student personality or values? Do practice, games, the coach, and other players influence or directly alter the participant's character? (See Figure 3.)

Figure 3: The Interaction Model

Student Input		Student Output
Prior Personality	Active Sports	Altered Personality
Values	Participation	Values

To evaluate this relationship we turn to a sampling of the empirical research in this area.

Changes in Student-Athlete Characteristics

In an early study by Shifers (1956), former high school athletes were asked to reflect upon their sports experiences. The vast majority of them claimed that sport helped them develop "calmness and poise under pressure (88%) and courage and self-confidence" (84%)." Schendel (1965) studied 334 athletes and nonathletes at levels from the ninth grade through college. He found that athletes ranked generally higher than nonathletes on the following personal and social characteristics: dominance, responsibility, sociability, self-acceptance, well-being, and tolerance. In Cooper's (1969) review of the literature on sports and personality change, he found that most studies found athletes were outgoing, socially confident and aggressive, less compulsive, less impulsive, and more able to withstand pain. Webb (1969) found that as athletes progressed through school they demonstrated higher levels of achievement orientation. These findings were corroborated by Mantel and VanderVelden (1981). Inconsistent findings are reported between studies by Paulhus, Molin, and Schuchts (1979) and the research by McKelvie and Huband (1980) on locus of control. In the former study of Ivy League athletes in football and tennis, sports participants reported a significantly greater perception of control over life events than did nonathletes. McKelvie and Huband, however, found no significant difference between athletes and nonathletes on the variables of anxiety and locus of control.

To summarize this research, athletes are generally, although not universally, different in personality from nonathletes. If character is defined as the possession of "positive" personality and value qualities, however, then sport participation — if it has a causative effect at all — may imbue "negative" traits. The same research by Mantel and Vander Velden (1971) and Leonard (1980) that showed differences between athletes and nonathletes in the desire to win, also demonstrated a greater tendency for athletes not to care about the process of winning as much as they valued winning itself. Distressingly, this relationship strengthened as athletes progressed through organized sport in school. Fun and fair play were less important for experienced athletes. Richardson (1962) has shown that those more successful in athletics, that is, letter winners and scholarship holders, were less concerned with sportsmanship. If character involves the desire for fair play, then perhaps participation in organized sport is not appropriate for the educational institution. This is true if we can assume that colleges should be concerned generally with the inculcation of the belief in fair play. Similarly, Sage has decried the educational process of sport that does not promote individual maturity but instead promotes conservative value orientations. According to Sage (1978:44): "The real achievement of organized sports programs consists of their ability to train participants to accept the prevailing social structure and their fate as workers within bureaucratic organizations." In Sage's view (1980), sport participation is educative only in that athletes are encouraged toward traditional values, an acceptance of authoritarian leadership styles, a willingness to become business- and product-oriented.

Matters of autonomy, choice, and self-determinism are not promoted by sport participation.[2]

If we may assume that the coach's leadership style communicates a message much as does the hidden curriculum of the traditional school program, then traditional styles of coaching generally employed do promote in a covert manner a character structure inconsistent with a view of education as the facilitator of individual autonomy and maturity. Snyder (1972) has suggested that locker room slogans are used as a means of value transmission. Slogans such as "Cooperate — remember the banana; every time it leaves the bunch it gets skinned" and "When they are drowning throw them an anchor" certainly promote a value system with which many educators would disagree. In a number of studies, coaches have been found to be manipulative and autocratic, concerned more about success than the process of achievement (Sage 1975; Ogilvie and Tutko 1966, 1970). Athletes do seem generally to differ from nonathletes on a number of personality variables. Questions remain, however, whether these characteristic differences are good or bad, whether they are consistent with the purpose of higher education, and whether these differences were actually caused by sport participation.

Proponents of the value of college sports participation have also claimed that compared to nonathletes, intercollegiate sport participants perform better academically and that their social mobility after sport is enhanced. Once again, a review of the sport studies research indicates inconsistent findings, which permit little generalization.

In early studies, Eidsmore (1961, 1963) found that male and female basketball players, and male football players, had higher grade point averages than nonathletes. Schafer and Armer (1968), after comparing a matched set of athletes and nonathletes controlled for intelligence and curriculum, found that athletes' grades were slightly higher. This effect was accentuated for athletes from lower social class backgrounds. Athletes also had higher educational aspirations, with 62% aspiring to complete four years of college, compared to 45% of nonathletes. Similar results were found by Bend (1968), Buhrman (1972), and Otto and Alwin (1977). Stuart (1985) compared a matched sample of football players and nonathletes at one large Midwestern university. Between 1977 and 1980, she found that football players entered the university significantly less well prepared than nonathletes. Their high school grade point averages were lower, they completed fewer math courses, and they scored lower on the standardized ACT examination. Despite athletes' preparation detriment, however, Stuart found no significant difference in the academic performance of football players and nonathletes. In measured mean college GPA, number of semester hours completed, average number of courses dropped or repeated, grades in English and the number of English courses completed there was no significant difference between the school performance of these big-time football players and the general student population.

Findings from these studies run counter to those of Hanks and Eckland (1976), who concluded that sport participation had neither a depressing nor elevating effect upon academic performance. In an earlier review of forty-one studies, Davis and Cooper (1934) found that, generally, nonathletes performed better in school and that athletes' grades rose after completion of the competitive season. Sack and Thiel (1979) studied Notre Dame athletes and concluded that they demonstrated significantly lower GPAs and went on to earn fewer advanced degrees. Messner and Groisser (1981), after controlling for academic aptitude and sociodemographic background, studied athlete and nonathlete performance in the core courses required at one Ivy League school. They found that athletes demonstrated slightly lower GPAs — one-tenth of one grade point.

In the past, athletes have been forced to interact with academic materials. At the University of New Mexico, varsity athletes are made to attend a "study table" four times a week for two hours. In search of higher grades, a staff of twelve tutors, academic counselors, and athletic coaches oversee fifty athletes (Middleton, June 9, 1982). Perhaps at some schools these sorts of practices have had an effect on grades; but the process is a far cry from sports as a discipline inducing higher grades, as advanced by proponents of the "scholar-athlete" concept.

Claims for enhanced academic performance do not fare well in the face of Webb's study (1968) of 300 Michigan State University scholarship athletes who played between 1958 and 1962. Five years after their class year had graduated, 49% of team and 60% of individual athletes had received their diplomas, compared with an overall graduation rate of 70% for the university. In a more recent study, Shapiro (1984) found that of 1,642 Michigan State letter-winners and nonletter-winners in the sports of football, men's basketball, baseball, and hockey, the proportion of athletes graduating seven years after initial enrollment has declined significantly since 1953. In that year, the athlete graduation rate was 80%, while the overall student graduation rate was 45%. By 1973, the graduation rate for athletes had fallen to 61%, as opposed to a rise in general student graduation rates to 62%. At the University of Utah between the years 1973 and 1982, the overall graduation rate was 49%, while 57% of football and 34% of male basketball players graduated. The overall athlete graduation rate was 45% (Henschen and Fry 1984).

Of interest in this regard is a study conducted by the College Football Association, composed of the biggest athletic powers in college sport. From surveys gathered at 47 of the 61 Association schools, it was found that 562 of 1,211 scholarship athletes, or 46%, had graduated within five years. In a similar study conducted by the American College Testing Program in 1981, it was found that 52% of male varsity athletes graduated within five years, compared with 42% of all male students. Wide discrepancy in graduation rates was found among college football athletes, however. As many as 84% of these athletes were found to have graduated, compared with a low figure of 15% at another big-time football school. Among conferences, wide discrepancies in graduation rates were also found for seniors who played regularly for their basketball teams. Graduation rates ranged from 100% of seniors at Ivy League schools, followed by 77% of Big East, 63% of Southern, 50% of Big Eight, 41% of PAC Ten, 40% of Southeastern, 37% of Atlantic Coast, and 30% of Big Ten basketball players (*Chronicle of Higher Education*, April 28, 1982:9).

Especially with early studies, however, one must cautiously interpret findings. Often samples used are not comparable, and not controlled. Another problem in these studies is illustrated by the 1981 NCAA survey of male athletes that found a 52% graduation rate, as opposed to an overall graduation rate of 42%. Because of sampling problems caused by a poor response rate (23%) and unreported data (distribution of schools among divisions, for example) results must be interpreted as merely suggestive (Waicukouski 1982:170).

An important contribution to this literature has been provided by the 1987–1988 report titled the "Studies of Intercollegiate Athletics" (1988). In an attempt to gain baseline data on which to base policy decisions, the Presidents' Commission of the NCAA sponsored a $1.75 million survey conducted by the American Institute for Research. In this study of 42 Division I schools 2925 athletes and 1158 students with strong extracurricular interests were studied. It was found that (1) football and basketball players scored lower on the SAT exam (883) than athletes in other sports (919) or than other students with extracurricular interests (990), (2) football and basketball players had lower college GPAs (2.46) than did athletes in other sports (2.61) or those students involved in extracurriculars (2.79), (3) 34% of football and basketball athletes in "more-successful" competitive programs have been on academic probation as opposed to 26% from "less successful" programs, and (4) in-season football and basketball athletes spend an average of 30 hours per week on sport and 25 hours per week on classes and academic preparation as opposed to the 20 hours per week spent on extracurriculars and 27 hours per week spent by students with extracurricular interests on their classes and academic preparation.

Overall, the mixed bag of inconsistent findings does little empirically to validate claims concerning the academic enhancement qualities of intercollegiate athletic participation. These claims are made more hollow by well-publicized accounts of transcript alterations, recruiting violations, grade forging, and the changing of athletes into gut courses which have been chronicled in the popular press (Underwood 1980).

A study by Adler and Adler (1985) looked at the academic progression of college athletes over four years. By observing the same group over this extended period, the researchers were able to demonstrate that athletes typically enter college with optimistic academic goals and attitudes. Faced with long practices, the demands of away game travel, the psychic investments required of competition, group membership in an athletic crowd and its peer pressures to conform to a lifestyle focusing on "a shot at the pros," student-athletes in big-time sports subsequently modified their self-image, typically emphasizing the athlete role. If sport participation had any effect on "character," athletics engendered norms of behavior and values which were counterproductive to academics. Growing detachment from academics often led to giving up once optimistic educational expectations, and, eventually, inferior academic performance might result. Freshmen often believed that by "puttin' time in" they would somehow receive their college degree as they had received their high school diplomas. As one student-athlete put it:

> We got to go two-a-days, get up early as the average student, go to school, then go to practice for three hours like nothing you have ever strained. . . . It's brutal 'cause you so tired. Fatigue is what makes a lot

of those guys say "Chuck it, I'm goin' to sleep!" You don't feel like sittin' there an' readin' a book, an' you not goin' comprehend that much anyway 'cause you so tired. (Adler and Adler 1985:244)

Regardless of academic performances, however, if it can be demonstrated that intercollegiate athletic participation is positively related to social mobility, then rationalization for sport may be made as a facilitator of economic (if not academic) success.

In early research, Husband (1957) studied 1,926 Dartmouth students twenty years after graduation. He found that letter-winners earned approximately $18,000, while nonathletes earned $14,280. Shupp (1952) similarly concluded that Minnesota letter-winners earned $1,360 more than nonletter-winners. Loy (1969) also found considerable occupational mobility among UCLA "Life-Pass Holders," that is, athletes who had earned at least three varsity letters. Otto and Alwin (1977) similarly found that athletic participation had a positive effect on occupational aspirations, attainment, and income. In their study, Sack and Thiel (1979) concluded that while both athlete and nonathlete graduates of Notre Dame experienced considerable upward mobility, first team players were significantly more upwardly mobile than nonfirst-teamers.

Contradicting this literature, however, are studies by Lebar (1973) and Dubois (1978, 1980), which indicated that college athletes were not significantly different from nonathletes in their economic attainment. According to Dubois (1980), college athletics should not be seen generally as a stepping stone to success. After controlling for education, age, ethnicity, academic average, years of work experience and father's occupational prestige in a sample of 160 senior male university athletes and 450 senior male nonathletes, athletic status had no significant effect on the dependent variables of occupational prestige and earnings. For freshman and sophomore males, Blann (1985) found that athletes did not formulate as mature educational and career plans as did nonathletes. While junior and senior athletes and nonathletes were comparable, among the underclassmen fully 28% of these athletes planned professional careers despite the enormous odds against their attainment of professional positions.

In their reviews of research on the subject of college athletic participation's effects, both Snyder and Spreitzer (1978) and Coakley (1978) support the view that the positive effects of sport on upward mobility are probably overrated.

At this time there is little empirical evidence that conclusively

validates the thesis that college athletic participation generally promotes character growth, academic performance, occupational and
economic aspiration of achievement. Like most other social
phenomena, the effects of college sport on individual participants is
mediated by a host of other variables, such as parents' socioeconomic
status, and student's intelligence and gender. Similarly, there is little
proof that participation in college sports is destructive to the individual, that is, that the athlete's school and life performance is
impaired. No rule to this effect is empirically defensible at this time.
There is enough evidence to warrant the conclusion that sport may
positively affect participants, given the proper conditions. But the
general utility of sports to build character, increase academic aspiration, promote occupational mobility, and increase earning power is not
empirically verifiable at this time.

In summary, empirically unsubstantiated claims for the positive
effects of college athletic participation have included the notions that
intercollegiate athletes earn higher grades, make more money, and/or
are more socially mobile than nonathletes. The most ardent supporters
of these notions have asserted that the discipline, physical fitness,
achievement orientation, and mental facility required for athletics are
developed through sport, and that these qualities are then transferred
to other academic, work, and social settings. This view conforms to the
"Interaction Model" (represented in Figure 3).

The Process of Impact by College Athletics on Students

A related theoretical question in higher education is verification of
the actual process through which the college effects changes in general
student characteristics. We have already noted that the process through
which college sport impacts change in athlete characteristics is unclear.
College sport controversies parallel the same controversies on the
wider campus scene. Many of the very same social, economic, and
political arguments in the athletic arena reflect controversies in higher
education on a larger scale. The similarity of this reflection is
demonstrated through brief consideration of the research on college
impacts.

The empirical research on the effects of college on students clearly
indicates that students change in a number of ways in college.
Authoritarianism and religiousness decline, while autonomy, self-
esteem, and political sophistication generally increase (Katz 1976).
But as Astin (1987) has noted, considerable question remains concern-

ing the cause of these changes. Paralleling the question of how athletics impacts on these students, there remains the issue of whether students' general maturation is the change agent or whether the college environment itself effected these changes. Astin's research on over two hundred-thousand students illustrates that the interactionist view (called by him "the industrial model") is oversimplistic, in viewing students as raw material entering the educational factory to be reshaped into a sophisticated graduate. Feldman and Newcomb (1969) have similarly called into question notions that contact with classroom teachers, tests, homework, and readings form the most essential part of the student-shaping process. According to Astin (1968, 1987), seniors' characteristics differ from their freshman profiles because of initial characteristics such as ability, gender and race, the rate of individual maturation, the larger environment independent of the school, factors within the school (such as the colleges' resident or commuter status, public or private governance, large or small, selective or nonselective admissions, single-sex or coed gender) as well as the effects of faculty and the formal curriculum. Therefore, to declare that colleges change students in a certain way is to grossly oversimplify, just as declaring that athletics change students is too simple an assertion. While overgeneralizations such as these may serve as public relations material, they are not valid.

Particularly relevant to claims concerning social mobility and earnings is a view very different from the interaction model. Rather than students or athletes being given the personality, values, and attitudes that will equip them with superior skills for competition in the economic battleground, college or sport participation may label these individuals as successes, the kind of person with whom other high-status individuals should affiliate. This labelling model is presented in Figure 4.

In this view, character is not actually changed through interaction with other students, athletes, teachers, and coaches in the rigors of the university. Instead, the student or athlete is defined as a high-status

Figure 4: The Labelling Model

Student Input		Student Output
Prior Characteristics	Athletic or College Participation	Maturation of Prior Characteristics and Label of Success

individual and labelled as one obviously possessed of superior qualities. Because others see students or athletes as superior, they may be treated more respectfully than others not so labelled. Futhermore, former athletes or students of certain institutions may acquire access to social circles of greater affluence and influence who may sponsor career mobility.[3]

Plainly, the interaction model is more consistent with the conventional wisdom concerning the manner in which higher education does its work. The interaction model proposes that student characteristics are actually altered by sports and academic participation. It is suggested that interaction with teachers, coaches, and other players and students on and off the field — participation in practice, and the physical, mental, and spiritual demands of the university — teach the skills and orientation conducive to success later in life.

We have seen, however, that research does not consistently validate this thesis. Sports participation at the intercollegiate level has not been identified as the primary cause agent behind altered individual personality and values. In addition, whatever changes that take place may be negative, that is, may not contribute to individual autonomy and maturity.

In his extensive review of socialization research, Stevenson (1975) finds no conclusive support for the notion that sports participation itself changes the athlete in any significant way. Similar, conclusions have been reached by Werner and Gotheil (1966), Rushall (1972), and Ogilvie and Tutko (1971). A primary concern of these reviews is the question of the independent or dependent nature of variables such as aspirations, achievement, and discipline. Is it because these variables are possessed in great strength that certain individuals are chosen as athletes, or is it that sports participation actually develops these characteristics? At this time, the weight of the literature appears to indicate the former. Apparently, the qualities associated with athletes are necessary for participation in sports. The more competitive the sport, the greater the strength of attributes required to compete successfully at that level. The more stringent the conditions of play, the fewer the number of athletes who possess these characteristics. It may be that college sports acts more as a filter than a facilitator of specific character attributes, such as discipline. (This relationship is depicted in Figure 5.)

Figure 5: The Filtering Model

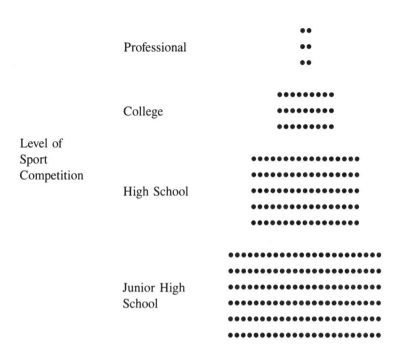

Numbers of qualified athletes = •••••

If indeed sport acts as a filter rather than a facilitator, questions concerning the propriety of intercollegiate sports in American education are appropriate. Despite the lack of evidence indicating sports participation as "character building," however, one must not out of hand condemn sport as dysfunctional. The sport that filters out may serve a function that parallels an important responsibility the school must fulfill for any society — the separation of elites from masses.

In different societies there is varying stress placed upon each of the numerous roles fulfilled by the school. Two of these functions are the school as "cultivator" and the school as "miner." In some societies, the high status of elite is more widely accepted than it is given the egalitarianism woven through American culture. English conceptions of the purpose of higher education, for example, plainly recognize the need for mining, that is, separating the "precious" from the "less precious," separating the elite necessary to lead society from those less capable. American egalitarianism, however, restricts such obvious elitism in our schools. Schools are seen more as the cultivator of raw materials. From humble seed grows flourishing life, given the proper nourishment over extended periods of time. Even in American society, however, there is the need to locate the elite, the more capable, the leaders.

In a very real sense, American higher education serves this allocation function. Alwin (1976), Sewell and Hauser (1975), and Astin (1968) have empirically demonstrated the importance of preexisting student characteristics for success in college. Students will achieve in school and hence be deemed superior largely on the basis of pre-existing qualities. School becomes a demonstration ground for ability, perhaps more so than a cultivator of all talent native to students.

American sports and the college itself may serve as filters to locate those with superior psychological and physical attributes, rather than as cultivators of those attributes in all would-be participants. As we have seen from the review of the empirical literature, to claim sports as a cultivator is, at this time, a view based less on fact than fancy. It is also a claim that may undermine acceptance of the legitimate filtering function of sport — a function consistent with the needs of society, and a role of higher education.

We have seen from the literature that there is little evidence to indicate that sports participation itself builds character, raises academic performance, or increases educational aspirations. If there is justification for intercollegiate sport based upon benefits to the individual, that rationale may lie in the labelling of athletes as possessors of superior traits. The labelling of individuals as bright or as leaders may then lead to their allocation to highly rewarded positions and the economic gain often associated with those positions. If, because of the biases of management, however, the talent-labelling process in higher education is undermined because of racial or other non-role-related criteria, then this justification for intercollegiate sport is to this degree less valid. If college sport is to function consistently with the mission of higher education as rational allocator of talent to necessary roles in society, then non-job-related criteria such as race or gender should have nothing to do with the allocation decision.

The Collegiate Institution as the Prime Beneficiary of Athletics

While some have justified intercollegiate sport because of its supposed benefits for individual participants, the suggestion has also been put forward that athletics were made a formal part of the university primarily to serve the educational institution. While we have seen that almost any sweeping statement concerning the diverse collection of schools that comprise American education merely tends to overgeneralize, it is possible in certain instances to address universities in the "big-time" sport category as a group. While some have suggested that athletics was incorporated within the responsibilities of the school in order to educate the newly entering masses of students at the turn of the twentieth century — if, indeed, the primary beneficiary of sport was to be the student — one may ask, then, why would college administration devote so much more of its scarce resources to intercollegiate sport than to intramural athletics? If college presidents sought to literally emulate the English public schools, why would they have not mandated many levels of athletic competition, a sport for every student, as opposed to diverting funds to building the large stadiums and hiring the athletic staffs to service only an elite few varsity athletes?

A strong argument can be made for the claim that the prime beneficiary of big-time athletics at the turn of the century was to be the university or college itself. The organization's needs superceded the needs of the individual student. Mass spectator sport supposedly benefitted the institution in various ways. By drawing in needed funds, it has been argued, intercollegiate sport performs "good work" for the organization, which requires funds to fuel the academic machine. Although purists may decry the inclusion within the formal structure of higher education of athletic programs whose prime purpose is not the education of the individual, such claims are based more on traditional European conceptions of the university whose material welfare could be assumed and less upon the American variant with its low economic confidence. Due to economic and enrollment difficulties, the derived organizational goal of survival must be a primary consideration for American higher education. Business concerns have had to be a priority for educational institutions.[4]

If we may assume the legitimacy of money-making operations as part of the formal structure of American higher education, then let us in the next section evaluate the validity of the thesis that intercollegiate sport serves the economic survival necessities of the institution. Does college sport perform "good works"? Does it provide funds necessary for brick and mortar and the operations of the academic institution?

The Economics of Intercollegiate Sport

> It appears from the record that there is a "tug of war" going over this plaintiff. The academics are pulling toward higher standards of achievement for all students while the athletic departments must tug in the direction of fielding teams who contribute to paying a substantial share of the university's budget. (United States Judge Miles W. Lord, quoted in Wehrwein 1982:5)

Some sport leaders openly acknowledge the importance of financial considerations in intercollegiate sport. According to Don Canham, Athletic Director at the University of Michigan:

> My job is poorly described by the term "athletic director." What I am is a sports promoter. . . . Either I promote our sports program solidly into the black or I'm out of a job (quoted in Weiner 1973:42)

Bo Schembechler, football coach at Michigan, clearly knows his objectives.

> Don (Canham) gave me two orders. One, produce a winner, and two, fill the stadium. I figure if I do the first, the second will happen automatically. (Weiner 1973:42)

Neither is Ted Bredehoft, Athletic Director at Wichita State, any less clear about his responsibilities. According to him, "We must be, in everything we do, profit-conscious and results-oriented" (Middleton March 3, 1982:6).

The student-controlled and student-financed sport of the nineteenth century has given way to a system of formalized institutional operation through full-time athletic directors and coaching staffs — a situation almost unique to the United States (Bennett, Howell, and Simri 1975). Such an organizational structure has developed to oversee the expenditure and receipt of sums of money considered too important for students to control. As early as 1903, Yale generated $106,000 from football — a sum equal to one-eighth the combined income for the university. Clearly, such amounts were significant to institutional finances. But what is the current economic condition of college sport? While it has been estimated that Patrick Ewing's $48,000 four-year athletic scholarship returned $12 million by tripling attendance at Georgetown (*Chronicle of Higher Education*, January 8, 1986:29), what of the hundreds of other college sport programs?

In almost all classes of men's intercollegiate competition, average total expenses are greater than revenues generated by sport ticket sales, student activities fees, guarantees, contributions, media payments, and government support (see Table 1). The size of average deficits in 1985 range from $53,000 in Division III nonfootball-playing schools (Class F) to $300,000 for Division II football colleges (Class B). Only at the big-time Division I football level (Class A) do average revenues exceed costs, with a surplus of $192,000in revenues.

Another way of looking at these costs is to examine costs relative to the number of intercollegiate athletes served. In Division I football (Class A), intercollegiate costs of $4,609,000 divided by the 385 athletes playing during fiscal year 1985 equals a cost of $12,947 per athlete served by intercollegiate sport, as opposed to the $9,500 per athlete cost of big-time sport in 1981 — an increase of $3,400 in four years. These costs can be compared to the $1,040 spent to field male athletes at Division III nonfootball institutions (Class F) ($182,000 divided by 175 participating athletes). In 1985, salaries and wages constituted the largest single expense accounting for 27% to 52% of total costs. Grants in aid represent between 6% and 30% of total expenses, but never exceeded salaries in any class of institution. (See Table 2.)

Women's athletics may be characterized as deficit-producing in almost every class of competition (see Table 3). There is a consistent relationship between the size of athletic program and the amount of the deficit. At the elite levels of play in 1985, Division I female sports lost an average of $511,000 at schools with football (Class A) and $188,000 at schools without football (Class D). Deficits are markedly smaller at the Division II level (Class B and E).

The stakes are certainly high for the Division I school. Apparently, the revenue-producing potential of the gridiron, with its large stadiums, far exceeds other sports. The investment that must be committed to finance the costly game of football, however, averaged $1,780,000, and consumed 39% of the total men's athletic budget of $4,609,000 in 1985 (Raiborn 1986:37).

Perhaps the most significant of all figures for the administrative leaders of higher education are those derived from combining average revenues and expenses for both men's and women's sport, yielding the average total costs and financial benefits of intercollegiate athletics (Raiborn 1986:50, 56). (See Table 4.)

Table 1: Comparative Averages for Total Revenues and Expenses in Men's Intercollegiate Athletic Programs by Class

Fiscal Years 1978–1985
(in Thousands)

Average Operating Results by Respondent Category	1978	1979	1980	1981	1982	1983	1984	1985
Class A Institutions (a)								
Total revenues	$ 2,368	$ 2,581	$ 2,959	$ 3,391	$ 3,533	$ 4,175	$ 4,597	$ 4,801
Total expenses	−2,238	−2,460	−2,875	−3,243	−3,491	−3,920	−4,271	−4,609
Implied profit (b)	130	121	84	148	42	255	326	192
Class B Institutions								
Total revenues	$ 164	$ 182	$ 212	$ 248	$ 288	$ 317	$ 359	$ 419
Total expenses	−287	−322	−355	−392	−510	−555	−609	−719
Implied deficit (c)	(123)	(140)	(143)	(144)	(222)	(238)	(250)	(300)
Class C Institutions								
Total revenues	$ 40	$ 45	$ 51	$ 56	$ 34	$ 43	$ 44	$ 71
Total expenses	−188	−201	−221	−249	−232	−262	−288	−339
Implied deficit	(148)	(156)	(170)	(193)	(198)	(219)	(244)	(268)
Class D Institutions								
Total revenues	$ 277	$ 343	$ 384	$ 476	$ 395	$ 454	$ 470	$ 598
Total expenses	−410	−476	−563	−631	−579	−625	−692	−878
Implied deficit	(133)	(133)	(179)	(155)	(184)	(171)	(222)	(280)

Average Operating Results by Respondent Category

	1978	1979	1980	1981	1982	1983	1984	1985
Class E Institutions								
Total revenues	$ 74	$ 77	$ 86	$ 102	$ 161	$ 182	$ 206	$ 282
Total expenses	−163	−166	−180	−232	−278	−314	−346	−418
Implied deficit	(89)	(89)	(94)	(130)	(117)	(132)	(140)	(136)
Class F Institutions								
Total revenues	$ 24	$ 26	$ 29	$ 30	$ 87	$ 78	$ 83	$ 129
Total expenses	−106	−121	−129	−144	−127	−134	−147	−182
Implied deficit	(82)	(95)	(100)	(114)	(40)	(56)	(64)	(53)

(a) Class A, B, C institutions refers to Division I, II, III (respectively) football playing NCAA level schools. Class D, E, F institutions refers to Division I, II, III (respectively) non-football playing NCAA level schools in which basketball is typically the most popular intercollegiate sport.

(b) *Profit* is used to describe an excess of revenues over expenses.

(c) *Deficit* is used to describe an excess of expenses over revenues.

Source: Raiborn 1986:50.

Table 2: Expenses by Object as a Percentage of Total Expenses in Intercollegiate Sports by Class

Fiscal Years 1977–1985

Respondent Category	Grants-in-Aid	Guarantees and Options	Salaries and Wages	Team and Other Travel	Equipment and Supplies	All Other Expenses	Total Expenses
Class A Institutions (a)							
Fiscal year 1985	17%	8%	30%	12%	5%	28%	100%
Fiscal year 1981	16	11	30	13	5	25	100
Fiscal year 1977	18	12	28	12	5	25	100
Class B Institutions							
Fiscal year 1985	29	1	29	14	8	19	100
Fiscal year 1981	26	5	23	15	8	23	100
Fiscal year 1977	29	2	32	14	9	14	100
Class C Institutions							
Fiscal year 1985	9	*	39	17	12	22	99
Fiscal year 1981	10	1	38	18	10	23	100
Fiscal year 1977	14	2	39	15	15	15	100
Class D Institutions							
Fiscal year 1985	27	3	29	14	6	21	100
Fiscal year 1981	25	3	32	17	6	17	100
Fiscal year 1977	27	4	27	13	6	23	100

Respondent Category	Grants-in-Aid	Guarantees and Options	Salaries and Wages	Team and Other Travel	Equipment and Supplies	All Other Expenses	Total Expenses
Class E Institutions							
Fiscal year 1985	30	2	32	15	7	14	100
Fiscal year 1981	26	1	30	16	9	18	100
Fiscal year 1977	28	1	34	14	8	15	100
Class F Institutions							
Fiscal year 1985	6	*	47	16	11	20	100
Fiscal year 1981	*	*	52	16	14	18	100
Fiscal year 1977	9	*	44	12	11	24	100

*Less than 1 percent of total expenses.

(a) Class A, B, C institutions refers to Division I, II, III (respectively) football playing NCAA level schools. Class D, E, F institutions refers to Division I, II, III (respectively) non-football playing NCAA level schools in which basketball is typically the most popular sport.

Source: Raiborn 1986:34.

Table 3: Total Revenues and Expenses of Women's Intercollegiate Athletic Programs by Class

Fiscal Years 1982–1985
(in Thousands)

Average Financial Results by Respondent Category (a)	*1982*	*1983*	*1984*	*1985*
Class A Institutions (b)				
Average total revenues	$ 105	$ 116	$ 117	$ 129
Average total expenses	−475	−526	−592	−640
Expenses paid by men's program	41%	39%	41%	42%
Class B Institutions				
Average total revenues	$ 47	$ 51	$ 57	$ 75
Average total expenses	−105	−118	−139	−155
Expenses paid by men's program	11%	11%	10%	6%
Class C Institutions				
Average total revenues	$ 3	$ 4	$ 4	$ 8
Average total expenses	−42	−47	−56	−65
Expenses paid by men's program	0%	0%	0%	0%
Class D Institutions				
Average total revenues	$ 28	$ 22	$ 18	$ 18
Average total expenses	−180	−210	−203	−206
Expenses paid by men's program	3%	3%	3%	9%
Class E Institutions				
Average total revenues	$ 119	$ 121	$ 115	$ 125
Average total expenses	−94	−113	−124	−148
Expenses paid by men's program	0%	0%	0%	0%
Class F Institutions				
Average total revenues	$ 54	$ 73	$ 42	$ 49
Average total expenses	−31	−39	−40	−42
Expenses paid by men's program	0%	0%	0%	0%

(a) Revenues exclude any direct or indirect support provided by the men's athletics program.

(b) Class A, B, C institutions refers to Division I, II, III (respectively) football playing NCAA level schools. Class D, E, F institutions refers to Division I, II, III (respectively) non-football playing NCAA level schools in which basketball is typically the most popular sport.

Source: Raiborn 1986:56.

Table 4: Total Expenses and Revenues for Men's and Women's Intercollegiate Sport, 1985

(in Thousands)

| Class | Women's Sports | | Men's Sports | | Total Difference |
	Expenses	Revenues	Expenses	Revenues	
A	$640	$129	$4,609	$4,801	−$319
B	155	75	719	419	−380
C	65	8	339	71	−325
D	206	18	878	598	−468
E	148	125	418	282	−159
F	42	49	182	129	−46

Source: Raiborn 1986:9, 56.

While male athletics played at the Class A football level of competition was the sole nondeficit situation, looking at the total costs of intercollegiate athletics, we see consistent deficits from total costs exceeding revenues in every class. While these figures are averages, and while there are specific institutions that are exceptions — the financial difficulties generally facing intercollegiate athletics are clearly demonstrated.

Obviously, the "doctrine of good works," the claim that intercollegiate sports produces income necessary for the welfare of the entire educational institution is untrue for the overwhelming majority of colleges and universities in America.[5] While the "doctrine of good works" may be used to justify sport's existence on college campuses in South Bend, Indiana, and Ann Arbor, Michigan, this rationale just does not hold true at almost all other American institutions. Intercollegiate athletics costs each general student more money than the student benefits directly from sport's gate receipts and media revenues. Even Notre Dame, which draws more than $4 million from football and basketball concessions and tickets sales, has been forced to economize. With growing costs and the outlays necessary to finance nonrevenue-producing sports, Notre Dame's 1980–1981 budget was a mere $29,000 in the black (Middleton, *Chronicle of Higher Education*, March 3, 1982:5, 6). Increasingly, schools are faced with the economic realities of costly intercollegiate sport. Recently, such

schools as the University of Colorado, Yale, Colorado State, and
Berkeley have been forced to reduce the number of their varsity sports.
Southern Methodist University has dropped baseball, and it has placed
golf on a nonscholarship basis in order to save the school $150,000
(Paul 1980).

Still, the argument may be made that collegiate sport serves to
draw alumni donations. The total $588 million of alumni contributions
for 1975–1976 equaled only 1.3% of the total higher educational
expenses of $44.8 billion (Hanford 1979), and the value of all private
gifts averaged only 5.3% of all revenues (*Chronicle of Higher Education*, April 1, 1987:2). Yet for some schools this money is crucial
(Hanford 1974). By maintaining former students' allegiance, it is suggested that the "doctrine of good works" may indeed be validated.
Indirect incomes generated by athletic team successes may be received
in the form of alumni contributions. The research on this subject once
again demonstrates the limits of generalizations concerning the utility
of intercollegiate athletics.

Early studies seemed to indicate little, if any, correlation between
alumni giving and athletic success. Marts (1934) found an endowment
increase of 105% in 16 schools which were building up their football
program. Sixteen other schools which had no football programs,
however, demonstrated an endowment increase of 126% during the
same 1921–1930 period. Felix Springer (Hanford 1974) found that for
the 151 schools that dropped football between 1939 and 1974 there was
little effect on alumni contributions. Despite initial concerns, there was
little significant economic deprivation caused by the deemphasis of
football. In fact, there were some cases where increased alumni giving
was positively correlated with the demise of football programs that had
consistently losing records. Budig (1976) found little statistical
evidence to support the notion that winning football and basketball
teams are positively related to increased alumni contributions at the 79
colleges and universities studied. Research by Sigelmand and Carter
(1979) and Sack and Watkins (1980) have come to similar conclusions.
In a more recent study, Gaski and Etzel (1987) looked at data from 99
universities, predominantly from NCAA Division IA, for the years
1970–1979. Using the basketball and football won/lost ratios as
independent variables, and alumni contributions, nonalumni contributions, as a proportion of alumni invited to donate, and money donated
per contributing alumni, the researchers found no apparent connection
between university major sport performance and donations.

A Study by Frey (1981) may shed some light on reasons for the apparent lack of correlation between athletic team success and alumni contributions. From a random sample of 52,000 alumni of Washington State University, Frey found little evidence for the notion that athletics are of preeminent importance to alumni.

In his sample of leaders and alumni, the items "recruitment of athletes" and "build and maintain athletic facilities and programs" were rated of less importance than the development of academic programs, facilities, and salary of faculty. It may be, then, that traditional academic matters are of greater importance to graduates than college athletics. Although alumni leadership held athletic concerns in higher regard than the general alumni body, even they ranked sports as of secondary importance.[6]

While most early research could not arrive at a generalizable statement concerning the relationship between alumni contributions and athletic success, a study by Brooker and Klastorin (1981) indicates the significance of football and basketball records to the balance sheets of particular types of schools. Reanalyzing the data of Sigelman and Carter (1979), Brooker and Klastorin classified schools according to their athletic conference, public versus private status, and size.

Table 5: Items of "Highest Priority" as Ranked by the Alumni General Body and Leader's Group

Concern	Alumni Rank	Alumni Leaders Rank
Maintaining traditional academic programs	1	1
Faculty salary increases	2	3
Building and maintaining classroom facilities	3	2
Expanding traditional academic programs	4	7
Financial assistance to students in need	5	6
Funding programs of social importance	6	8
Special programs for disadvantaged	7	11
Recruitment of athletes	8	5
Building and maintaining athletic facilities and programs	9	4
Special activities such as music and drama	10	9.5
Recreation facilities for all students	11	9.5
Recruitment of minorities	12	12

Source: Frey 1981:57.

In the Big 10 Conference, the percentage of football games won was significantly related to the percentage of alumni who made some donation, and to the average gift made to the annual fund. In the Ivy League, the percentage of football victories was positively related to the size of gift per alumnus and to the percentage of the alumni who contributed money. In large private universities, percentage of football victories was related to the size of the donation made to the annual fund. In high-quality private schools, football success rates were positively related to the size of gift per alumnus, to the percentage of alumni donors, and to the size of donations made to the annual fund (Brooker and Klastorin 1981).

They found no significant relationships between athletic records and alumni giving for the major schools that were not members of athletic conferences, small public universities, and those only emphasizing basketball. But significant findings were discovered for other schools. Brooker and Klastorin summarize that athletic performance is indeed related to alumni contributions, *but* this relationship is dependent upon a number of "institutional factors" (1981:746). Athletic success is more important for contributions directed toward private as opposed to public and to religiously oriented schools.

The combined weight of research on the subject of athletic success and donations does not permit the generalization that football and basketball victory is necessary for the economic health of higher education. While early studies of numerous institutions have found little to support the "doctrine of good works," when considered against the more sophisticated analysis by Brooker and Klastorin (1981), it appears that the strength of the relationship between football/basketball prowess and alumni contributions is dependent upon the situation of the particular institution.

Summary

In previous sections, the matter of rationalization has been examined. Intercollegiate athletics, like all programs within the higher educational organization, must be justified as within the roles, responsibilities, and methods deemed appropriate by the task environment. Students, alumni, faculty, education critics, and legislators, among others, must be convinced that athletics fit within their general understanding of what the American college and university should do. Only with an assumption of the legitimacy of the institution will the organization receive the resources of students, money, and status necessary for survival.

Empirical research that has been conducted to evaluate the rationalizations for intercollegiate sport has been examined. These justifications have been that (1) sport builds character, (2) sport participation is conducive to academic performance, aspiration, and social-occupational mobility, and (3) sport economically benefits institutions of higher education. We have seen that although a particular sort of sports character building may exist, questions remain about whether sports builds character or whether it serves as a filter. The effect of sport participation on school performance and expectations, as well as mobility in later life, is largely dependent upon other individual factors; the process through which mobility occurs may fit less the interactive model — that the athlete develops positive qualities through practice, competition, coaches, and peer interaction — than a labelling model where the elite status of sports participant is generalized into a leadership label applied to other social situations. We have also seen that the validity of the "doctrine of good works" is once again dependent upon a host of situational factors in each institution.

In the face of inconclusive research, it is clear that at this time, the rationalization for college sport based upon individual and institutional benefits is founded on very limited empirical evidence. While benefits to the individual or the school may actually exist, research employing inappropriate models of the effects of sport, and oversimplified analysis, have not to date demonstrated that intercollegiate athletics should be part of the American college because of its beneficial effects. Consistent with the pluralism from which American education arose, there exist multiple models of curriculum, governance, types of students, and holders of resources. To generalize the rationalizations of character, mobility, and economics across all institutions, populations, and environments is foolish.

Intercollegiate athletics does not exist in a vacuum at the university. Simple truths, too often overlooked, sometimes offer the greatest insight. The very same diversity of opinion concerning the effects of the organization, controversies concerning the model through which changes (if any) are effected, the appropriateness of methods employed and goals sought in athletics mirror similar concerns in the university. Does sport or the university liberalize or bureaucratize? Do the organizations mold and educate, or do they filter and allocate? Is sport, and the university that supports it, too business- and ends-oriented? Intercollegiate sport provides the spectator a ready seat to observe the very same controversies that exist on a larger, though less visible, scale on the campus outside the sports arena.

The Condition of Higher Education and Athletics in America

In this chapter, we will look closely at some of the major problems facing the academic world and their particular manifestation in sports. Racism, sexism, unethical behavior, and external intrusions into the autonomy of the college provide parallel challenges for higher education and those concerned with athletics.

Racism, Sexism and Unethical Behavior

All societies are faced with the problem of allocating the most talented individuals for positions of leadership. While in early societies, blood succession or the will of God may have served as legitimate criteria for selection, positions of high reward in contemporary society require selection processes more consistent with a modern world view that demands specific reasons and qualifications for choosing those who will be carrying out leadership functions.

Both the college and its sports have been considered as means of talent location. The most able (and some less able, for that matter) are labelled as more capable, and thereby chosen for positions of responsibility and high reward. The filtering that occurs, however, if it is not to be functional only in the sense that it allocates those with superficially elite characteristics, must be based upon objective merit, skills, and dispositions required for leadership. Only then will it fulfill the allocation function of higher education unbiased by social class, race, or sexual concerns. If schools are to locate individuals with the unique skills and dispositions thought appropriate for the particular upper-level positions of society, then the college or university must seek to locate these individuals without regard for nonrole-specific criteria. If, for example, discipline, perserverance, aggressiveness, and managerial skills are deemed appropriate for positions of business leadership, it is imperative for schools to locate these individuals based upon their possession of these role-specific traits and to allocate them to those positions. Criteria unrelated to role performance should not enter into the calculus in the perfectly fair institution of higher education. In the following sections, we will look at the behavior of college sport and general personnel. From this review, it will become evident that college athletics exhibits the very same problems that confront the larger institution that supports it.

The Black College Athlete

As studies by Williams and Youssef (1972, 1975), Chu and Segrave (1980), and others have indicated, nontask-relevant criteria have apparently been applied to the selection of intercollegiate athletes and coaches. According to the college coaches interviewed by Williams and Youssef, white players are characterized by thinking ability, mental comprehension, and reliability. Blacks were stereotyped as possessing superior physical speed, physical quickness, and high achievement motivation. Because of these stereotyped racial differences, white players were usually assigned to positions of leadership (that is, to positions of quarterback and offensive center). Chu and Segrave found support for the racial stereotyping thesis in college basketball. White ball players more often were assigned to the leadership position of guard — the position that is overwhelmingly considered to lead to appointment as basketball coach after the athlete's playing career is over. And among all players that were assigned to guard during their playing days, white guards compared to black guards were fifteen times more likely to reach coaching positions. From a 71% return of 380 questionnaires mailed to half the 726 NCAA basketball member schools, it was also found that 92% of Division I, 86% of Division II, and 95% of Division III coaches were white. These figures are more striking when compared to the 33% of 1,977 college basketball players that were black. Only 2% of all coaching staffs had a black head coach and a white assistant coach, while 17% of the teams had a white head coach and a black assistant coach. Edwards (1982) has noted that among the basketball teams playing in 1980 at the highest levels of competition, Division IA, there was but one head football coach who was black, despite the 90% turnover in coaching positions during the 1970s.

Clearly, leadership opportunities for blacks are not as plentiful as for whites in intercollegiate sport. That this situation is the result of the smaller number of blacks who have completed their college playing careers and who therefore have contributed to a smaller pool of potential coaches appears unlikely, since black sport participation rates have generally increased during the last twenty years. This is especially so at the big-time level of play. Covert racism cannot be discounted as a factor. But other variables also enter into the situation.

Since college coaching positions are often associated with college degree requirements, especially in the less competitive Divisions II and III, the lower black athlete graduation rates (relative to white athlete graduation rate) will reduce the eligible pool of potential coaches. Shapiro (1984) notes a 17% lower graduation rate for blacks compared to whites at Michigan State University, while Underwood (1980) cites a general black athlete graduation rate one-half or less that of white athletes. Edwards (1982) estimates that of all black athletes awarded sport scholarships, 75% do not graduate.

Disparities between black and white intercollegiate sport experience and positions are indicative not only of differences in the sports they play but also of differences in the student experience outside the sport arena. An athletic scholarship does not ensure graduation, nor does enrollment at college indicate readiness for college-level work. The black student entering the predominantly white culture of higher education may be well prepared to play sport but ill prepared for academic performance. The black student who already suffers from educational disadvantage may be sought for the institution's athletic program. Basketball star Chris Washburn was admitted to North Carolina State with a combined SAT score of 470 — only 10 points above the minimum of 460; at the University of Southern California between 1970 and 1980, the athletic department was authorized to admit 330 students that fell below normal admissions standards (Waicukauski 1982).

As former Clemson basketball coach Tates Locke (1982) has chronicled, believing that the necessary social and educational supports exist. Upon matriculation, however, the athlete finds "educational support" whose primary purpose is the maintenance of eligibility as opposed to the student's educational gain. Under the liberal banner, minorities have been admitted to the university so that they may better their lot. Without necessary support, however, graduation rates evidence the lack of academic success of these students. Out of the freshman classes of 1976–1978 at North Carolina State University, only 12 of 80 football and none of the 15 basketball players graduated (Asher 1985). Flexible admissions policies so popular during the 1960s and 1970s as a means of getting minorities into higher education have been abused by coaches more interested in the athletic ability of black athletes than the athletes' academic preparation for their probable future outside of sport.

As Underwood (1980) has pointed out permission for poor academic performance in college is given by athletic personnel. The coach at the University of New Mexico arranged for illegal transfer credits from Oxnard College; an "academic advisor" at the University of Southern California was involved in the phony enrollment of twenty-eight athletes in Speech Communications 380 — a course open only to members of the debating team.

The downgrading of academic performance by black athletes extends beyond that, in a system of higher education that is not secure financially, in student enrollments, nor sure of the confidence of the American public. It is a higher educational system that craves exposure, the sort of visibility that labels an institution as in the "big leagues." And it is an educational system in a society where athletic success gains more exposure than academic accomplishments. Black athletes like Billy Harris learn early in their college careers that they are important people, because the athlete helps with the school organization's critical relations with the public — important enough to have a probable "F" deleted in Billy Harris' case because he was an athlete (Underwood 1980).

These athletes dream of big-money professional careers. Emulating the primary role models in the black community, they often place education on the bench. Bill McGill did just that. A high school star in Los Angeles, and the University of Utah's leading scorer at 38.8 points per game, he was taken as number one by the Chicago Zephyrs of the National Basketball Association. Given a $5,000 bonus, and $17,000 for the first and $10,000 for the second year, Bill McGill by age 28 was earning $84 per week working for a janitorial service just ten years after the beginning of his professional career. Bill McGill was unaware of the statistics: of seven hundred thousand high school basketball players and fifteen thousand college players, only two hundred are drafted by the National Basketball Association. Of the fifty or so that make a team, the average playing career is 3.4 seasons.

There are fewer than one thousand blacks making their livings as professional athletes. The odds, therefore, of any one of the 3 million black youths age 13–22 making his living as a professional athlete are worse than 20,000 to 1.

At least from the 1950s the belief has been prevalent that sport demonstrates the best of the American Dream. It was thought that the racial integration of sports would serve as the cutting edge in slashing the last constraints of segregation. Integration in professional baseball initiated by Jackie Robinson, by J.C. Caroline at the University of Illinois, and by Prentice Gautt at the University of Oklahoma would spill over into American society generally. What the public saw during the turbulent first years of school integration, however, was evidence that the campus was less a leader of integration than it was the site of continued segregationist efforts. Not to be upstaged by George Wallace's stand at the University of Alabama, Marvin Griffin, Governor of Georgia, requested that Georgia Tech reject its Sugar Bowl bid because of the University of Pittsburgh's black player, Bobby Grier. After the governor's request was dismissed by the University, the Georgia Board of Regents banned its schools from future bowl games in the South that did not follow segregationist laws and customs (Grundman 1985).

The popular American view of sport as integrated was jolted by the 1968 boycott of the Mexico Olympic Games. Led by Harry Edwards, the boycott protested the condition of blacks in American society. In Edward's view, the black athlete was used in the international arena to extol the virtues of the American political-economic system, but that success enjoyed by black athletes was not mirrored in American society.

In retrospect, the Mexico City Boycott and public outrage at the rationale for the protest illustrates the degree to which the black experience was misunderstood. Grundman (1985) contends that the dominant liberal belief of the era arose from the assumption that equalizing access to opportunity would lead to legitimate success or failure in the competitive economic and political marketplace. By providing access to higher education, for example, liberals could congratulate themselves with providing the opportunity for black students to succeed or fail academically on their own accord. After all, success handed on a silver spoon ran counter to the American meritocratic ideal.

More recent examination of this assumption shows its naivete. The economic, political, and education marketplace, with all its competition, may be less color-blind than was assumed in the 1950s and 1960s. Evaluations of performance must be judged relative to some criteria, and more often than not those criteria are white middle-class ones. Certainly, the educational structure mirrors the value system that supports it. Today, it is recognized that for many disadvantaged black youngsters to do well in school, support is necessary to acquire the skills necessary for success in an unfamiliar culture. While in the arena the black athlete may succeed with sport's more objective evaluation system. But that same black athlete may require educational and social support to do well in the dominant white cultural system of the university, where evaluation is a good deal more complex and conducted with more hidden agendas than the ability to run fast, hit well, or put the ball through a hoop.

Proposition 48, which upon its passage by the NCAA convention became rule 5-1-J, is an attempt to provide standards across the flexible chaos of thousands of college admissions requirements and it provides a ready example of future problems facing intercollegiate athletic administration. Considering the institutional autonomy of American colleges and universities, the passage of regulations defining minimal high school grade point average, SAT/ACT scores, and core curriculum courses is somewhat remarkable. When applied to incoming classes, however, these standards would disqualify a large percentage of black athletes who eventually graduate. In the NCAA-sponsored study, undertaken after the protests of black college presidents, it was found that applying rule 5-1-J standards to the sixteen thousand Division I freshmen receiving athletic scholarships in 1977–1982 would have disqualified 69% of blacks and 54% of whites who went on to graduate (Farrell, September 5, 1984:1, 31). In a survey of Division I membership conducted after the first year of 5-1-J implementation, it was found that of 424 athletes meeting the core curriculum and GPA requirements, but not standardized test requirements, 299 were black and 104 were white (*NCAA News*, April 29, 1987). Predominantly black colleges have been the most severely affected, with 34% of all Mid-Eastern Athletic Conference and 27% of all Southwestern Athletic Conference freshman student-athletics ineligible (Becker and Weinberg 1986).

As black athletes have found themselves having to succeed in a culture dominated by white leadership and standards, women have similarly had to work within a sports system controlled by men. As there are questions concerning the composition of leadership and the allocation of rewards to black student-athletes, so too are there questions concerning the criteria employed for the selection of women's sports leaders and the disbursement of athletic funds.

Women's College Athletics

Although the first recorded intercollegiate contest for women was a basketball game between Stanford and Berkeley in 1896, most female athletic activity took some form other than the highly competitive, organized structure of men's intercollegiate sport. Early women's sport was typically the responsibility of physical educators who were opposed to the commercial excesses of male spectator-oriented inter-collegiate athletics and/or who feared for the development of unfeminine traits (such as aggressiveness) or damage to female reproductive capacities in the face of overly strenuous activity.

By 1936, only 17% of 77 schools in one survey reported female varsity athletics, while 74% reported "telegraphic meets" (schools wiring results of some sport performance to other schools for comparison) and 70% reported "playdays," which were a form of competition where women from participating schools were pooled to produce teams composed of players from many schools (Gerber 1975; Acosta and Carpenter 1985). These early women's sport leaders saw their mission as preserving the participant orientation of athletics so that the benefits of moderately strenuous sport could be extended to females. Sport activity was rationalized as being a physically healthful activity for women so long as competition was controlled.[1]

Until 1971, there was no organization to oversee women's sport which paralleled the NCAA in its national scope. In that year, the Commission on Intercollegiate Athletics for Women was formed. Eventually, the organization became the Association for Intercollegiate Athletics for Women — a group which even to its last moments prior to the takeover of women's sport by the NCAA was dominated by physical educators firmly committed to safeguarding women from the abuses apparent everywhere evident in men's sport. With increasing pressure from feminist and education groups, the NCAA, heretofore solely governors of men's college sport, engaged in dialogue with the AIAW to coordinate the governance of all intercollegiate athletics. In the face of continued AIAW efforts to enforce federal Title IX legislation, however, the NCAA at its 1980 convention voted to offer women's championship competitions. Given the inducement of expenses-paid competitions, few of the major powers in women's sport could resist the NCAA championship format, which required NCAA membership and adherence to its rules. After the loss of an antitrust suit in February 1983, the AIAW all but ceased to exist, having had its responsibilities and membership taken over by the more financially powerful NCAA.

Title IX, which was passed in 1972, was the catalyst for change in women's sport. With its threatened cutoff of federal funds to those institutions discriminating in their educational services on the basis of gender, the legislation had a major effect on sport opportunities for women. Whereas in 1973 the average number of college sports for women was 2.5 per school, five years later the average number was 6.5 (Acosta and Carpenter 1985). Whereas women's athletic budgets constituted only 2% of the $500 million spent per year on intercollegiate sport prior to Title IX, Raiborn's (1982) NCAA-sponsored study indicates that women's college sport 1981 expenses ranged from 12% to 31% of college male athletic budgets.

While Title IX has been credited with a rapid alteration of the intercollegiate athletic scene, beyond prohibiting unequal institutional funds allocation on the basis of gender it is hardly revolutionary. In fact, Title IX does little to question the fundamental assumption of intercollegiate sport — the appropriateness of the link between sport and the educational institution. The legislation also does not raise questions about the legitimacy of mass spectator sports, since it does not require the allocation of equal funds on anything like a per capita basis, which would lead to the expansion of intramural sports. Title IX does nothing to question the convention of males playing against other males, while women play only against women. Instead, the legislation only requires that money for meals be the same; that uniforms, equipment, and dressing facilities be similar and that transportation be of the same quality. Evaluation of program quality is based on the existing components of the male sport system. Instead of requiring standardized tests to assess the educational qualities of sport, Title IX implementing guidelines essentially measure the quality of women's sport programs relative to male sport standards. Do the women play as many games as the men? Are women given an equal number of scholarships? The very basis for no-need scholarships is left unquestioned. Furthermore, the sport establishment in higher education was left intact through the exception of big-time football from many of the enactment policies.

While the popular impression may be that Title IX has considerably altered intercollegiate sport, Carpenter and Acosta (1985) have done empirical research on some of the leadership ramifications of the legislation. Their study, covered the period from one year preceding the mandatory compliance date of 1977 to four years after compliance was supposed to have been enforced in 1982. Data were gathered from more than two-thirds of all AIAW and NCAA schools fielding women's teams. Some of the findings between the years of 1977 and 1982 are listed below:

(1). There has been an increase in the number of sports offered on each campus for women, from 5.61 to 6.59 sports.

(2). There has been an increase of 13.8% in the total of varsity and junior varsity women's teams.

(3). The percentage of women coaching women's teams has actually decreased from 58.2% to 52.4%.

(4). At the entry level for coaching women's teams, that is, at the junior varsity level, there has been a 5.7% decrease in the number of women's teams.

(5). More than 80% of women's athletic programs are under the supervision of a male athletic director (80.1% of all athletic directors in 1979–1980).

(6). There is no female involvement in the administration of women's sport at over one-third of all colleges and universities.

(7). In sports of interest to males, the percentage of women coaching is often decreasing. Whereas women's basketball in 1977–1978 was coached by a female 79.4% of the time, in 1981–1982 the figure had fallen to 71.2%. In tennis, women coached 72.9% of teams in 1977–1978, and only 65.3% in 1981–1982. In volleyball the decrease in females coaching women's teams was from 86.6% in 1977–1978 to 74.8% in 1981–1982.

While it generally appears that the number of women's sport opportunities had increased between the years 1977 and 1982, there also seemed to be a decrease in the percentage of women in administrative and coaching positions. Given the value and normative system predominantly found in men's sport, these statistics argue for the probability of continued alteration of the once "sport for all," "moderate competition" philosophy of women's sport.

Uhlir (1982) reports that of 1,768 new coaching positions for women's teams established between the years 1974 and 1979, 724 went to men. Of 35 institutional mergers of formerly separate male and female athletic departments, only one woman was named to head the combined departments following the merger. And of 609 AIAW schools, 80.5% had a male administrative head by 1979–1980.

As in the case of the black athlete, increasing rates of participation do not necessarily mean increased leadership opportunities. While women are playing in numbers greater than their pre-Title IX rates, the allocation process seems to be still selecting leaders based on nontask-relevant criteria, or at least on criteria which are biased in favor of those already in control of intercollegiate athletics. To assume that only one of 35 women was more qualified than a man to serve as overall athletic director is clearly ridiculous.

Rationales such as greater male experience with large budgets, numbers of personnel, and the particular problems and pressures of football and basketball may be offered to justify the male choice. But how valid are such criteria as being able to run an athletic program on a limited budget, or for that matter running an educationally based athletic program — criteria that would seem to favor the female candidates among those 35 merged departments?

Additional information concerning the present status and future trends in intercollegiate sport for women is available from reanalysis of statistics from Raiborn's 1982 and 1986 NCAA-sponsored reports, "Revenues and Expenses of Intercollegiate Athletic Programs."
A number of observations can be made (see Table 6). Most telling is the very fact that while the percentage of females attending higher educational institutions in the United States exceeded 50% in the early 1980s, women constituted, at best, 35% of all college athletes. While this is much better than pre-Title IX participation rates, these figures indicate the extent to which further college female sport opportunities must be provided. Secondly, it seems safe to say that judging from this time frame, the period of explosive growth in college women's sports opportunities appears over. Third, college sports opportunities for men have not decreased as sports has become more available to women. Despite the popular impression, this was not a case of robbing Peter

Table 6: Women's Intercollegiate Sport Programs Compared to Men's, 1981/1985, by Class

| | Class (a) | | | | | | | | | | | |
| | A | | B | | C | | D | | E | | F | |
	1981	1985	1981	1985	1981	1985	1981	1985	1981	1985	1981	1985
Average Number of Sports												
(women/men)	(8/12)	(8/12)	(6/10)	(7/10)	(8/11)	(7/12)	(5/9)	(6/12)	(6/8)	(5/9)	(5/9)	(6/10)
Percentage of women's sports relative to total number of sports	40%	40%	38%	42%	42%	37%	36%	33%	43%	36%	36%	38%
Number of Participants												
Women	123	118	86	102	102	101	67	61	60	70	80	95
Men	343	356	305	271	294	297	150	175	147	151	169	175
Percentage of women relative to total number of participants	26%	25%	22%	27%	26%	25%	31%	26%	29%	32%	32%	35%
Expenses												
Women (in thousands)	$ 392	$ 640	$101	$155	$ 48	$ 65	$188	$206	$ 72	$148	$ 37	$ 42
Men (in thousands)	3,243	4,609	392	719	249	339	631	878	232	418	144	182
Percentage of women's expenses relative to total athletic expenses	11%	12%	21%	18%	16%	16%	23%	19%	24%	26%	20%	19%

(a) Class A, B, C institutions refers to Division I, II, III (respectively) football playing NCAA level schools. Class D, E, F institutions refers to Division I, II, III (respectively) non-football playing NCAA level schools in which basketball is typically the most popular intercollegiate sport.

Source: Raiborn 1986:9, 56.

to pay Paula. This finding may be further corroborated by reference to pre-1981 data (Raiborn 1982). In almost every class, male sport opportunities have remained the same or increased, as measured by the average number of teams available to male athletes per school, and in most cases by the average number of males participating in sport at each school. It seems, then, that both male and female college sport have expanded in this time frame, as measured by number of teams and participants.

Relative cost changes for both men's and women's sport between the years 1978 and 1985 (Raiborn 1982, 1986) are interesting in that they illustrate the relative increase in overall expenses for men's and women's athletics (see Table 7). Athletic directors in Raiborn's 1982 study identified the "expansion of women's programs as the major cause of increased operating costs" and the second leading cause of cost inflation in the 1986 study. Yet the data clearly show the source of budget additions in absolute dollar amounts — often hidden by statistical manipulation — and the percentage increase of women's budgets over the short-term: in Class A Division I football playing schools, while the cost of women's sport rose $479,000, the cost of men's programs increased by more than $2 million. Men's increased expenses ranged from more than two times to more than four and a half times the increase in women's athletic programs (as measured in absolute dollars). This must be viewed in light of the fact that in almost every class, with the possible exception of Division I football-playing schools, men's as well as women's athletic programs lose money. It seems, then, that blame for the rising costs of doing business in intercollegiate sport is misplaced. Dollar losses are overwhelmingly due to increased costs in the men's athletic program.

The condition of women's athletics may be viewed currently as glass half empty or a glass half filled. While women's sport has clearly expanded since Title IX and the egalitarianism of the late 1960s and early 1970s. Certain facts remain undisputed: (1) women constitute but one-quarter of the population of intercollegiate athletics; (2) budgets for women's athletics range between 12% to 31% of male athletic budgets; (3) while the number of sport opportunities appears to be increasing, there has been a proportional decrease in the availability of leadership positions for women athletic administrators and coaches.

The extent to which Title IX will continue to serve as a catalyst appears uncertain. In the Grove City College case, the Supreme Court,

Table 7: Increase for Women's and Men's Intercollegiate Sport by Class between 1978 and 1985 (in Thousands of Dollars)

Class	Women			Men		
	1978	1985	Increase	1978	1985	Increase
A (a)	161	640	479	2238	4609	2371
B	62	155	93	287	719	432
C	28	65	37	188	339	151
D	95	206	111	410	878	468
E	36	148	112	163	418	255
F	26	42	16	106	182	76

(a) Class A, B, C institutions refers to Division I, II, III (respectively) football playing NCAA level schools. Class D, E, F institutions refers to Division I, II, III (respectively) non-football playing NCAA level schools in which basketball is typically the most popular sport.

Source: Raiborn 1982:23, 46, 1986:9, 56.

voting 6 to 3, ruled that the entire college's programs are not subject to federal statutes barring sexual discrimination in the use of federal funding. Only in programs for which such monies are received are federal regulations applicable. The NCAA has cautioned, however, that sport scholarships may still be covered under Title IX, since federal dollars are supplied for financial aid (Vance and Fields 1984). While the ultimate effect of this blunting of Title IX is not yet clear, to the NCAA's credit, action has apparently been taken to equalize sport participation and leadership opportunities. By the academic year 1986–1987, it declared Division I schools must offer the same minimum number of sports for men and women (Vance, January 4, 1983:98). In addition, the NCAA has established a subcommittee composed of the thirteen female members of the NCAA Council to review all proposed rule changes and to recommend action on any that may be harmful to women's sport (Vance, September 28, 1983:24). Whether the NCAA and its member institutions will demonstrate a continued commitment to women's athletics remains unclear. Without federal pressure in the form of legislation modifying Title IX to broaden its jurisdiction, or without judicial decisions explicitly covering women's sport, further enlargement of opportunities for female athletes must come from within the academic-athletic community. The acceptability of future levels of women's athletic budgets, participation rates, and leadership structure remains to be seen.

Unethical Behavior

So much publicity has been given to the seemingly endless flood of unethical behavior in college sport that only a limited review will be provided here. "Unethical behavior" here refers to violation of right principles of conduct in higher education and its programs. In this brief look at institutional behaviors, the focus will be on those initiated by the university and its agents. Illegal betting and game fixing, the scalping of complimentary athletic tickets, and student-initiated crime are not the subjects of this discussion. Although the athletic and educational system in this country may condone or encourage such individual behaviors, it is institutionally initiated behaviors we will discuss here.

For the college or university, unethical behavior usually begins at the recruiting stage. Given the lack of a "farm system," comparable to that in baseball to prepare future professionals, would-be football and basketball stars must almost always play "amateur" athletics at some institution of higher education. Graduation, however, is clearly *not* a requirement. In 1986 the University of Miami football team remained in serious contention for the national championship until its title match against Pennsylvania State University. From that University of Miami team only one starting senior did not graduate. Heisman trophy winner Vinny Testaverde never satisfied graduation requirements during his five years of college. Of first-round National Basketball Association draft choices in 1986, only 7 of 18 graduated with their classes (*Chronicle of Higher Education*, July 2, 1986:17). Only 4 of 47 College Football Association schools in 1986 (Duke, Notre Dame, Virginia, and Wyoming) and only 3 of 53 schools in 1987 graduated at least 75% of their players. This figure is complemented by the 8 of 53 institutions of higher learning which graduated less than 25% of their student-athletes (Asher 1985). Of 188 National Football League athletes from the Pacific 10 Conference during the 1979 season, two-thirds had not graduated from college. Of all National Basketball Association players in that year, 80% had not gained their degrees (Underwood 1980). Competition for the very best players rages between agents of higher educational institutions. Practices such as the hiring of "coaches" strictly for recruiting purposes, writing literally hundreds of recruiting letters to potential players in order to gain one enrolled athlete, and having a fleet of aircraft specifically earmarked for the pursuit of players are not uncommon among the biggest schools. Regardless of their level of academic preparation, budding stars are typically sought. Even at prestigious Tulane University, admissions standards for admitted athletes were lowered 600 to 700 points below those for the average Tulane freshman (Asher 1985). A report signed by the president of the University of Southern California found that 330 athletes were admitted between 1970 and 1980 who did not meet the university's minimum requirements. The primary criterion for admission was their "athletic prowess, as judged by the Athletic Department" and the review was conducted "without normal Admissions Office review" (Sage 1986:48).

Is it really any wonder that our distinguished universities fail so miserably at that for which they ostensibly exist? Should we expect any graduation rate so different from these figures when school officers place so much pressure on the shoulders of eighteen- and nineteen-year-olds? Many basketball teams schedule over thirty games per season. At the University of Maryland, one-third of a basketball player's classes could be missed because of travel to contests. Before he died of a cocaine overdose while celebrating his first-round selection by the Boston Celtics, Len Bias had withdrawn from three classes, failed two others, and had flunked out along with four other team members that Spring (Farrell, July 9, 1986:19, 23). What message are our schools giving athletes about the priority of academic work when a star running back such as Auburn's Brent Fullwood is permitted to play in the Florida Citrus Bowl despite his failure to attend classes for the three months preceding the contest (*Chronicle of Higher Education*, January 7, 1987:34)?

To Walter Byers, the Executive Director of the NCAA, abuses in college sport have reached epidemic proportions. Not counting the institutions that act unethically if not illegally relative to NCAA regulations, Byers estimates that 30% of those in big-time athletics cheat (Kirschenbaum 1984:11). He adds that,

> there seems to be a growing number of coaches and administrators who look upon NCAA penalties as the price of doing business. If you get punished, that's unfortunate, but that's part of the cost of getting along. (Farrell, September 2, 1984:29)

There have been a great many documented cases of school's offering illegal inducements for enrollment. Many of these recruiting abuses are chronicled by star basketball center Wayne "Tree" Rollins (Locke and Ibach 1982). Rollins describes the extent to which not only the athlete but his family may be courted.

> It started back with the first school that tried to recruit me: Gardner-Webb College. They brought a car to my home and parked it out front. Told me it was mine if I signed with them. I remember the University of Georgia was recruiting me. A guy who owned a lumber company was an alumnus of Georgia and they built my mom her home in Cordele for practically nothing. The final price was ridiculous . . . just because they thought I was going to their school. (Locke and Ibach 1982:66)

It is the norm for big name athletes such as Tree Rollins to be asked by the coaches to help attract future players. After failing to recruit Phil Ford to Clemson. Rollins asked why he had chosen North Carolina. Ford's reply: "I got a better deal at Carolina" (Locke and Ibach 1982:65). Rollins continues:

> Like I said, I think all the schools cheat. Really. Once your reach the pros you sort of joke about it amongst yourselves. You say, "Who got the best deal while they were in school?" (Locke and Ibach 1982:65–66)

An irate Digger Phelps, basketball coach at Notre Dame University, has acknowledged the existence of an unbroken code of silence among college coaches, about paying basketball players. According to Phelps,

> there is a going underground price for players. It is $10,000 a year and $40,000 for their varsity careers. And if the NCAA continues to levy such weak punishments on colleges for violations the going rate is sure to climb to $100,000 a career in a couple of years. It's worth it to take a risk. Already in football, a good running back can get $10,000 or $25,000 a year. (Wilder, 1982:120)

Even "legal" expenses associated with the recruiting of athletes may be highly suspect for an institution whose societal charter is supposed to center around the education of the young — an institution that continually laments the shortage of resources. The privately financed corporation that controls varsity sports at the University of Georgia recently incurred the following expenses: $2,500 for five hundred bobwhite quail necessary for shooting sessions for recruits and a $3,373 helicopter rental fee for four days' transportation of potential athletes from Atlanta's Hartsfield Airport to the Athens, Georgia, football field. In sum, it is estimated to cost $16,500 to turn each potential recruit into a Bulldog varsity athlete (*Chronicle of Higher Education*, March 26, 1986:34).

Once the athlete has been enrolled, abuses follow from the necessity for athletes' academic "good standing" (as independently defined by each NCAA member) in order to maintain their athletic eligibility. While accounts of forged transcripts, phony credits, substitute test-takers, and the like are legion, the case of Billy Mullins provides a particularly interesting example of legerdemain in the search for athletic talent. Billy Mullins was the University of Southern California's NCAA 400-meter champion in 1978. On March 10, 1980, he was found to have a transcript that contained credits from Rio Hondo Community College for Economics 1A meeting at 8 A.M.; another credit for 9 A.M. Chemistry 22 class at Pasadena Community College, 20 miles away; and another credit from Literature 1B back at Rio Hondo which met at 10 A.M. (Underwood 1980). Then there is the case of Gary Moss, who recovered a fumble to win a Cotton Bowl game for Texas even though he had flunked out of the University twenty-four days before (Vecsey 1984).

Coaches who are more interested in maintaining eligibility than in educating athletic youngsters, and neophyte intercollegiate athletes who too often are ill-prepared for university level work, have typically followed a particular eligibility strategy: by avoiding core courses required for graduation, athletes may skirt some of the more difficult courses in the university. By so doing, they also maintain the flexibility to change majors often. Changing majors ensures that upper-level junior and senior-level courses may be avoided. In addition, athletes may take every kind of physical education activity course and "gut" courses in other departments, where good grades are much more likely. Athletes, of course, share knowledge of these sorts of courses (Underwood 1980). Never mind that all these courses do not amount to a meaningful course load, one necessary for graduation and a career after college.

Many of the problems of college sport are exhibited in recent cases at the University of Georgia and Southern Methodist University. As Coordinator and Instructor in Georgia's Remedial English Program, Jan Kemp eventually came to see the relative importance of her academic program compared to big-time sports. Before she was fired, Ms. Kemp had been ordered to change the failing grades of 5 athletes to incompletes. Following her protests after the transfer of 9 football players from the remedial to the standard academic programs because of their repeated failures in parts of the program, she was first demoted and then eventually dismissed. In response, Ms. Kemp sued Virginia T. Trotter, the university's Academic Vice-President, and Leroy Ervin, the Director of Developmental Studies, alleging that she had been fired because of her protests over the preferential treatment accorded athletes. The court ultimately found for Kemp, awarding $2.57 million in February 1986 — a settlement later reduced to $1.08 million — and reinstatement in her former position as English Coordinator.

Clearly, the mentality of big-time sport had diseased the academic administration at the University of Georgia. At the trial, University President Fred C. Davison was asked what the admission of students barely meeting a 2.0 high school GPA meant to the University. He replied that to do otherwise would be to "unilaterally disarm" in the race for student athletic talent (Monaghan, 1986:38–40). In the Board of Regents review of Georgia's remedial programs, it was revealed that since 1981 athletes had been admitted to the Developmental Studies program who were ineligible and that special efforts had been made to maintain the eligibility of athletes by such means as listing professors who would give preferential treatment to athletes.

In a secretly recorded conversation, Kemp's academic superior demonstrated an insight into big-time sport and its abuse of the academic ethic:

> I know for a fact that these kids would not be here if it were not for their utility to the institution. There is no real sound academic reason for their being here other than to be utilized to produce income. They are used as a kind of raw material in the production of some goods to be sold as whatever product, and they get nothing in return. (Footnotes, 1987:10)

Clearly, the university administrator understood the nonacademic values that place fund raising for the institution before the school's maintenance of its social contract with the citizens of the society — the social contract which requires that parties to an agreement fulfill their obligations to each other and that they negotiate in good faith. The university would admit students into a remedial program who could not legitimately satisfy even its reduced standards. Student eligibility would then be maintained by almost any means necessary, including abuse of the basic academic freedom of professorial autonomy. At Ms. Kemp's protests, her academic head, told her, "I'll break you physically, financially and emotionally. I'll run you out of money and run you out of town" (*Footnotes*, 1987:10). Despite a university defense case that included unfounded accusations against Ms. Kemp of plagiarism and sexual misconduct in the classroom, she ultimately prevailed and was honored by the American Association of University Professors for her defense of the rights of the professoriate.

Far from uncommon is the evidence of NCAA rule violations at Southern Methodist University. Following its seventh violation since 1958 and its fourth sanction since 1974, the university was the first to be punished by the "death penalty." With evidence of $61,000 in illegal payoffs to athletes since its last probation in August 1985, SMU was prohibited from fielding a football team in 1987 and was told that it would be permitted to play only a limited schedule of games away from home the following season (Lederman, March 4, 1987). Given difficulties associated with recruiting athletes and other problems, the university subsequently decided to give up any football competition until the academic year 1989–1990.

The dimensions of the ethical problem at Southern Methodist University were exemplified by Texas Governor William Clements' confirmation that he had approved of continued illegal payments to athletes while he served as chair of the university Board of Regents (Farrell 1987), and that the university Regents attempted a cover-up, ordering a halt to its own probe. Clearly, unethical behavior is not solely the province of relatively minor college officials. Instead, at this school the pursuit of athletic victory through illegal means extends to its highest-ranking officers. As David Berst, Director of the NCAA's enforcement division has observed in reference to Governor Clements, "If he is typical of people who are in charge at the highest level, then there really isn't any hope for integrity in collegiate athletics" (Lederman, March 18, 1987:49).

Given such nationally publicized problems, for good reason Southern Methodist has become very concerned with its image. If indeed the reputation of the institution is critical to the school's ability to confer on its students heightened status, then it is only natural that Southern Methodist should fear its loss of attractiveness. Without a football program to bolster its image and with publicly recognized unethical behavior on the part of university leadership the university lost a great deal of its precious stature. Though the depressed Texas economy may have something to do with declining applications, SMU found it necessary to admit 15% fewer students into the freshman class for the academic year 1987–1988. Without lowering the entrance standards that the school has made so much effort to raise, a greatly diminished applicant pool has seriously jeopardized this most vital of all institutional resources. The power of university athletics to do bad as well as good for the institution is evidenced by this apparent result of administrative disregard for the principles of higher learning. While affecting the larger legitimacy of higher education in the long run, athletic improprieties at SMU have had serious tangible repercussions in the short run. A shortfall of only one hundred students out of a class of one thousand two hundred will directly lead to the loss of $1.3 million in revenue for the university over four years. In addition, the diminished stature of the entire university seems to have discouraged alumni support as well, since there has been a 10% drop in contributions from this group — a loss of approximately another $1 million (Lederman, May 6, 1987).

One may ask how all this is possible. How can an academic institution stoop to such levels of behavior? First, it must be recognized that this is not a new phenomenon. Rader (1983:139) notes that legendary coach Fielding H. Yost liked to use experienced players on his squad. As star, of the undefeated Kansas team of 1899, Yost was an experienced player who had five years of service at West Virginia University to supplement his one year of professional experience. Moving to the University of Michigan in 1901, he brought along with him as a player one Willie Heston, who was already a graduate of San Jose State University.

Abuses such as this are possible for a number of reasons. These reasons extend far beyond the coach's room into the very meaning of higher education in America. (1) Because of the lack of stable federal and local support to higher education, there remains the continued need for monetary and student resources. This encourages attempts to gain favorable position in the competitive market through sport success, and makes more attractive the seductive advances of money-bearing external groups. (2) The search for athletes who are critical to sport success and a ranking of the institution in the top echelons is so important that the relatively minor sanctions for illicit actions do little to deter such behavior. (3) The tradition of institutional autonomy coupled with the enormous size of many schools has led to difficulties in regulating universities at the national level, as well as in governance from within the organization. (4) Business-minded leadership of these institutions evaluates the success of the schools' programs in terms of such concrete measures as profit and winning, as opposed to vaguer, less measurable factors such as student maturity. (5) The media, satisfying greater societal interest in sports than in education, provides instant national exposure for successful teams of schools seeking to enhance their reputations (for example, small Chaminade College defeating previously the unbeaten University of Virginia in basketball during Ralph Sampson's senior year).

To Underwood(1980), parents of athletically talented youngsters are too often concerned with the youngster's performance and advancement in sports as opposed to other school programs. Coaches fearing for their jobs in a win-or-you-are-fired situation have taken advantage of affirmative action programs to admit students who really do not have the preparation to succeed in college. Over crowded classrooms, the mass processing, passing and graduating of students without confirmation of academic abilities, and cutbacks in faculty and staff have all led to students who may be strong, swift, or tall, but who are unprepared for or by college-level work. Presidents of schools do not want to be told what to do by some national agency that does not contribute much to the school's financial welfare; but that same president must listen intently to the booster who says he can hire some hot-shot coach or recruit some "impact" player.

Actually, the root of the present condition of intercollegiate sport goes deeper than this. It goes to the very values of our society, to an epistemology that says leave men alone to seek their own fortune and they in concert will succeed for the nation. This is an American world view that says anyone can succeed in this land of opportunity so long as he or she has talent and works hard. So we have institutional autonomy. So we have schools constantly searching for the means to survive in a competitive market for students and money. So we have the scramble for the means to succeed in that market — in a society that values visible demonstrations of success and that likes to see it on television from the comfort of an armchair. It is a society that has learned to recognize a Boiler Maker, Hoosier, Trojan, Spartan, Eagle, Longhorn, Razorback, and even a Hoya. Is it any wonder that abuses in college sports are so widespread in a society that values sport success so much and intellectuality so little?

When Jackie Sherrill was hired by Texas A & M University for $267,000 per year (which includes salary and fringe benefits)

$1,602,000 over the six-year term of the contract — President Frank Vandiver was asked to compare this to his own $90,000 salary.

Q. Do you think the priorities are out of whack?

A. That's reasonable to say. No, wait, let's say that priorities are different for different people.

Q. So how do you feel about the priority given football around here?

A. I can deplore it but I also can understand it.

Q. But did the university debase itself as an academic institution?

A. No, it only embarrassed itself. (Looney 1982:29).

President Vandiver's answers, while humorous, are also insightful, for they recognize the diversity of groups in the task environment that must be pleased with the programs and goals of the university, as well as the difficulty of this task, the powerlessness of his office in this matter, and the extent to which the institution is willing to risk embarrassment in order to promote winning football. Howard Schellenberger's more recent contract shows that the value of top-rank coaches is increasing rapidly. On top of Schellenberger's $72,100 base salary are added an $80,000/year minimum television and radio guarantee, a one-third share of profits above $160,000, a $500,000 five-year annuity, a $12,500 bonus for a bowl game appearance, country club memberships, and two late-model "quality automobiles" (Weiberg 1986).

As we will see in the next section, however, the current state of big-time sports is but one embarrassment for American higher education. Though football and basketball are more visible than the composition of faculty and administrative staffs and the reward structures in which they operate, intercollegiate sport is a component of wider problems that must be addressed by higher education in America.

The Reflection of Wider Issues in Higher Education

To isolate the issues of racism, sexism, and unethical behavior an intercollegiate sport invites focusing too much attention upon merely one set of problems among what should be more pervasive concerns of the academic world. While the salience of sports makes criticism easy, improper behavior by functionaries of the university are symptomatic of larger issues.

We must remember that racism in the academy did not begin or end with James Meredith at the University of Mississippi. The academic world dependent upon the environment for its institutional survival, typically mirrors the values, attitudes, and normative behaviors of the legislature, community, and alumni who are so important for its survival. While the United States of the 1920s was congratulating itself on the prosperity it could offer, Synnot (1979) notes that Harvard, Yale, and Princeton were reacting to the "Jewish Invasion" by erecting overt and covert barriers. At Harvard, President A. Lawrence Lowell instituted quota system for admitting Jews and Yale President James Rowland Angel acquiesced in demands for limits on the number of Jewish students.

While discrimination may not take such overt form today, the institution that does not recognize and help compensate for the educational disadvantage of many minority youths dropped into the white middle-class culture of the typical college is merely propping up the class structure as it presently exists. The college or university does no great service to minorities enrolled under flexible admissions guidelines if those students, who are all too often ill-prepared for college-level work, are allowed to flounder about on their own without educational and social support services.

Statistically, it appears that while blacks have gained some access to higher education there is certainly room for further progress. Blacks in 1984 made up 9.8% of enrollment (*Chronicle of Higher Education*, January 16, 1985:15), much below the roughly 13% of American youth age 18–24 who are black (Anderson 1981). Between 1978 and 1980, black enrollment had risen some 4.9%, from 1,054,325 to 1,106,445 (U.S. Department of Education, 1982). But as of 1984, black enrollment had fallen back to 1,070,000, while white students numbered 9,767,000 (*Chronicle of Higher Education*, July 23, 1986).

More careful inspection of enrollment patterns indicates that minority students attend institutions with fewer physical resources to devote to education. Whereas expenditures per white student averages $2,024 for "instruction," schools attended by black students devote an average of $1,942 and Hispanic students, $1,807, for "instruction." More striking are differences between the average per student value of physical plant and facilities for students of white, black, and Hispanic origins. Whereas white students average $13,144 worth of school plant and facilities per student, blacks average $11,197, and Hispanics but $8,029 (Astin 1985:90). These figures indicate a stratified pattern of college attendance. While minorities may enroll at rates that indicate progress, on the whole they do not seem to enroll in the same sort of schools as whites. Minorities attend poorer schools, schools with less to devote to instruction and support services. While humanities may be taught just as well in an old classroom, science certainly cannot be taught using obsolete equipment.

Insofar as college leadership is concerned, in 1961, while 3% of all college faculty were black, by 1975–1976 that figure had risen to 4.4% (Menges and Exum 1983). In 1977, of 47,138 college and university trustees, 11% of public but only 5% of private institutions' trustees were black (Wallenfeldt 1983:10–17). The need to increase black participation in higher education in student, faculty, administrative and trustee roles is made all the more pressing by the increasing proportion of blacks as a percentage of the college-age population (Anderson 1981). Despite this fact, however, since 1975 there has been a decline in the number of black college faculty. By 1981, blacks constituted but 4.2% of the professoriate (Heller 1985).

The condition of women in sports parallels their situation in American higher education. The apparent discrimination and gains in the sports area reflect rising concerns of women on campus.

Flexner (1972) records 1841 as the year a women first graduated from a full course of college study in the United States. At that time, educators typically believed that the female brain was smaller in capacity and ability than the male brain. The education provided them was not to be the taxing sort aimed at the preparation of leaders; instead, the goal was to make women better wives and mothers. The few upper-class women who could afford college typically took a shortened course of study suitable for their assumed limitations.

Even Oberlin, given credit as the first coeducational institution in America, demonstrated the conventional wisdom of the mid-1800s concerning the sort of higher learning appropriate for the female.

Oberlin's attitude was that women's high calling was to be the mothers of the race, and that they should stay within that special sphere in order that future generations should not suffer from the want of devoted and undistracted mother care. If women became lawyers, ministers, physicians, lecturers, politicians or any sort of "public character," the home would suffer from neglect. . . . Washing the men's clothes, caring for their rooms, serving them at table, listening to their orations, but themselves remaining respectfully silent in public assemblages, the Oberlin "coeds" were being prepared for intelligent motherhood and a properly subservient wifehood. (Fletcher 1943:373).

It is Conable's contention (1977) that the admission of women to Cornell University from its inception in 1864 was not an example of the progressive spirit. Far from being an act of enlightened liberalism, the decision to admit women was more an expedient economic measure in the face of economically influential benefactors who pressed for female admissions. At the outset, women were seen as inherently different from men in their interests, capacities, and legitimate career opportunities. Even at prestigious Vassar, chartered in 1865, the most distinguished member of the faculty, Maria Mitchell, felt that the male president and all-male board of trustees preferred men for higher academic posts, resisted the equalization of salaries, and were reluctant to appoint women to faculty committees (Flexner 1972).

While there was a 10.9% jump in female college attendance between the years 1978–1980, so that by 1980 women constituted 52% of all college enrollees, patterns of enrollment indicate significant differences between men and women (Anderson 1981; U.S. Department of Education, 1982). Bernard (1964) reported that female graduate students were generally underrepresented at high-quality universities, despite their higher grades as undergraduates. While 51.5% of women attained a GPA of B+ or better, as opposed to 36.5% of men, only 25.9% of women graduate students attended "high-quality" universities, as opposed to 74.1% of males. Women attending graduate school at the time of the study tended to enroll at medium- and low-quality colleges. By 1970, of those pursuing advanced study, only 13.3% of all doctoral degrees were gained by women (Feldman 1974).

As in intercollegiate athletics, where allocation of high-status positions deviated from the ideal academic model, there appears to be deviation from academic standards of leader choice in the greater academic world. While one might suspect that leaders will be chosen from those demonstrating the most academic success as undergraduates, and in some quantity similar to their proportions in the college population, women are underrepresented at higher-quality institutions, in the number of doctorates produced, as well as in the proportion of faculty, presidents, and trustees. Clearly, other factors than poor quality are at work. Like the coaches who stereotyped black athletes, who thought they knew what these athletes were best suited for even before seeing them, so too do expectations work to the disadvantage of women in higher education Bernard (1964:48) quotes a department head's justification for his quota system.

My own practice is to appoint women to about 50% of our graduate assistantships and to about 30% of our instructorships. My fear that this is too large a proportion of women appointees arises from the consideration: (1) that women are less likely to complete the degree program upon which they embark; (2) that even if they do, marriage is very likely to intervene and to prevent or considerably delay their entry into the teaching profession; (3) that even when they do become full-time teachers (at whatever level, including the university), their primary sense of responsibility is to their homes, so that they become professional only to a limited degree; (4) that they are far less likely than are men to achieve positions of leadership in their professions, either through research and publication or through activity in academic organizations.

Perrucci (1970) has noted that even in the most rational fields of higher education, engineering and science, the ideal model of reward for demonstrated merit falls short of the reality. More is expected of women upon their entry into the labor market, and these differences are further reflected in differences in rank and remuneration throughout their careers.

As a result, by in1972–1973, 22.3% of faculty at the nation's colleges and universities were women. By 1979–1980, there had only been an increase to 25.9%. Furthermore there had only been an increase to 25.9%. Furthermore, according to Fox (1981), distinct reward criteria for the sexes are operating in American higher education. Her research at a large Midwestern university on 5,450 academic personnel (83% male and 16% female), which she controlled for experience, educational attainment, rank, and years at the university, indicated that compared to men, women with the same levels of educational rank and attainment cannot expect to receive equal compensation. In a broader survey of higher education in 1983, salary differentials were reported indicating that males on average were paid at least six and a half percent more than women at a comparable academic level (see Table 8).

Fields (1982) reports that the average female faculty member earned $4,835 less per year than her male counterparts. Astin and Bayer (1972), looking at men and women making similar career choices (such as marriage and its timing, education, and the like), found that women make less than men in the same educational institutions.

Similarly, as Table 9 indicates women have a lower probability of tenure and senior ranking than do men in academia. Astin and Bayer

Table 8: U.S. College and University Salaries by Rank and Gender, 1983

	Women	Men	Percentage Difference
Professor	$33,730	$37,860	+12.24%
Associate Professor	$26,870	$28,610	+6.48%
Assistant Professor	$22,050	$23,870	+8.25%
Instructor	$17,960	$19,410	+8.07%
Lecturer	$19,150	$22,050	+15.14%

Source: ACADEME 1984:12.

(1972) reported that women with doctorates from the most prestigious schools and of great scholarly productivity could not expect to be promoted to high rank as quickly as males. Gender was a better predictor of academic rank than years of education, years employed, or books published. In 1977–1978, the modal rank for men was "professor," while the most common rank for women was "assistant professor." In 1980–1981, 74% of all faculty were male of which 70% were tenured; whereas 50% of females had gained the freedom of tenure (Menges and Exum 1983). By 1982, Fields reports that 10% of all female faculty had become full professors, which was little better than the 9% figure of ten years before. By 1983, women's proportion at each academic level was at least twenty-one percentage points lower than men's (see Table 9).

Table 9: Percentage of U.S. College and University Faculty Tenured by Gender and Institutional Type, 1983

	Women	Men
Public	50%	71%
Private	52%	73%
Church-Affiliated	41%	66%
All Institutions	40%	63%

Source: ACADEME 1984:14.

While some might argue that the condition of women in higher education has improved, a more forceful argument may be made against this proposition. True, the number of women teaching at college has increased. In 1969–1970, there were 206,000 women faculty, as opposed to 376,000 in 1980. Relative to their male counterparts, however, we have seen that women have not advanced as high, are not paid as much, and have not achieved the security of tenure as much as men.

And what does tenure mean? Of course, it means security — not only economic security but the political security to speak out on important issues. Tenure is the academic freedom to call to public attention hiring improprieties, to have the time and energy to devote to research which may not be politically popular. Without tenure, women and blacks must too often consider the costs of politically unpopular criticisms of the existent systems for hiring, promoting, and rewarding academic behavior.

Incremental progress is indicated by the proportion of women in college administration. Between the years 1975 and 1979 there had been only an increase from 4.8% to 6.4% in the proportion of women serving as college presidents (Anderson 1981). By 1984, 286 colleges and universities reported female presidents (Watkins 1985). In 1983, only 15% of all private college and university trustees were women (Wallenfeldt 1983).

The percentage of female deans at an institution is related to the probability of female faculty members at the institution (Bach and Perucci 1984). Yet as the percentage of black basketball players does not find proportional representation among leaders in college sport, so the high-status administrative positions in higher education are not populated by women in the proportion one might expect given the rate of their college attendance.

It is easy to point a finger at racist, sexist, and unethical behavior in intercollegiate sport. In the previous sections, however, we have seen that racism and sexism in athletics mirror discrimination on the broader campus. Visible exploits on the athletic field may bring more public glory and greater shame than the less visible hand of discrimination in the administrative and academic offices on campus; but it is the very invisibility of discriminatory behavior across the campus which makes it so difficult to combat and so insidious in its effects. Perhaps bread and circuses do deflect the masses' attention.

Some of the most damaging behaviors are the most common — the sorts of behaviors to which academics and experienced students have become almost oblivious because of their wide acceptance. But this is an acceptance of practices whose price has been cynicism about the process and integrity of higher education. What does Stuart Craft, a junior mathematics science major from one of the "hot" schools of the 1970s, Stanford University, see at there?

> Teaching assistants instructing too many courses and doing a poor job at it . . . professors more concerned with their resumes than with the intellectual growth of their students. . . . I have seen middle to advanced courses filled to standing room only, with a teacher–student ratio well in excess of 50 to 1. I have seen world-famous research professors who are abysmal at teaching and yet whose departments continue to let them teach. (Craft 1984)

While the comments of this science major may be passed off as expression of undergraduate energy, this letter contains more than a kernel of truth. How many times have we witnessed abominable teaching just as we have seen displays of poor sporting character or ego-gratifying administrative power mongering? With the push to publish, how often have classes suffered at the hands of an ill-prepared or overly tired lecturer? For that matter, how often have we witnessed whimsical grading based upon nebulous criteria? We trumpet the importance of teaching in catalogs, from convocation to commencement, yet students as well as faculty at many schools soon learn the truth. At Harvard, Stephen Jay Gould observes that "To be perfectly honest, though lip service is given to teaching, I have never seriously heard teaching considered in any meeting for promotion" (*Chronicle of Higher Education*, April 15, 1987:15). Professors learn and pass on to their students a hypocrisy about teaching's "importance," and then through their silence they socialize the young to keep silent about this hypocrisy.

While the heart of higher education is teaching, how many professors have studied the art and science of teaching? Too few have even observed their own style, despite the ubiquity of video machines. There is the assumption that somehow we will pass down to a future generation the *veritas* and style appropriate for the profession, despite the inability of most of us to define what it is that we fundamentally need to instill in our students.

Then there is the commitment to research. What proportion of the professoriate even submits one article for publication in a year? How much of the work is theoretically or socially meaningful, as opposed to merely printable? How many in the profession have a commitment to finding things out, to keeping an open mind to other points of view, and to separating academic egos from egoless knowledge?

Too many of us have witnessed such behavior in our own professors or our colleagues. For every class a professor skips or for which he or she arrives late, for every ill-prepared session, for every boring lecture, for every meeting that is little more than memory or regurgitation devoid of deeper comprehension, there develops a cynicism concerning the integrity of higher learning. Perhaps, it may be thought, the university really is a business. Less important is the process than the product. Just get the grade, just get the degree, just get the job.

Scandalous behavior is not limited to the football or basketball arenas. At the University of Florida in 1969, 26% of female undergraduates and 31% of female graduate students reported sexual harassment by the faculty. In the same year at the University of Rhode Island, 53% of those reporting sexual harassment indicated that it was their professors who had initiated it: 8% of incidents by graduate assistants, 6% by staff and administration, 14% by other employees, and 14% by other students. Furthermore, in 58% of reported cases of sexual harassment, grades or exams were an issue. At Iowa State University, 43% of female students reported flirtation by faculty, and 13% explicitly avoided courses because certain faculty were known in the community as sexual harassers. At Arizona State University, 13% of female students reported harassment — a figure which in absolute numbers amounts to 2,300 students on one campus (Dziech and Weiner 1984). National research has indicated that between 20 and 30% of all female students experience sexual harassment, but that only 2 to 3% of women report it (*Chronicle of Higher Education*, July 10, 1981). In a survey of 464 women, it was reported that one in six female graduate psychology majors indicated having some sexual contact with a professor. While working toward their degrees, one-third of women doctorate holders reported that they had been subjected to inappropriate sexual advances, with one-half of them reporting some retaliation by professors when their advances were rejected (Heller 1986).

The figures reported above are all the more striking considering the inhibition naturally felt by female students to report inappropriate sexual behavior on the part of faculty who hold such power over them. It is the imbalance of power in the relationship which makes women easy prey for the "leering professor," and it is the extent to which academic personnel take advantage of their charges that is scandalous. This sort of behavior, though less visible than abuses reported in the sports pages, provokes the same loss of respect for the integrity of higher education among those involved. But does the relative invisibility of lecherous behavior make it any less embarrassing to the institution? Do these "private secrets" publicly known on campus make them any less ethically scandalous?

In Warren Bryan Martin's consideration (1982:27) of the "college of character," he notes intercollegiate athletic scandals as one of the problems confronting American higher education with ethical ramifications and moral dilemmas. Clearly, the problem of college sport is but one example — albeit a particularly visible one — of campus problems on a larger scale.

Perhaps because of the diversity of American life since the nation's birth, the social tolerance required to accommodate so many peoples and beliefs contributed to a pluralism gone wild. According to Martin (1982:33–34) pluralism came to be seen as an end in itself. Rather than assuming that accepting so much diversity was a prerequisite to establishing an ethical basis for the entire culture, pluralism instead became an end in itself. The ethical crisis in higher education, of which the scandalous coach and professor are prime examples, goes back to the very origins of the nation and the interrupted search for cultural unity. Instead of searching for the one set of principles by which we could all live, in higher education and elsewhere, the search was prematurely interrupted by an overindulgence of individual and group extremes. The logic and economy of capitalism, whereby things are left alone, with the assumption that they should be left to fall or succeed on their own, did not recognize the deviance that such worship of the market, victory in the competition, could engender. Right standards by which higher education's professors, coaches, students, athletes, and administrators should live have become diluted by bloated principles of tolerance and laissez faire.

To tolerate all policies and to totally deregulate higher education from the constraints of ethics frees the university to pursue all manner of behavior. Given the highly flexible charter of higher education in this country, there is an enormous range of institutional policies and programs possible within its responsibilities. The range of institutional options is only limited to and set by the world view of those who run the university. And who runs the university?

We know that most trustees are white, male, in their fifties, well educated, wealthy, and most often business executives with ties to prestigious occupations (Hartnett 1974). It is the perspective of the wealthy business upper class, with its ties to corporate resources essential to university survival, which dominates the leadership of higher education. And it is just this tie to the interests of the upper class which has so affected the character of American higher education, as well as the problems facing academia.

Hall (1982) contends that Jefferson's 1800 election symbolized the erosion of New England's "Standing Order" - the elite of merchants, ministers, lawyers, and doctors who dominated the region's politics in the late eighteenth century. In order to perpetuate its power, the Standing Order established means other than electoral. It developed the private institution, that is, business corporations, professional societies, charitable trusts, and private colleges and universities as the earmarks of legitimate power. The introduction of "character education" at Harvard and Yale, according to Hall, was an attempt to develop an educational leadership cadre that would extend the cultural hegemony of the Standing Order throughout the nation's colleges. The university was to provide the hub of a new control system in America — an aristocracy of talent and virtue would be established through the legitimizing of selected youth in the country's finest schools. The social and moral authority that had been diminished by populist victories would be reestablished.

With the seal of approval of the prestigious universities, their graduates were afforded the presumption of appropriateness for high position. It was assumed that these graduates would and should be the leaders of business, society, and education. It was their access to others of similar position, and to the same means of production and the dissemination of ideas that provided "the ideological framework and intellectual instruments through which reality was defined and acted on" (Hall 1982:1).[2]

The leftist interpretation of collegiate history in the United States parallels the neo-Marxist critique of intercollegiate sport. The athletic program, with its emphasis on order, character, discipline, performance, obedience, and teamwork, is a more visible display of the socialization generally available through higher education. While sport and education both mouth the virtues of the meritocracy of talent, both demonstrate the racism and sexism that contribute to the maintenance of the existing class structure.

As early as the mid-1880s, the identification of the Vanderbilts with Yale, the Whitneys, Sloanes, Alexanders, and Scribners with Princeton demonstrated to the nouveau riche the necessity of university ties for social status (Rader 1983:177). Wealth was clearly important, but by the end of the nineteenth century social acceptance of elevated status became more and more equated with the legitimizing effects of university attendance. With the invention of "adolescence" in the period 1900–1920 (Kett 1977) there developed an even more pressing need to legitimize the inherited status of this new group of wealthy young men and women who had not earned their own positions. The establishment of ties with the university through donations, trustee service, graduation, and sports participation were some means through which these youths' legitimacy was enhanced. The university, mythologized as a classless objective proving ground for talent, provided a site through which the upper classes of society could justify their status by instilling in the consciousness of the public an understanding of their high character and ability apart from the advantages of inheritance.

The public was fed a diet of sporting news that was based on an assumption of the university as a proving ground for talent apart from the advantages of money and position. As expressed by Frank Merriwell, the fictional Yale football captain, in his criticism of Harvard.

A man's real worth does not carry him so far as in Yale or Princeton. Here [Yale] a man is accepted for just what he proves himself to be; there, he is accepted for what he has the reputation of being. Aristocracy cuts a mighty small figure at Yale, but in Harvard the bloods are the ones who play ball, row and so forth. A fellow whose parents are nobodies has a poor show in Harvard, but here he gets where he is able to place himself by merit. That is why Yale has triumphed over Harvard so often, and that is why Harvard receives so little sympathy when she meets defeat. (Standish 1904)

An American public nurtured on a view of the meritocratic society, found reassurance that her leaders would not only be those lucky enough to be wealthy but also those most capable. Success in sport and at college in general demonstrated superior talent and ability to the public. Never mind that academic success in the humanities might have little to do with political or economic leadership. Never mind that the upper classes were only those exposed to the advantages of pre-college education and the network of influential sponsors. "Demonstrated" talent and ability in the college's programs, especially in its most visible program of sports, provided reassurance for the public about its leadership and its entertainment of the masses, and promoted conscious as well as unconscious acceptance of higher education.

Despite Frank Merriwell's romantic view, however, higher education in America has historically been the province of the wealthy. As the ground-breaking research by Burke demonstrates, socioeconomic stratification has been a fact since at least the postbellum period. Regardless of American mythology to the contrary, social and economic position is reproduced in the educational system. In the period after the Civil War, when $10,000 per annum was a considerable sum, 68% of all Williams College and 47% of all Yale University students' families earned that much. Only normal schools and some private coeducational colleges admitted students from families of skilled and unskilled workers. The proportion of students from professional families was six times what one might expect relative to their proportion in the population (Burke 1982).

This same pattern of disproportionate upper-class representation in American colleges and universities continued in the early twentieth century. If one assumes that those testing at or above the 94% to 95% level on the Army's intelligence exams were capable of college level work, then enrollments were underrepresented by 50%. If all of the relevant population that was one standard deviation above or below the mean test level were included in the college population, enrollments should have risen 250% (Burke 1982:228–239).

The exclusiveness of higher education in contemporary America is corroborated by Sewell and Hauser (1976). Their research found that students from high socioeconomic families were two and a half times more likely to continue their education after high school than low socioeconomic class students. High socioeconomic status (SES) students are four times more likely to enter college, six times more likely to graduate from college, and nine times more likely to attend graduate school. High-ability students from a high SES group are three and a half times more likely to obtain graduate education, four times more likely to attend college, and nine times more likely to graduate from college than their lower-class counterparts of similar intelligence (as measured by the Henmon-Nelson Test of Mental Maturity). While sports have been criticized by neo-Marxists for reproducing the existing class system in America, there is considerable evidence that contemporary American higher education has similarly manifested the class structure of this society. Just as women and blacks are underrepresented in academic leadership positions, just as women generally do not receive equal support in the athletic budget, just as both blacks and women suffer from insidious discrimination in college sport programs and facilities, so too does other historical and contemporary research support the view that higher education in America is the province of the upper classes and a reinforcement for culture and ideology that is supportive of the status quo. The abuses in college sport are no more or less scandalous than those on the larger campus. The sexist coach has his counterpart in the leering professor. The athletic director whose primary concern is filling the stadium is paralleled by the university administrator who panders to the wishes of wealthy alumni and trustees. And the very same over-acceptance of diverse behavior and unwillingness to judge the ethical behavior of coaches have contributed to the power vacuum found in the leadership of American higher education today.

The Control of the Campus and the Arena

As has been discussed in the previous section, many of the problems found in college sport are but reflections of issues facing American higher education in general. Gender and racial stratification in sport and higher education have, according to critics, perpetuated the existing social structure. The rewards available in the university and its programs are not solely dependent upon intellectual or athletic performance. To focus undivided attention on the abuses in sport is to divert attention from the larger issue. Similarly, questions about the governance of intercollegiate sport are mirrored by concerns about who controls the campus. Just as the president of a university such as Texas

A & M may have little control over hiring its football coach, so chief executive officers of many institutions appear to be less involved also in the academic work of the school than they once were. Presidential attention to external constituencies, whether they be corporate or government or alumni sources of money has increasingly diverted the chief executive's attention to the wishes of these extrainstitutional groups. Academic freedom as well as the very integrity of academia are at stake here.

In the first section we will look at the governance of college sport historically and sociologically. While it may appear that conventional governance procedures for college sports place athletics under the direction of faculty and other academic officers, the reality of governance in many cases has placed sport largely outside the authority of the institution's central administration. Curiously, the most publicly visible single program bearing the university's standard often falls outside the control of its academic leadership.

The Governance of College Athletics

Athletics of the middle nineteenth century usually took the form of student-organized, -financed, and -coached teams — a pattern of management resembling the organizational structure of the English school sport system.[3] Concerned alumni might help advise, and at other times coaches might be hired by the students on a seasonal basis (Sage 1975:404). While college officials might cast an interested eye at the roughhousing of their charges, primary responsibility for athletic supervision and planning still rested with the students.

Early athleticism was often carried out over the objections of faculty who saw sport as distracting from the real work of the college. With student mismanagement, overzealous play, and the growing popularity of campus sport, eventually the American college took its students' athletic activities within its formal control and financial structure.

By the end of the nineteenth century one observer noted the apparent differences between the English system of student-run extra-curricular athletics and the fanatic all-too-consuming athletics of American institutionally administered sport. American football players saw the game as central to their reason for being in college.

> The sight, familiar to us, of members of a defeated eleven throwing themselves prostrate on the ground in agony or bitter disappointment would indeed make Englishmen stare in wonderment (Whitney 1895:90, 92).

Apparently, the English school games varied from their American counterparts in style as well as structure of governance.

The Call for Faculty Control. The original curriculum of the physical education discipline had little to do with organized sport, emphasizing health and fitness through calisthenics and gymnastics. But given the strong resistance encountered by fledgling departments of physical education, resource acquisition and legitimation were pressing concerns of the new field's leadership (Hartwell 1893). Physical education personnel increased the visibility afforded them by the incorporation of athletics into the curriculum by adding the formal duty of managing intercollegiate athletics (Chu 1979). In 1892, Amos Alonzo Stagg at the University of Chicago became the first college coach to be given faculty recognition. In the first third of the twentieth century, most faculty from the newly emergent field of physical education were also given responsibility for intercollegiate sport. Physical educators quickly assumed responsibility over a new curriculum of sports activities and the extracurricular intercollegiate teams. By 1929, 78% of directors of physical education were also responsible for intercollegiate programs.

Incorporation of intercollegiate athletics within the formal responsibilities of the faculty (more specifically, the physical education faculty) was, in the minds of many professors, an answer to the abuses associated with campus sport. In response to the growing salience of campus sport the American Association of University Professors issued a number of reports and recommendations. In 1926, the Committee on Intercollegiate Football of the American Association of University Professors (AAUP) reported that,

> the responsibility for the educational welfare of our college students lies primarily with our faculties, which have therefore the right and duty to determine under what conditions any college activity should be carried out. (*AAUP Bulletin* 1926:228)

The faculty's solution to football's ills was for them to guide it. Indeed, with the proper philosophy of education, morally and ethically disciplined, and relatively innocent of the corrupting influence of business considerations, the faculty should run the entire intercollegiate sport enterprise (*AAUP Bulletin* 1931:331–337). In 1927, a committee of the AAUP developed a set of goals for intercollegiate sport. One of the most important recommendations was that coaches should be full-time faculty typically assigned to the department of physical education (*AAUP Bulletin* 1927). Under public pressure to reform football, and with the need for public, faculty, and sometimes state government support, college leadership developed control structures through which athletic improprieties would be, they hoped, eliminated. Faculty would play a watchful role, and governance of athletics would be through official college channels rather than the helter-skelter of the previous student-alumni structures.

The American college and university at the turn of this century formally incorporated sport within its control and financial structures in order to maximize the flow of resources while minimizing loss of prestige from athletic scandal. Athletic personnel would be employed as physical education faculty and provide the necessary oversight. While winning sports presumably drew money and students, internal tranquility, essential to public perception of institutional quality, would be ensured through faculty control of athletics — or so it could be claimed by college leaders interested in maintaining resource flow.

The question remains, however, as to the real extent to which faculty were afforded control over intercollegiate sport. While responsible in title, were they governing? By 1929, it was reported that of 177 directors of comprehensive departments of physical education and athletics, only 23 had majored in physical education as undergraduates, and 85% reported that their success as football coaches was instrumental to their appointments as directors (*Carnegie Bulletin* 1929). Whereas the intention of faculty presumably was to exercise real control over athletic programs, questions remain as to how real this control was. Did the faculty, presumably steeped in the philosophy of higher education and sensitive to deviations from educational purpose, really control college sport, or were they merely coopted?

Selznick (1972) defines cooptation as an organizational response to environmental pressure. In order to reduce pressure from the environment, the organization many make token changes in its structure. Apparent accommodations in the direction desired by critical groups reduces pressure and maintains the appearance of the organization as rational and reasonable.

Thus, the appearance of faculty support for administratively sanctioned programs is important to the school which seeks to maintain its prestige. A school torn by faculty–administrative warfare runs the risk of a tarnished public image and an eventual reduction in the supply of students and monies. By accepting the form of the AAUP recommendations for faculty control of intercollegiate athletics, while in actuality maintaining the superiority of athletic success over educational training criteria in the selection of sports directors, administrators were able to quell the criticisms of faculty and groups concerned with education while keeping athletic personnel primarily concerned with producing winning sports teams. A faculty divided into disciplinary cells and with relatively little power vis-a-vis the administration could do little to ensure the educational focus of all programs.

Governance Structures. The early-twentieth-century controversy over the control of intercollegiate sport is illustrative of both the extent to which college administrations have control over program development and the significance of a facade of formal structure (as opposed to the realities) of governance applied to collegiate work.

As indicated earlier, American college presidents have developed much power vis-a-vis the faculty. This is not the case with the European models. Oxbridge governance is much less centralized in powerful administrators. Instead, governance is characterized by faculty control. In the traditional German system, rectors and pro-rectors are elected to one-year terms by the professors (Burns et al. 1971:165–196). American faculty, originally groups of transient tutors, have historically exercised less control over the substance of education programs included within American higher education than their European counterparts.

Although American faculties have not always abdicated power willingly — as we have seen through the AAUP controversies over the control of intercollegiate sport — the college administration has been able to coopt faculty to quell criticisms while maintaining real control. As Paulsen has noted, the American college president is historically an administrator with great power to change programs. The president often alters programs because of felt pressure and from fear of losing appropriations (Paulsen 1906:viii). As evidenced by differences between University of Chicago Presidents Harper and Hutchins, the American college president has in the past been able to completely alter athletic policy to suit his particular educational philosophy (Lawson and Ingham 1980). Without substantial faculty input into decision making on programs, college presidents have stood relatively free to pursue programs with the potential for financial or prestige gains, with only secondary regard for the appropriateness of such programs for the traditional mission of higher education.

Controversies over the control of intercollegiate sport in the early twentieth century are also illustrative of the confidence placed in formal bureaucratic blueprints for governance of educational programs. Following the AAUP recommendations, faculty were placed in positions of direct governance over athletic programs. It was assumed that such positioning in the bureaucratic hierarchy, coupled with the faculty's proper educational philosophy and sensitivity, would guarantee consistency of athletic programs with educational objectives. Instead of real control, however, there was a formal fulfillment of faculty demands for control, while in reality faculty control was not exercised. Instead, athletic personnel in many instances were merely given faculty titles.

Confidence in formal designs of bureaucratic control is a distinctive feature of modern society. The rational ordering of roles, with carefully explicated relationships, lines of authority, and specific organizational goals, give a sense of the organization as modern, efficient, and legitimate.

A number of structures have been developed which differ as to which organizational officers control intercollegiate sport (see Figure 6). In all structures, however, theoretical accountability to the ultimate overseers of college operations, the board of trustees, is designed as the guarantee of the educational merit of organizational programs.

Intraorganizational governance structures can be separated into four types, depending on the degree to which each structure resembles the traditional means through which academic departments in the college or university are governed. Primary differences between the models concern (1) the number of officers that have some control over athletics and (2) the degree to which their daily responsibilities concern business as opposed to curricular and other academic matters. As we move away from sports governance structures more closely approximating traditional academic control structures, (model A in Figure 6), there are progressively fewer levels of personnel able to exercise control over athletics and there is more of a business emphasis in the responsibilities of officers. While in the academic model athletics are governed as an area of academic concern through the Academic Dean or a similar officer, in the opposite structures (models C and D in Figure 6) this control is lacking. While the Academic Dean must, of course, be concerned with dollars, this officer is not as concerned with such matters as the Vice-President for Business Affairs must be (as in

Figure 6: Alternative Governance Structures for Intercollegiate Sport

Structures within Traditional Academic Framework		Structures outside Traditional Academic Framework	
Board of Trustees	Board of Trustees	Board of Trustees	Board of Trustees
President	President	President	
Vice-Presidents	Vice-Presidents		Board of Directors
Provost	Provost		
Academic Dean	Dean of Student Affairs	Vice President for Business Affairs	
Chair of Physical Education			
Athletic Director	Athletic Director	Athletic Director	Athletic Director
Coaches	Coaches	Coaches	Coaches
Intercollegiate Sports	Intercollegiate Sports	Intercollegiate Sports	Intercollegiate Sports
(A)	(B)	(C)	(D)

model C). Substituted for the academic and curricular concerns of the Dean are the hard criteria of cost-benefit analysis applied through the Business Office. Academic control is almost entirely bypassed in the most nonacademic structure (model D), which excludes even the president of the institution. Athletic structures such as these may be private corporations. These sport departments may be affiliated with the university and act as symbolic representations of the institution, yet athletics may not be governed by the same rules as other programs of the school (Frey 1982).

Accompanying the difference in governance structure has been a growing reliance upon "boosters" funds. Alumni and "friends of the university" typically join to form the booster organization. These clubs sponsor tailgate parties and awards banquets; although only unofficially related to the university, the ability of boosters to raise funds gives them a certain degree of influence in the college community. With spiraling costs for sport, there has been a greater urgency to find money from untapped sources. This has led to significant increase in the flow of donations earmarked for athletic purposes. While donations accounted for 5% of athletic budgets for big-time schools in 1965, in 1977, average booster donations accounted for $246,000, or 10%, of total athletic budgets. More recent research indicates continuation of this trend toward greater reliance upon booster-generated funds to cover athletic costs. In a 19801–981 survey to 58 major universities, it was found that donations per institution averaged $1.34 million (*Chronicle of Higher Education*, March 3, 1982:5).

While booster groups have increasingly demonstrated their fund-raising effectiveness and have thus become increasingly popular among colleges and universities, the potential for abuse has also increased. While such organizations may raise much-needed money for the support of athletics, the external nature of booster groups inherently distances such groups from the central philosophic tendencies of the institution with which they are affiliated. While booster groups may direct all their energies toward the acquisition of one institutional goal (dollars, star players, or coaches), boosters unassociated and unsupervised by central administrative leadership may, unwittingly or not, supplant the primary educational goals of the college or university with the secondary goal of resource acquisition. With the drying up of funds from federal and state sources and the growing popularity of outside booster fund-raising groups, the potential for abuse increases.[4] The internal governance structures employed at much-penalized Wichita State and Texas A & M most clearly resemble the forms without academic control (models C and D). In the extreme case (model D), the influence of booster groups, that is, outside promoters of college sport, is maximized and uninhibited by even a minimum of intrauniversity personnel.

Although educational control over intercollegiate sport is still theoretically provided by trustees supervision in all four models, nevertheless because of their nature in models that bypass traditional academic offices there is less input by officers specifically concerned with the curriculum and the education of students. Rather than being concerned with educational programs and individual students, incumbents of elevated bureaucratic positions typically concern themselves with more global concerns, such as resource acquisition and relations with significant elements in the task environment. To delegate the control of intercollegiate sport to business officers and trustees is to guarantee that sport will be evaluated in terms of the contribution it makes to these officers' concern for resource acquisition for the organization. If indeed "we are what we do," then those who constantly deal with matters of dollars and budgets, red ink and black, will naturally tend to generalize these concerns to the programs they oversee.

It may be, then, that the educational control that such structures are intended to provide for intercollegiate athletics is only theoretical. Blueprints for efficient internal governance of academic programs, although they may indicate rational direction of the organization's programs toward the achievement of stated educational objectives, may not in fact function effectively to provide that educational guidance.

The National Collegiate Athletic Association. The ineffectiveness with which sport has been educationally directed through internal college and university structures has been paralleled by an extraorganizational control structure which, to date, has similarly not ensured educational direction for intercollegiate sport. The National Collegiate Athletic Association (NCAA), which presently governs the athletic programs of some eight hundred institutions, evolved from the 38 schools that in 1906 formed the Intercollegiate Athletic Association. The Association was originally formed in response to public criticisms of the brutalities of football. It was reorganized into the NCAA in 1910, with a constitution that called for "studying college athletics and promoting measures to make college sport dignified and ethical."

According to Stern (1979:252-259), the NCAA grew for a number of reasons from a loose confederation into the primary governing organization for intercollegiate sport. The growing numbers of schools involved in sporting competitions increased the need for standardizing rules, communications, and coordination. These functions became increasingly centralized under the auspices of the NCAA. Championship competitions became more important to schools with big-time athletic programs, and this increased the strength of the NCAA, which staged these championships. With the rise of television with its strong interest in college sport, the NCAA organized the bargaining efforts of individual schools, coordinated bowl championships, and served as sanctioning agent to legitimize approved competitions. With continued appearances on behalf of college sport through its spokespersons, press releases and reports, the NCAA gained recognition and legitimation as official spokesperson for college athletics.

Like other organizations, the NCAA has had to adapt to its environment in order to survive. Despite policy to the contrary, for example, member schools were allowed to play against institutions unaffiliated with the NCAA, and many of its competitions included unaffiliated colleges. In 1935, a decision by the Southeastern Conference to give scholarships ran directly in opposition to national association policy. When the costs and benefits of the scholarship system became apparent to other conferences, and other schools adopted this practice, the NCAA repealed the "need" criterion previously in effect (Stern 1979:255).

Discrepancy between stated policy and permitted behavior is an example of "loose coupling." By not tightly following officially sanctioned rules, frictions within the larger organization are decreased and overall support for organizations such as the NCAA is maintained. Loose coupling is practiced by many formal organizations that deem the cost of adherence to official policy too great.

With repeated public disclosures of scandals in intercollegiate sport in the early 1950s (*New York Times*, March 21, 1951:1; August 5, 1951:1; August 12, 1951:Sec. 5), with unsuccessful periodic attempts at regulation, and with the threat of the American Council on Education's recommending deemphasis of sports, the "enforcement decision" of 1952 was reached, which gave the NCAA control over rule making and the enforcement of sanctions against violators of recruiting, eligibility, and other rules (Stern 1979). Between 1952 and 1977, 993 charges of rule infractions were brought to the NCAA, with disciplinary action taken in 548 cases. Of the 144 Division I football schools, 74 were penalized by the NCAA during that period (NCAA Enforcement Program 1978).[5]

Schools that have sought legal redress from alleged NCAA interference with internal university concerns (for example, California State University at Sacramento, Howard University, Centenary College, University of Denver, and University of Minnesota) have been generally unsuccessful (Gerber 1979). The courts have usually upheld the right of the NCAA to govern intercollegiate sport because of the inability of colleges and universities to control abuses in their sports (El-Khawas 197:511). In addition, the 1951 authorization of the NCAA to negotiate television rights for all of college sport gave the association leverage for a time against violators interested in increasing television revenues.

Despite sanction powers given to it by the 1952 enforcement decision, and subsequent support of its jurisdiction by the courts, the NCAA continues to draw criticism. In the thirty years that have elapsed since enforcement powers were increased, the NCAA has not been able to stem the tide of illegal recruiting violations and eligibility transgressions. To this day, the NCAA maintains that it is the interorganizational guardian of amateur collegiate athletics. In the face of these claims comes a seemingly daily torrent of transcript frauds, admissions criteria and test-score changing, and under-the-table money from alumni and college boosters. Big-time college sport is criticized as anything but educational and amateur. Instead, the NCAA is cited as a vehicle through which competition is restricted and profits maximized for the university "firms" engaged in the business of intercollegiate athletics (Koch and Leonard 1978).

Discrepancy between the lofty mission of higher education and the low level of ethical conduct which seems to pervade big-time intercollegiate sport was largely responsible for the Carnegie Foundation report of 1929 and the two investigations of 1952and 1974 funded by the American Council on Education (ACE). With a mission as rational and moral as that given to higher education, it seemed inconsistent that methods perhaps more appropriate for criminal intercourse should be employed by collegiate sports. Summarizing the results of a more recent ACE study, Hanford reports that,

> the results of the inquiry suggest that most of the rules for the conduct of intercollegiate sport were written to protect institutions from each other and that the interests of the athletes themselves as individuals come second (Hanford 1974:127).

Despite pages and pages of rules and officially sanctioned procedure, member institutions continually violate those rules in the recruiting and eligibility maintenance of athletes. Why?

Organizations characteristically develop norms of behavior with which they are comfortable. As individuals associate with others with whom they are similar, and as their interactions are governed by norms of behavior with which they are personally comfortable, organizations like colleges and universities employ in their interactions normative patterns of behavior that are based upon assumptions concerning the behavior of the professionals in the organization. For example, while it might be the norm to punch a time clock in some organizations, assumptions concerning personal commitment to teaching and learning mitigate against the appearance of a time clock in the academic department office.

Similarly, schools that find a need to cooperate employ norms of behavior similar to those characteristic of the academic professions. As previously noted, "loose coupling" (the disconnection of policies from outcomes, and structures and rules from actual activities) in the school permits the organization to operate amidst the wide range of goals and processes of the university (Meyer and Scott 1983:182–183). By not enforcing all policies and by not searching for inconsistencies in philosophy and programs, the university is able to present a rational, efficient facade to the environment that supports it.

Despite the thirty-some years since the NCAA enforcement decision of the early 1950s, the need for strong institutional enforcement — that is, an NCAA with real capabilities to police the behavior of individual schools — there has been relatively little done to counter the historical institutional autonomy of the American academic world nor the loose coupling which has become the norm in higher education. American schools have historically guarded their independence with zeal, while encouraging the assumption that the profession will police itself without the enforcement structures seemingly more appropriate for nonprofessional workers. Because of the tradition of institutional autonomy and the academic norm of loose coupling (which itself is dependent upon the assumption of a self-policing professoriate) extrainstitutional organizations such as the NCAA have little teeth when it comes to the enforcement of association policies.[1]

As Hanford (1974) has noted, enforcement resources of the NCAA have been minimal. Even with its recently enlarged staff of 12 full-time and 26 part-time investigators, the potential cost of rule violation has not been high. To the coaches whose livelihoods depend upon winning, the pressure is great to get an edge in this competition, to recruit the "franchise" - to do what is necessary to please alumni, money-minded university business officers, and prestige-hungry boosters of the teams. Without adequate enforcement personnel, the probabilities are small of presenting sufficient deterrence to radically reduce the number of violations among some eight hundred NCAA members and, in particular, among the 177 Division I schools.

The legality of one of the most important sanctions available to the NCAA has been called into question by recent lawsuits aimed at wresting from the NCAA authority for the negotiation of television contracts. In the court's initial decision, Judge Juan Burciaga, after noting the "classic cartel behavior" of the NCAA, ruled that the body does not have the right to be the sole negotiator of television contracts for college football. Ruling in favor of big-time athletic directors, the court declared that only the individual college or university has the right to market its telecasts (*New York Times*, 1982:819, 824). In the summer of 1984, the Supreme Court concurred with the lower court ruling and in its 7–2 decision declared that intercollegiate big-time sport is first and foremost a business venture that is engaged in for profit and that the NCAA "restricted rather than enhanced the place of intercollegiate athletics in the nation's life" (Farrell, July 5, 1984:1, 22). According to Justice Stevens, it was evident that the NCAA possessed market power to restrain trade because "college football constitutes a separate market for which there is no reasonable substitute."[7]

The question remains, however, why have rules not been more strongly enforced? The columnist David Anderson described the ineffectiveness of sanctions.

> Being on probation is almost fashionable. Being on probation is proof for the alumni and the boosters that a college is trying to win. And being on probation is even a source of laughs now. (Anderson 1982:53)

Walter Byers, Executive Director of the NCAA, admits that violations are widespread: "The rewards have escalated so fast and the penalties have not increased at the same rate. Probation is considered the price of doing business by some schools." Estimating that payments to top "amateur" athletes run as high as $20,000 per year, Byers also senses decreased cooperation by coaches, little power by presidents to act, and little remorse by violators placed on probation (Alfano 1984:1, 48).

If the issue of consistency of college sports practices with institutional educational mission and method is important, why have member schools not demanded more enforcement, and supported that demand with added funds? As Harold Enarson, former President of Ohio State

University, has remarked, "The NCAA naturally can be only as effective as its members make it . . . " (Enarson 1980:26). Clearly the control of college sport is highly problematic. As G. Alexander Heard, Chancellor of Vanderbilt University, has declared:

> Can controls be effective in a system characterized by the incentives for abuse that exist in intercollegiate spectator sports? American society has, for a long time, sought to control complex social phenomena and highly motivated individual behavior through regulations, rules, and statutes, sometimes with satisfactory results and sometimes not. There may be no way to contain the pressures in the system short of a full and radical revision of it. (Enarson 1980:25)

The present system of intercollegiate sport and its governance is not working. The system is designed to serve the survival needs of big-time schools and not the educational needs of its players. Existing external and internal institutional governance systems serve less as means for maintaining educational direction for collegiate sport than they serve as "evidence" to the public that mechanisms exist to "guarantee" the educational consistency of sport programs. Token surveillance along with punishment of rule violators is less a deterrence to future transgression than it is symbolic evidence of sincerity on the part of the NCAA to keep intercollegiate sport "educational." But then again, considering the minimal power and resources given the NCAA to enforce its regulations, do the schools that compose its membership really want enforcement of the codes that they have agreed to?

There is clearly a perception among NCAA member schools that they receive more resources in the way of money and prestige without tight enforcement than they would gain with it. By supporting only a token enforcement of official rules, institutions of higher education may play sports at the big-time level, provide entertainment, and earn the dollars and prestige of a major institution, while maintaining the fiction that enforcement mechanisms exist to punish wrongdoers and ensure the educational mission of these schools. Certainly, the level of enforcement so far sanctioned has not served to redirect the athletic programs away from emphasizing winning and toward educating the individual student-athlete. Token enforcement has instead acted as a component of the myth of educational sports.

In a similar fashion, both the intrainstitutional and interinstitutional governance structures for intercollegiate sport resemble the formal structure discussed by sociologists Meyer and Rowan. Formal structure is described as

> a blue print for activities which includes, first of all, the table of organization: a listing of offices, departments, positions and programs. These elements are linked by explicit goals and policies that make up a rational theory of how, and to what end, activities are to be fitted together. (Meyer and Rowan 1977:342)

It is often assumed that the primary purpose of formal structures is to ensure rational and coordinated means of efficient production. In the case of the control of athletics, the product is supposed to be sport which is educational, sport which is controlled by the school and the NCAA, and sport which is therefore ostensibly consistent with the stated educational philosophy of colleges and universities.

If we assume that the prime purpose for formal structure is efficient production, then with the incorporation of necessary changes to the structure, production should be more efficient. Tinkering by changing a role relationship, adding personnel here and a new program there, should increase productivity. This may be the case, however, only if the *real* function of formal structure is to reach the stated goals of production. If the real goal is different, if the formal structure is primarily a skeleton for public perusal, but which will be given little substance, then tinkering with this structure will do little to facilitate education. Member schools of the NCAA, for example, may not support the enforcement efforts of the Association because they do not wish greater enforcement. With few personnel to discover and punish rule violators, the main body of violations is not uncovered. Therefore, the publicized sanctions imposed provide evidence of the efforts by the schools and the NCAA to maintain consistency between educational purpose and athletics.

According to Meyer and Rowan, policies and procedures may be adopted by organizations less to increase productivity than to obtain greater legitimacy and to enhance the survival prospects of the organization in society. Internal and external athletic governance structures may exist not to govern the educational propiety of sports programs but to present the image of educational appropriateness of the sports programs.

We have seen in the history of the NCAA instances where formal policy has been loosely coupled with actual allowable member behavior. NCAA members have played nonmember schools despite prohibitions. No-need scholarships have been awarded despite policy against this. In a similar manner, enforcement efforts have not been effective. Without strong enforcement there is little deterrence against rule-breaking behavior.

In many formal organizations, there is evidence of loose coupling.

structural elements are often only loosely linked to each other and to activities, rules are often violated, decisions are often unimplemented, or if implemented have uncertain consequences, technologies are of problematic efficiency, and evaluation and inspection systems are subverted or rendered so vague as to provide little coordination (Meyer and Rowan 1977:342-343).

There is already sufficient evidence that schools are loosely coupled organizations (Meyer and Rowan 1975). Educational organizations lack internal coordination. Academic instruction, although presumably sequential, is rarely evaluated. Quality of academic performance is not systematically controlled and there is little hard evidence that the methods efficiently and specifically lead to the stated goals of the organization.

Because schools have little way to prove that they teach efficiently and rationally, there is the need for institutionalized rules that promote trust and confidence. The formal structure of educational organizations, although rarely intended for strict implementation, plays an important function for the organization. Formal structure that buttresses the myths in the institutional environment serves as a demonstration that the organization is acting in a proper and adequate manner (Meyer and Rowan 1977:349). The organization that wants to draw resources from groups in the environment will develop a formal structure that appeases as many of these groups as possible. Bureaucratic flow charts are developed and appropriate educational personnel are included so as to "ensure" educational accountability. Policies concerning recruiting and eligibility rules are drawn up and publicized, and sanctions are announced for offenses. In so doing, the educational organization engenders a public assumption of its rationality and legitimacy, which is necessary for institutional survival. However, the organization may not actually function according to this formal structure. Policy statements are hollow unless enforced.

In organizations such as schools that demonstrate loose coupling between their formal structure and their actual behavior, it may be the case that rigid coordination and adherence to policy standards will promote too much internal friction. Rules and standards that are designed primarily to appeal to the environment outside the school may conflict with the actual needs or wants of the school staff. To enforce vigorously an eligibility rule, for example, that was specifically adopted to appease some outside education concern group may cause great dissension among the majority of athletic personnel inside big-time sport who understand the normality of eligibility rules' violation. As a result, little or no enforcement of rules may be supported. Token enforcement leads to minimal internal friction and the maintenance of a veneer of legitimacy in the eyes of outside concern groups.

Owing to the diversity of higher education's task environment, a number of ceremonial rules are enacted. Rules of governance structure and policy are "ceremonial" in the sense that they are primarily for consumption by those viewing them, and do not really affect internal governance of the educational organization. Because of the number of important resource-bearing groups in the environment, it is understandable that some of these ceremonial rules may conflict with each other. Alumni and booster groups want winning athletic teams if they are to support the school financially. Students want the prestige of winning sports, as do state legislators. But faculty and educational concern groups point to more traditional understandings of what the academy should be and do. The public has a vague notion that school programs should educate.

Notions of academic freedom and institutional autonomy further undermine chances for extra-institutional governance to control and limit excesses in college sport. College administrators zealously guard against such intrusions into their independence, such as that represented by the proposal sponsored by the American Council on Education, which would have set up a decision-making council of forty-four presidents. Instead, on January 10, 1984, the proposal before the NCAA Convention was defeated 328–313 in favor of the NCAA-sponsored proposal that called for the formation of a council of presidents given merely the power to advise on NCAA legislation to be reviewed by the full NCAA convention — a convention dominated by the athletic directors and faculty representatives (themselves often boosters of college sport) who constitute the vast majority of all delegates (Vance, November 30, 1983:21; Bok 1983:33; White 1984:85, 87).

The diversity of American higher education's task environment and the depth of its resource insecurities have contributed to a complex web of formal structure and policy which is at times conflicting and generally confusing. Programs and policy statements designed to appeal to and draw resources from one group may seem to contradict the policy and programs designed to appease some other groups. Formal structures to oversee athletics are set up, but somehow athletics takes an noneducational turn. Unethical behavior is supposed to be deterred, but somehow continues to occur. "Student first and athlete second" is the claim, but somehow this becomes a fiction in big-time athletics.

Because of the web of conflicting rules, policies which if implemented will lead to internal friction, offices that are only ceremonially included in bureaucratic control charts, and other examples of organizational cross purposes, obfuscation, and confusion, there develops the "logic of good faith" — the notion that programs will function well enough so long as officers do not look too closely for organizational inconsistency and do not try to radically alter the system. Confidence is expressed in high organizational officers whose duty it is to oversee athletics. These officers then need not deal more with this conflicting web of policy and programs. College presidents and trustees gladly leave responsibility for sports programs to the athletic director, who in turn expresses faith in the coaches. Although most blueprints for the formal structure of internal college governance indicate the ultimate responsibility of the president and/or trustees — hypothetically able to meld economic and educational concerns — because of confusion in program and conflicting policies, these officers often abdicate that responsibility.

The College President. The chief executive officer of the college or university enjoyed real power at least until the end of the nineteenth century. The trustees historically bequeathed the real power to the president of the college, given their part-time status, their other work commitments, their lack of direct sources of information concerning the college, their dependence upon the resident administrators for information and access to the governance structure of the institution. The small number of faculty in the late nineteenth century, enabled the president to directly and almost immediately influence institutional programs. In 1870 ten faculty and ninety students in the average college permitted an intimate relationship among leadership, staff, and students.

With the rapid growth of the academic world in the twentieth century, the role of the president has changed markedly. The average
number of students and faculty had quadrupled by 1910 (Carnegie
Foundation 1982:16). Presidents faced with populations of one thousand, two thousand, or forty thousand students, with faculty number-
ing upwards of two thousand, with sciences, programs in technology,
social sciences, and the humanities, with graduate, undergraduate, and
part-time students, are confronted by a very different task today than
in the simpler nineteenth century. The college president today must be
much more concerned with the nurturing of the campus and its protection from the environment than with academic matters within the
campus. With faculty specialization into many disciplines and with the
part-time status of trustees, it is theoretically the president who must
oversee the delicate balance between the internal needs and moral principles of the campus against the resources available from the environment. The increasingly outward push of the president's role, however,
has made this oversight responsibility all the more problematic. Control over the campus, its programs, and the moral image reflected by
the behavior of institutional agents, has therefore been left to specialized faculty and staff. But business managers and development personnel concerned with the fiscal state of the institution will naturally see
program efficiency in terms of a program's contributions to the
economic welfare of the institution. Department chairs, while they may
express concern over athletic abuses or irresponsible investment or
building programs, because they are primarily concerned with their
department's welfare, are left out of the ordinary governance processes
of the institution.

The combination of all-college administration with perspectives
too often limited to the budget, faculty whose power and responsibilities are commonly isolated within the corridors of their discipline,
and, finally, the president whose responsibilities to external constituents (such as potential benefactors) have supplanted historical concerns with the academic programs and integrity of the institution, have
all contributed to a power vacuum on the campus. This void has created
opportunities for misguided agents of the institution to fulfill their own
specialized interests — such as winning football, or looking for faculty
who do the "right" sort of research — without the guidance of strong
overall institutional leadership.

From an organizational perspective, given the size of the institution and the web of conflicting noncoordinated goals and programs of

the university, it is no small wonder that leadership has changed its role from an internal to an external focus. Meyer and Scott (1983), among others, have noted that organizations such as the university so dependent upon the outside environment for resources will often direct their attention toward maintaining conformity with "socially standard-ized categories of the educational system while little effort is expended in the control and coordination of instructional activities" (Meyer and Scott 1983:49). In order to maintain the support of accrediting bodies, federal watchdog, agencies, private foundations, state legislatures, and potential benefactors, the university must above all else look like a university. Leadership is focused on the number of volumes in the library, the higher degrees of the faculty, the appearance of buildings, which provide material evidence of the appropriateness and hence the legitimacy of the institution.

While the college president (or more specifically, the chief execu-tive officer — CEO) typically stands at the head of the organization's resident administrative structure, the nature and effectiveness of the position seem to have changed quite markedly from the days of power-ful presidents such as Harper and Hutchins. Rather than being able to almost single-handedly alter the character of an institution, modern presidents often find themselves constrained in their behaviors toward athletics or other institutional concerns by forces both within and out-side of the college. Although one might naively accuse the CEO of unethically supporting an immoral intercollegiate sport system, these leaders are not all-powerful autocrats. Rather, they may be quite fearful for their jobs and have so many other immediately threatening fires to fight that issues other than those currently burning may be ignored.

While the first college presidents were recruited from the ministry and were concerned every day with "the ethical dimension," according to Enarson (1984:25), for the new business leadership, "Nowhere do ethical concerns and and capacities fit into the job description." Now instead of leading the university, presidents too often are managers, who, perhaps owing to the pluralism of the school and of society, are unwilling to make decisions based on moral and ethical considerations. Instead, these presidents play the game with the rules as they are presently written. They avoid wrongdoing and the appearance of wrongdoing because it is reasoned that an image of a harmonious effi-cient organization permits them the resources to do good works for the institution. Attending to the routine of bureaucracy, maintaining good public relations, and appearing "presidential" have become of paramount importance. Conflict within the institution and the bad publicity that can be engendered are to be avoided at all times. But as Enarson (1984:25) notes, "playing the game" and the avoidance of wrongdoing "are very different from promoting the highest values of the institution, the self and the society."

Presidents whose conservative orientations have been almost ensured by passage through layers of bureaucratic filters have been socialized to see their job in bureaucratic terms. But according to Wood (1984:42)

> From an idealistic perspective, higher education suffers when bureaucratic means begin to dominate the intellectual and heroic ends of educational leadership. . . . It is clear that today's social and economic environment encourages trustees, presidents and faculty members, those who both reflect and mold prevailing ideas about the presidential role, to value managerial and political skills more than a continuing intellectual engagement with what Mathew Arnold once called "the best that is known and thought in the world."

Beneath the level of sociability between the trustees and the president, Wood identifies a tension — a tension found in business, where the turnover of chief leadership is nearly unequalled. This performance pressure has led to caution on the part of presidents. The precariousness of the president's position has spoken against exercising dynamic leadership and toward "good management." And what is good management? Good management is evaluated by the trustees, who, like their predecessors, are primarily from the business class. Ninety percent of the forty-eight thousand voting trustees in the spring of 1985 were white, 80% were men, and 70% were at least fifty years old. While black trustees in public institutions has doubled from 5.9% in 1976 to 11.4% in 1986, blacks still compose but 5.5% of all trustees in American private colleges and universities (Jacobson 1986:23).

But good management — which, as Enarson (1984) notes, may be value-neutral — may not be good leadership, which is almost never neutral. While good management places a premium on the smooth flow of resources to the efficiently operating components of the organization, the cautious management role of the contemporary president shrinks from the confrontation with issues that are bound to upset some elements of the institution's environment and so upset the harmonious facade of the university. This is so whether the issue is intercollegiate sport or investments in South Africa, the hiring or firing of a coach or of female, black, or Marxist faculty. When the efficient management of the university becomes of paramount importance to the sole agent with the oversight and authority to maintain the moral course of the institution, then there is no one to oversee the "good character" of the academic environment.

The academic world is buffeted by external agents which threaten its treasured autonomy. As boosters have undermined the athletic program from without and single-minded athletic directors and coaches have chased money and winning beyond ethical limits, without strong oversight from moral leadership, then state and federal government bureaucracy, the courts, and the logic of specialized interest groups within the university threaten academic freedom and responsibility.

Cohen and March (1974:2) have noted that the college "presidency is an illusion." While images of the white-haired patriarch of the university imply omnipotence, on closer examination the effect of the president has become increasingly decoupled from the decision-making process. Whereas presidents of an older day typically presided over small schools with few faculty and students, over an institution that may have had a more focused mission than today's behemoth campuses, and over a college more isolated from external forces of government, unions, courts, industry, and accrediting agencies, today's realities have undermined and vitiated the personal influence of the president over such issues as college sport.

In *The Confidence Crisis*, Dressell, Johnson, and Marcus (1970) illustrate the effect of disciplinary departmentalization on the university. Faculties ensconced in their own particular fiefdoms vigorously defend their budgets and personnel, placing departmental priorities above those of the institution. Becoming more concerned with their own ways of thinking, political viewpoints, and priorities, the insulated disciplinary department checks the freedom with which the president may change the institution. The same feudalistic attitude pervades the American academic organization composed of specialist offices each demanding input prior to decision making.

Growth in the size of the university has further inhibited dynamic institutional behavior by imposing layer upon layer of bureaucracy on the organization between the president and what is actually going on. Rapid decision making and action on policy decisions is curtailed not only by still somewhat influential faculty and department heads, but also by the many offices, officials, forms, committees, through whom decisions and information must pass to and from and the chief executive officer. Because of the size of the institution and the growth in the bureaucracy of governance, the contemporary college president has passed through many filters to reach his office (Cohen and March 1974:2). In his passage through the status of student, graduate student, faculty member, department head, dean, vice-president, and then president, overly radical behavior and demeanor at any stop may eliminate the would-be chief executive officer. Conservative presidents result from this filtering process, concerned with maintaining their school's reputation and in minimizing the conflict that might do damage to their own reputations as well as the institution's.

With the increased influence of more internal as well as external constituencies, the work of the president has become more administrative and fire fighting than leadership and long-range planning (Boyer 1977; Keller 1983). Furthermore, the presidency has become more concerned with external agencies and pressure groups, to the detriment of the president's leadership capacities within the institution. Presidents have had to respond to greater external political pressure and intrusion; more than two-thirds of the CEOs in a 1983–1984 study stated that fund raising consumed more time and effort than ever (Evangelauf 1986:1). In another study conducted by Clark Kerr (Winkler, January 25, 1984), based on interviews with over seven hundred presidents, it was found that only 2% felt they were "fully involved and play a central role in academic life." In Kerr's estimation, the role of the college president has changed from "academic leader" to "manager." E. Bruce Heilman, President of the University of Richmond, feels that this change in role has been caused by the pressure to raise money, recruit students, spend time in the state capital, be involved in federal politics, and respond to the demands of governing boards. Academic priorities are no longer set by the presidents of the nation's colleges.

And what is the result of this change of presidential role due to the demands of internal and external constituencies? Based on interviews with nearly eight hundred fifty presidents and other leaders of colleges and universities, it seems that higher education in America is suffering from a "pervasive lack of strong presidential leadership" (Jacobson, September 26, 1984:1). "Kind of going day by day" has replaced long-term planning. Procuring resources is more important than academic leadership.

It is no small wonder, then, that a president encountering a successful football or basketball coach is reluctant to question too deeply that coach's method or demeanor. After all, the coach may be speaking to the very same constituencies that the president does. Students, legislators, and diverse faculties may all be united behind the coach's team. The school banner is waved nationally before the proud eyes of trustees and potential donors. The reputation of the school may be enhanced, and sine the president typically is no longer concerned with academic questions, it is financial and recruitment matters that are the president's greatest concerns.

The altered focus of the president's role has coincided with dramatic change in big-time college sport. Koppett (1984) notes that in the last ten years competition between the top 80 football schools in the country has required that they model this mode of operation after the intensive recruiting and labor practices of the elite football powers. Academically oriented private schools such as Stanford are now faced with three choices: (1) to change admissions procedures, recruiting methods, fund-raising strategies, athletic staff pay scales, and general attitudes toward intercollegiate sports in order to compete with the football elite; (2) to adjust the schedule so as not to play these schools; (3) to do neither, and continue to lose. At Rice University, another selective private university, the president has supported spending $300,000 to hire a "supercoach," develop football facilities, and incorporate a new business curriculum to appeal to the more pragmatically minded student-athletes (Vance November 2, 1983:21–22). Apparently, the image of the university requires bolstering through the improvement of the football team. Money and curriculum will be directed toward this end.

The reluctance of college presidents to take a strong hand in reforming sports abuses is explained by the relative power of the successful coach, through structures of governance which place sport outside the authority of the president, and through the changing role of the president, from academic leader to business chief. The winning coach is powerful because of the sport's visibility and the status accorded winners in our society. Chief executive officers may be reluctant to carefully scrutinize their own athletic programs even though they may suspect athletic improprieties (Hanford 1974). Without direct authority to hire or fire athletic personnel, college and university presidents who find themselves with a winning but unethical coach must confront trustee, alumni, and booster groups more directly concerned with the tangible pleasures of winning than with abstractions such as ethics and lofty academic purposes. Finally, presidents whose responsibilities demand a limited view of the institution, whose roles are concerned with money and students and not with the integrity of the school, will do little to curb the excesses of the very sport programs that label that president's tenure as successful.

President William Atchley of Clemson University tried to gain control of athletics at his institution. In addition, he was a proponent for reform within the NCAA and the College Football Association. Clemson, which won football's national championship in 1981, had twice been given severe sanctions in men's basketball (1975–1978) and football (1982–1984). More recently, the campus had been shocked by revelations of drug abuse and the influence of boosters who donated over $5 million annually but who undermined the integrity of the athletic program through illegal payments to athletes and recruiting violations. When President Atchley asked for a vote of confidence so that the University might clean its own house, the trustees refused and forced him to resign. Apparently, college sport was not deemed by the trustees to be within the jurisdiction of the president. Central administrative control of internal university affairs were thus undermined at Clemson (Monaghan 1985).

The Control of the Campus. As the problems of unethical behavior, and racial, sexual, and economic stratification in sports mirror those of the wider campus, problems in the effective governance of intercollegiate sport are reflections of concerns for the institutional and national governance of the academic world. Outside interest groups intrude on the autonomy of higher education to shape academic policy, and the malaise in the presidential role affects the reform of sport as well as educational leadership. Factors such as American academe's historical lack of resources, its tradition of community service from the latter nineteenth century, the broad definition of the purposes and programs of higher education, and a governance structure that mirrored the business-minded bureaucratic leadership of the nation have engendered the peculiarly American relationship between the campus and the community — a relationship that though apparently beneficial in the short run, may indeed threaten the future integrity of the academy.

Historically, the Dartmouth College decision of 1819 affirmed the independence of higher education institutions from the state. The board of governors of the college and its corporate body were to be seen as the holders of college property and its ultimate decision makers. With the exclusion of the state from direct control, the academy apparently gained autonomy from government. Coupled with the failures of the faculty to wrest control from the administration, this ensured the trustees their preeminent position in college governance.

In *The Control of the Campus* (1982), the Carnegie Foundation identifies a number of concerns in the governance of higher education in America. State legislatures and governors have been increasingly isolated from the needs of the campus by the burgeoning state of educational bureaucracy. Bureaucratic budget considerations and oversight have become threateningly intrusive into the academic decision-making process. In all fifty states, "sunshine laws" mandating public disclosure in the decision-making process have been reported to constrain discourse and candor in personnel evaluations, inhibit the quantity and quality of information used in decision making, increase reliance on procedure at the expense of leadership, discourage new ideas and innovation, and ultimately encourage mediocrity, making it exceedingly difficult to dismiss incompetent administration and faculty because of fear of defamation suits and bad publicity to the college (Jacobson, October 3, 1984:11). Specialized outside accrediting boards tend to isolate particular departments from the wider interests of the institution. The federal government, whose relationship with higher education was so optimistically expanded with the GI Bill and the Higher Education Act of 1965, and which is the university's major patron for research ($40 million in 1940, $138 million in 1953, $3.4 billion in 1979), has also increased its oversight of the academic world. Federal support has been matched by its restrictions on human subjects experiments, DNA explorations, and the free dissemination of research owing to "national security" considerations. Academic freedom is further threatened by universities that measure faculty productivity by success in grant applications. While it might be natural to expect government agency support of politically conservative as well as popular research topics. The courts have also increased their intrusion into the business of higher education. While Titles VI, VII, and IX of the 1964 Civil Rights Act have for the most part catalyzed long overdue shifts in the university's populations, in some cases litigation in the courts has led to time- and money-consuming battles.

The government money that prioritizes and legitimizes research topics and procedures is matched, by the increasingly intimate relationship of business to higher education.[8] Conflicts of interest are not uncommon between the teaching, research, and publishing of professors and their work as consultants, or even owners, of industry. How can the professor who owns a gene-splicing business argue against the ethics and practical dangers of that investment? How can the faculty's search for truth remain unbiased by the retainer of the business that hires the professor to find better ways to sell deodorant? And how well can professors serve society and fulfill their professional responsibility when they are being paid to develop pump toothpastes and similar improvements to the human condition?

In the face of boosters and special interest groups bearing money, with the court's civil rights legislation directing sport and hiring policies, with state legislators pushing for high-technology center clones of Silicon Valley as they measure the value of the university by the industry it attracts and the record of the football team, in light of insulated self-serving coaches, and faculty more concerned with their consulting careers than with their student-athletes, it is strong presidential leadership that is needed. In the absence of presidential control there is a dangerous void, a void unfillable by managers more concerned with the facade of efficiency and the hard measures of productivity. Management is not leadership.

Clearly, leadership was lacking from a Methodist university in Texas. This was a school with high ambitions to vault to the first rank of American universities — a school making progress in hiring distinguished faculty to teach higher-caliber students recently attracted to the institution. Yet it was a school that exhibited many of the governance problems considered in these pages. Southern Methodist University's ambitious plans were largely the result of the Dallas businessmen who dominate its Board of Governors. The Board imposed a corporate hierarchy and mindset on the University. According to Edwin Cox, a Dallas oilman on the Board:

> A university is run by a combination of people. . . . All should report to the board. Of course, the board does have final say. We want input but that doesn't always mean we'll take what they say and put it in force. (Lederman, January 7, 1987:37)

Southern Methodist University was run as a corporation. It was the business mindset of the organization that failed to remember that this was an institution of higher learning affiliated with the Methodist Church. Instead of fostering the academic oversight that the president could offer over all university programs, the board ensured that educational leadership would be lacking by creating an atmosphere so unattractive that Southern Methodist has seen seven presidents in fourteen years. As the Southern Methodist case illustrates, if higher education is run with a business mentality and its bottom line accountability, then the standards of rights and processes that are the norm of the social institution of higher education may very well suffer. Fair play, in the spirit as well as the letter of the law, does not always win in business or in athletics. While a strong board does not necessarily mean its school is a renegade athletic institution, nevertheless when trustees limit the athletic oversight authority of the president or make consistent presidential leadership impossible, then in such universities will there be the ever-present danger of athletic abuse and institutional humiliation.

Leader must require that their personnel demonstrate moral commitment in the institution's behavior. Leadership requires not only the ability to attract money but the ability to resist fiscal seduction. The economic survival of the college is of little significance when institutional behaviors required for that survival have altered the very substance of the organization and rendered it something other than a social institution that unbiasedly seeks truth, disseminates it liberally, to the benefit of the student and society. Leadership involves not only an understanding of the benefits of the flexible charter of American higher education but also the necessity for internally imposed discipline which that flexible charter demands. Whether the questions concern athletic or academic matters, the president must have a clear understanding of what the institution can do, what it may do, and what it must not ever do.

Sport and the Mission of American Higher Education

Notre Dame without a comprehensive athletic program would seem to be almost a contradiction in terms. Without athletics the university would not be the same as we have known it. The camaraderie of the various teams, not just football, contributes to the famed Notre Dame spirit. (from Notre Dame University publication, quoted in *Chronicle of Higher Education*, March 3, 1982:5)

How can we contribute to the building of a decent, law-abiding society in this country if educational institutions are willing to suffer their principles to be prostituted and involve young people in that prostitution for any purpose, and much less for the purposes of winning some games and developing an ill-gotten recognition and income (Rev. John LoSchiavo, President of the University of San Francisco, in *Chronicle of Higher Education*, August 11, 1982:1, 11).

Conventional wisdom prescribes remedies to cure ills uncovered. However, I will not offer wide-ranging panaceas. Instead, I suggest that those concerned with intercollegiate athletics should consider the contributions — both spiritual and material — which higher education can make, the different models for the process of education, and the governance crisis in sport and higher education before designating changes in the sport system. In conclusion, I argue for a return to the high goals of the American college and university, for intercollegiate sport in particular and for higher education in general.

To propose as radical a step as the abolition of intercollegiate sport is as nonsensical as arguing for removal of the heart of one suffering from cardiac distress. Even if recognizably impaired, the diseased heart still performs important functions. Intercollegiate sport, even in its diseased state, serves important functions for higher education and the society in which they are embedded.

To appreciate the function of intercollegiate sport, we must first accept the importance of symbolic, as opposed to material, resources. We have seen that intercollegiate sport does not seem to draw economic resources to the majority of schools. To invest the resources to bring monetary benefits is, however, also to make more probable the risks seemingly inherent in the big-time sport model of operation. Despite this fact, it would be unwise to merely evaluate such programs in terms of dollars and cents. Should we justify the existence of this college program on a materialistic basis when no other department of the college is asked to be self-supporting? Of course, the costs of some sports especially big-time programs are exorbitant and should be reduced. The hypocrisy of feigned amateurism should clearly be dispensed with. While there are those who would shudder to think of colleges and universities affiliated with overtly professional sports representatives, I offer that they have less to fear than they might believe. Big-time intercollegiate sports teams, especially in football and basketball, already clearly mimic their professional counterparts in form and substance. To admit this would call only for (1) a conscious recognition of what is already the case or (2) rationalization of the professional affiliation as a necessary economic condition for survival. When history shows that schools such as Denison, Bowdoin, and Rutgers sold their names for money and yet survived and thrived, it is not hard to believe that the open charter of American higher education could accommodate either professional or semiprofessional sports team affiliation.

Sport has clearly assisted the institutional image of certain schools. Notre Dame and the University of Southern California are two notable examples where successful sports teams have been directly responsible for the prestigious image of these institutions. While the American value system, with its emphasis on ability and competition to win would have us believe otherwise, those students labelled as "successful" merely by their affiliation with well-known institutions may very well benefit. If the self-fulfilling prophecy works in education, perhaps, those from whom success in schooling is expected may very well live up to those expectations. While recognizing the host of factors that would have to be controlled, it may be safe to say that the school that has earned prestige, even through its sports, has more to offer its students than the school without such prestige.

Clearly gender and racial stratification should be ameliorated. Women should be hired if at all possible for leadership positions as athletic directors and coaches. There is absolutely no reason what-soever for the hiring of male coaches for women's teams, given the probability of finding qualified female coaches. Similarly, there is no reason to hire so many white coaches for sports in which there is a large pool of qualified black coaches. The situations in basketball and football must be remedied as quickly as possible through affirmative action proceedings. Prestige can rise as quickly with a black coach that wins and plays the game well as that institution's prestige may fall with a white coach who loses and/or who plays the game outside of the rules. There must be considerations other than the record of wins and losses in the hiring of university athletic personnel. There are educa-tional criteria that are at least as important. And equity and justice must always be served.

Prestige has little to do with having two platoons or three squads of football specialists. Given national equalization of policy concerning the number of scholarship players on football teams, colleges and universities will not only save money but also compete just as vig-orously for the esteem of the public as they currently do in the overspecialized, overpriced arena of "amateur sport."

As Goode (1978:3-7) has point out, prestige defined as "the esteem, respect or approval that is granted by an individual or a collec-tivity for performances or qualities they consider above average" is allocated on the basis of perceived qualities. Regardless of the slippery reality of the effects of college, the allocation of status by those with whom the college comes into contact is more dependent upon the image, the impression of institutional goodness, than on any empirical accounting of college effects. Given the pervasiveness of sport and the enthusiasm of the sports media, it is clearly in the best interests of the institution to guard the quality of its institutional image — not only as a winner in sport but in its reputation for integrity and morality. The exposes of university athletic abuses have become so commonplace that the public is hard pressed to escape acknowledging this problem. Institutions of higher education must now deal forcefully with these problems in their own houses or their institutional stock of prestige so carefully built up after many years of concerted effort will be quickly depleted. While schools may be rapidly labelled "big-time" for the athletic company they keep, they may even more rapidly be labelled one of the renegade schools that cares little for ethical matters. Why send a son or daughter to such a school when there are so many others with better reputations?

Intercollegiate athletics, although it is generally an economic drain upon college operating funds, may promote the overall survivability of the institution because of the fact that sport has become an integral part of the image of higher education. Historically, we have seen the rapidity with which new curricular programs have been accepted into American higher education. So has it been for intercollegiate sport. In the 130 years since the first intercollegiate event, athletics has become part of the charter of American higher education. Although there are schools that have deemphasized it, there are few if any schools that have no form of intercollegiate athletics. It is not only accepted, it is *expected* that highly competitive athletics will be found at most institutions of American higher education. One is asked to explain its absence more than one is asked to explain its presence on the modern American campus. It is seen by the general population as part and parcel of college. To be without it is to invite criticism that the institution is not a bona fide member of the higher education fraternity.

We have seen that sport does not seem to satisfy the mission of higher education in any rational way. Economically, it usually loses money. It does not directly alter personality to the good but only may filter the fit from the unfit. Still, sport fits with higher education. It is accepted and deliriously promoted by alumni and other boosters. The reasons, I believe, lie in sport's ability to answer a need created by our pluralistic society and to help fulfill the peculiar mission of American higher education by (1) providing a vehicle for a sense of community, (2) promoting student commitment to the institution, (3) helping label its graduates as successful, and (4) elevating individuals beyond the limits of mundane realities to show them what they can be.

The Need for Community

> It's kind of hard to rally around a math class.
> Quote attributed to the legendary
> Alabama coach "Bear" Bryant

Is there something in the human character that demands affiliation? Whether learned or inborn, the desire to commune with others stands as an assumption of the human condition. Although existentially we may be ultimately alone in the universe, in the meantime we seek to commiserate with others over our condition.

Particular difficulties faced the American immigrant. Wide expanses of land and diversity in cultural background, values, and norms of behavior made community formation more difficult than in more homogeneous, closely spaced settings. Mobility into new territories and influx into developing industrial centers further exacerbated the problem of finding common interests about which to form community. Without traditional family roots in the village community, without a long history to tie ancestral blood to particular stone and soil, there was little tradition to strengthen feelings of community.

These problems of community became particularly acute in institutions of higher education as more students sought entry in college. Unlike its European counterparts, which appealed strictly to an intellectual and socioeconomic elite, the American university and, in particular, the public land-grant institutions were faced with a community-building task of immense proportions — how to gain commitment to a university and its spirit from the children of farmers and merchants, Protestants and Catholics, the rich and the common?

Benjamin Rader (1978) has identified sport as that common ground on which to affiliate. Standing in stark contrast to the boring bookish curriculum, athletics was popular with the physically vigorous population. Because sport did not threaten deeply held beliefs yet still provided common ground, it was a safe vehicle for affiliation. Without commonality of religion or culture, the diverse American peoples, as represented on the campus, could be joined in the worship of sport. After all, sport represented the best of America. Its values were the ideals of America: hard work and success; individual effort for the good of all; all created equally, with success dependent only upon talent and hard work. Sport could unify the campus as sport could unify the populations represented by college athletic teams. As early as 1906, Yale President Hadley reported that football has "hold of the emotions of the student body in such a way as to make class distinctions relatively unimportant" (Hadley 1906).

Particularly in the large expanses of the Midwest and West, particularly in those areas without competing symbolic representatives in the form of professional sport teams, college sport flourishes. Whether it be Kansas, Nebraska, Oklahoma, or Texas, in football or basketball, the fortunes of college sport teams are followed avidly. As a cynical friend of Ohio State President Harold Enarson once remarked, "Now that public hangings are forbidden, where else can you go and enjoy the contagion of the crowd and its excitement?" (Enarson 1980:23). Intercollegiate athletics draws people together — to care for common purpose in an atmosphere of exhilaration. With few tangible means of evaluating institutional or regional quality, the exploits of sports teams serve as quality indicators visible to all.

Athletics and the rituals of pep rallies and "Big Game" week are examples of "rites of intensification." Through these rituals, group solidarity is reordered, commitments to the institution, its values, and its people are reinforced. Identification with the school is engendered (Miracle 1980). Whereas formal religion may have served this unifying purpose in other times and places, for the American taste, formal religions, despite their universal aims, are too sectarian. Their symbols and liturgies cannot unite as many as sport does (Novak 1976:284).

While it may be that athletes are recruited and their eligibility maintained illegally, while it may be that they are in reality students second and athletes first, and while it may be that the education of the individual is not the primary concern of coaches, athletic directors, and other school personnel, still, sport teams are symbolic representatives of a school and a region. By affiliating with that team, by caring for its scores, we declare allegiance to an interest greater than oneself — the community. If Cady (1978:52) is correct, that we are all to some extent *homo fraternalis*, then sport provides an important avenue for fraternity, drawing together on the campus into a local and statewide community many peoples of divergent beliefs and norms of behavior. There is great value in that.

Effects of Student Involvement

College sport provides one of the few vehicles through which a diverse American population of students, otherwise isolated faculty, and administration may join with alumni and the community in some common interest. With diverse definitions of their reasons for being at the college, with various expectations for their economic, political, and social pasts and futures, the emotional bond engendered by sport seems to have filled a particular American need.

While empirical research has not substantiated a cause and effect relationship between sport participation and the development of personality traits, reliance upon the "input-out" model of student development may indeed hide some real effects of college attendance. To suggest that athletic participation or class attendance in themselves are capable of inculcating student changes may miss the mark. As Dreeben (1967), Feldman and Newcomb (1969), and Arnove (1980) have argued, the effects of schools range far beyond the formal curriculum — its classes, its professors, its homework, its tests and the like. Before discussing the effects of school image and prestige, the athlete as human model, and sport as ritual, in this section the role of sport as an agent of student commitment will be considered.

Any experienced professor has noted the remarkable difference between students who are committed to their education and those merely going through the motions. As recent educational psychology and research on teaching has conclusively illustrated, the effects of a school are at best as dependent upon the characteristics of students before they enter the school and their willingness to engage themselves in the activities of the school as are the school's effects the result of the formal curriculum. You can lead a horse to water by rewarding school attendance through a linkage of high-reward occupational and social positions with a college degree, but in order to have an impact on students there must be an active student involvement in the activities of the school. Astin (1985) refers to "student involvement" as the amount of physical and psychological energy that the student devotes to the academic experience. Research suggests that the student-involvement variable is positively related to greater-than-average changes in student characteristics, and for certain outcomes, student involvement is more closely related to changes than are the knowledge level of entering freshmen or the characteristics of the institution.

As the nineteenth century American college masters became well aware, merely requiring strict attention to studies is not enough to gain student commitment. Reinforcement through corporal punishment was insufficient as well. It was through the happy accident of sport, however, that student involvement in the life of the institution was engendered. And it may be that school sport, not only for the athlete but also for the spectator, remains a particularly American means of gaining student involvement in the life of the college.

Critical to an appreciation of the effects of student involvement in college sports is an examination of the important longitudinal research of Alexander Astin (1985, 1987). In the national studies coordinated by Astin, it was found that efforts to involve students, through residential and extracurricular life, for example, correlated statistically with

persistence in college. Particularly interesting to the academic traditionalist should be the finding that "athletic involvement" shows a pattern of effects on student development closely paralleling those
associated with "academic involvement." The relationship of both
types of commitment to the institution are similar — political
liberalism tends to increase and there is greater student satisfaction
with the institution's academic reputation, intellectual environment,
student friendships, and administration.

Athletic involvement, then, seems to have a positive effect on the
work of the institution. While there can be no quarrel from me that the
excesses of big-time sport require remedy, or with the fact of continued
discrimination in sport as well as higher education in general, athletics
seem to be one of the primary means through which the college may
effect change in students. Athletics engender an identification of the
individual with the academic community and the image of what that
particular community stands for. Novak (1976:286), for example, has
identified the kind of spirit that characterizes Notre Dame. It is playing
with "desperate seriousness and intense delight, with achieving not just
excellence but a certain kind of flair that must be thought of as gift and
grace." Through this identification of self with the institution and what
the school stands for, the individual is able to incorporate the values
and attitudes perceived to be at the heart of institutional character.

The Label of Success

Accompanying the role of intercollegiate sport as a focus for the com-
munal human and as a vehicle for institutional commitment, there is
another more individual, abstract, yet somehow tangible potential
benefit of such programs. Though it cannot be demonstrated empirically that sport causes character change through any scientifically
verifiable process, the association of students (not necessarily athletes)
with prestigious institutions may have positive effects for
those students.

It is the contention of this book that while originally based upon
European models of higher education, American institutions have had
to adapt themselves to the American environment — harsh economic
realities and a lack of great regard for higher learning. With an openness of charter which gave them the freedom to reshape goals and programs, American colleges and universities made changes necessary for
survival. Accompanying these changes, however, has been a continuity

in societal beliefs concerning the legitimate means through which higher education should do its work and the process by which success should be achieved in America.

Anthropological examination of American culture identifies "effort-optimism" as a focal value. The belief that "through hard work and vigor the individual may harness the universe for his utilitarian purpose" found expression in the Protestant Ethic (Corwin 1975:23): Success is based upon and measured by individual work. From the early incorporation of these beliefs in the relatively modest efforts toward egalitarian education proposed by Jefferson in the post-revolutionary period, to the mid-nineteenth century conception of education as the great equalizer of the inequities of birth, education in America has been traditionally valued for the success opportunities afforded capable individuals (McClellan 1980:123–124). The English system of mobility, whereby entry to the upper strata was available only through sponsorship by some member of the elite, was unacceptable. The American ideal was the fair contest. Status should be awarded according to talent and effort, not by the class to which one is born or sponsored (Turner 1968:219–220). The school is ideally seen as a provider of equal opportunity and a site for the demonstration of talent.

It has been conventionally reasoned that interaction between students and faculty, primarily in the classrooms, will educate students. They will be socialized to new skills, knowledge, and dispositions. Given these newly earned characteristics, the individual may then succeed in the contest of life. Regardless of social class, race, or gender, the American Dream is possible for all, given talent and hard work. This is how we have been taught to believe America works and how higher education should work. Despite radical changes in the programs incorporated in higher education in America, there has not been an accompanying change of view concerning the process through which that organization should do its work or the legitimate focus of that work. The American Dream necessitates the notion that the individual, given talent and perseverance, may learn at school that which when coupled with necessary talent and hard work is sufficient to better one's place in life.[1]

The continued acceptance of this model, however, has inhibited the acceptance of a very real benefit of college athletics. While athletic participation itself has not been proven to be an educational experience in the sense that the student is shaped through the process of athletic participation, there is reason to believe that labelling works to the benefit of students branded as successful, particularly those at prestigious institutions.

To appreciate this potential contribution of sport to social mobility through higher education in America, it may be necessary to alter the fundamental understanding of the primary process through which the school does its work. It is generally held that schools provide experience that instill knowledge, skills, and attitudes that facilitate heightened achievement. Research has, however, found that schools confer success and failure quite apart from the socializing effects that may take place (Blau and Duncan 1967; Collins 1971; Duncan, Featherman, and Duncan 1972; Bowles and Gintis 1976). Instead, people in society may be allocated to adult roles on the basis of years and types of education, apart from any learning they might have acquired or not acquired in school. Individuals deemed capable by their school graduation are allocated to roles and statuses seen as rational and legitimate for them (that is, it is assumed that they must have learned what is required for heightened performance on the job). Myths such as those that hold that teachers shape raw student material into educated products, and that attendance and graduation are direct indicators of this rational processing, are legitimating myths that help transform that status of the student. This redefinition of "student" to "college graduate" with all its attendant status changes occurs independently of any actual changes in competence that might have occurred (Kamens 1977).

Because it is believed by the members of American society that this is how schools work, they assume that this is how school programs should work. School sport must be rationalized not only for consistency with the goals of higher education but with the process through which these goals are pursued. Sport is rationalized as a socializing ground imbuing standards of individual effort, success, and mobility through demonstrated performance.

In his discussion of "diffuse socialization" (that is, shifts in individual values, personality, significant social roles, identities, and self-conceptions), however, John Meyer (1970:574) has noted that one of the many factors that control the extent to which students successfully internalize values and orientations of a school is the prestige of the institution. Because "prestigious schools can offer students both general status gains and the knowledge that these gains will be legitimated at many points in the system" (Meyer 1970:574), students who have not been thoroughly socialized through the traditionally conceived interactive process with teacher and other students in classes nevertheless may still acquire the school's important values and orientations. Prestigious colleges and universities may have a great impact on student characteristics, not because of the formal socialization process of school classes and assignments, but because the school is perceived by both students and the general public to be of high quality. The prestige of the school is translated into an assumption by the public and the students about the quality of the learning that must have taken place, regardless of the actual degree of socialization that may have occurred. Therefore, students who believe that they have learned something important, that their values and attitudes have been transformed by a highly respected college or university, may alter their own values and attitudes quite apart from the formal socializing process. Because students know that their school is highly regarded and that they will gain status from association with the school, students may actually alter their values and attitudes in the direction of the school's institutional image.[2]

For example, in a school chartered to produce the most capable scholars, like Oxford or Cambridge, graduates — regardless of the success or lack of success of formal socializing processes — may believe they are unquestionably bright. Since the wisdom of Oxbridge students is assumed, entrants as well as graduates may actually incorporate notions of their own enhanced intelligence, self-worth and, perhaps, aspirations without any impact of the formal schooling process. With greater self-expectation and the benefits of deference from other members of the society that so respects Oxbridge graduates, the new entrant to the labor market may benefit through enhanced mobility. Without this institutional prestige, neither the society at large nor the student would assume the student's possession of superior qualities and highly esteemed traits.

So it may be that prestige is a significant symbolic asset of American institutions of higher education. The impact of prestige may be felt at both the individual student and larger organizational levels. On the individual level, colleges and universities may develop prestige in many ways. Athletic success is one means of acquiring important institutional status. It may very well be that intercollegiate sport serves as an important "legitimating myth" about the quality of an institution and its graduates. A school's athletic successes as well as its roster of sports teams become indicators of its high status of schools. When asked why the Trinity University football team travels 1,200 miles to play the University of Chicago and 1,400 miles to play Occidental, President Ronald K. Calgaard replied, "We're interested in the right kind of visibility." While one might question Trinity's free substitution of the jet for the school bus, Trinity is one of the growing number of colleges that feels that the sort of schools it associates with athletically has an effect on its academic reputation. According to William A. Kinnison, President of Wittenberg University:

> Colleges are looking at all their activities in terms of marketing and positioning, beginning in sports. You don't want to play the wrong kind of schools because it might put you in the wrong class in someone's view. (Fiske 1983:A14)

As Hanford has noted (1974:54), "prominence in sports is equated in the public minds with academic reputation and prestige." Generalizing high status achieved in one program to the entire image of the institution is made more possible by the tremendous visibility of the intercollegiate sports program.

The very same prestige associated with winning athletics may very well attract a larger student application pool from which admissions directors may select the very best enrollees. In a study by Chu and Solomon (1986), application rates at NCAA conference champions were compared to those at schools that did not win league crowns in either football or basketball. In freshman applications between 1981 and 1985, significant differences were found between championship schools and competing institutions. Depending on the conference, the average increase in new applications for this period was at least doubled for conference champions. For example, whereas Big Ten schools that did not win championships in football or basketball saw an average increase of 376 applications for each year in the period 1981 through 1985, schools that won a championship in either sport saw their applications rise an average of 730. For basketball champions in the Big East Conference, mean applications increased by 553, while nonchampionship schools saw an average yearly rise in application rates of only 196.[3] While no conclusions should be drawn from this pilot study, the findings are highly suggestive. The prestige of athletics may serve to label an institution as a school with which students will wish to be associated - regardless of their status as participants or spectators. From this larger pool of applicants, schools may then select the best-qualified students. As McCormick and Tinsley (1986) have documented, there does seem to be a relationship between the individual's athletic success in football and higher SAT scores for entering freshmen.

For many schools, the visibility may serve both as symbolic evidence of general institutions quality and as a means to attract higher-quality students on which schools may build to enhance institutional and student prestige. While schools such as the University of Chicago and Yale with traditionally strong established images may not need symbolic representations of quality, for most schools excellence in sport serves as vivid evidence of the willingness and the ability of the school to develop excellence in some field. Though athletes may be abused or obtain no really useful education as they represent the institution, students and the public may very well generalize championships as symbolic demonstration that the college or university cares not just about their intellects but also as spiritual, emotional, social, and physical beings. Winning teams may mean to the students that choose to identify with them that they themselves can win, that they can be as perfect as that championship team.

On an individual level, the highly successful sports program promotes an image of the total institutional quality, which affects the student. This is especially so when clearer indicators of academic quality are not available, not visible, or unimportant to those assessing institutional quality. The successful football team that is held in high esteem for important institutionally mandated characteristics such as high achievement expectations, cooperation, poise, and so forth, stands as a model for students. It is not difficult to imagine that the student who so strongly identifies with Saturday's heroes may also internalize the perceived characteristics of these highly significant others. This may be especially so when others expect to find in that individual the characteristics for which the school has a reputation. Classwork may have less impact upon diffuse socialization than the sports team that wins and demonstrates character amid all the temptations for abuse in intercollegiate athletics. Because they are part of a school whose general prestige is enhanced by its sports team, students may shape their own values, personality, and self-concept toward the institutional qualities demonstrated by the school's sports teams. Whether or not this self-shaping occurs, public expectations for a school's graduates will affect its evaluation of the graduates' character and performance. Notre Dame graduates who have not incorporated her mythical grace under pressure will nevertheless benefit from public expectations to that effect. Former students who have developed this spirit reinforce such expectations in the public.

Of course, the potential validity of this thesis is affected by a host of factors. Meyer believes that schools vary in their ability to induce diffuse socialization, depending on the level of elite status offered by the school, the directness of access from school to high status, the extent of it monopoly over access, just to name a few of these variables (Meyer 1970:569–570). Controlling for these factors, however, one may still speculate that sport success enhances the school's institutional image for many in its varied publics.

While individual effects of institutional sports' prestige remain highly speculative, the effects of sport success on the school itself are more widely accepted. Football at Notre Dame was consciously developed in the late 1890s as an agency of institution building (Rudolph 1962:385). Professor Gregory Sojka reports that the evolution of small private Fairmont College into Wichita State, an urban university of sixteen thousand students, is closely tied to the fortunes of the "Shocker" basketball team (Middleton, March 3, 1982:6). As Hanford (1974:58) has noted, while other components of higher education are difficult to evaluate, to the naive public the apparent quality of institutions is readily measurable by the relative successes of their athletic teams.

The importance of institutional image is further evidenced by the economic model of higher education developed by David Garvin.

> An institution's actual quality is often less important than its prestige, or reputation for quality, because it is the university's perceived excellence which in fact guides the decisions of prospective students. . . . Perceptions are critical, for quality and prestige do not always move hand in hand. (Scully 1982:14)

The perception of high status, according to Garvin, is quite separate from actual quality. The school that acquires high status through its sports is in a much better position in the peculiarly American supply-and-demand market of colleges and students.

From this model of higher education, it is reasonable that colleges should take actions that will enhance their prestige. The fielding of sports teams is one means of seeking institutional prestige. The extent of status increase should, however, be affected by a number of factors. Some of these factors might include the relative valuation of the sport in which success occurs (football versus polo), the value system of the perceiver (how important is sports versus academic success?), the visibility of that success and the means through which success was achieved (through fair hard work and the demonstration of character or through questionable practices?). It must always be remembered, however, that institutional prestige can as easily be lost through sports as it can be gained. Highly visible unethical behavior in sports may have major repercussions stemming from the school's public, if that constituency has high regard for the truth ideals of the academy. This is particularly so if that public's evaluations are critical to institutional resource flow.

Glimpses of What Can Be

In addition to the community developed by campus sport, the commitment it may engender to the school's qualities, and the labelling that may result from sport's symbolic demonstration of institutional status, both participation in and observation of athletics may give glimpses of what humans can achieve.

According to Brubacher and Rudy (1958:317), "The history of American college life resembles the swinging of a pendulum in a wide arc." During the early era of church-dominated institutions, educational philosophy espoused concern for the "whole student." Then, with the influence of German scientism, a certain portion of American higher learning came to see solely the development of intellectual skills as its responsibility. After 1850, with the elevation of scholarship above good character among the faculty, the importance of moral education declined (Bok 1982:118). In the period 1865–1918, there developed the "bifurcated college," with a formal curriculum shadowed by the student-initiated informal extracurriculum. Finally, coinciding with the period of World War I there grew among American educators a renewed concern for the physical, social, and emotional, as well as the intellectual, welfare of the student (Brubacher and Rudy 1958:321).

Unlike the earliest English models, which professed concern for character but which left actual responsibility for total development to the student or to informal school agencies, the American church-related college up through the first half of the nineteenth century demonstrated a deep concern for the student's soul and moral life as well as the official commitment of school resources to overall student development. These early schools, first demonstrated the responsibility characteristically assumed by American colleges to formally oversee much more than student intellectual life. The first sectarian schools were instead interested in guiding the development of spirit and character.

During the later half of the nineteenth century, however, a faculty psychology became popular which posited a dualism of mind and matter. Through mental discipline, faculties of judgement, will, and imagination could be developed. This continental European interpretation of higher education was intellectualistic and impersonal in attitude. In retrospect, however, this period of little regard for the nonintellectual character of the student appears to have been but a brief episode. According to Charles Eliot, President of Western Reserve University, religion during this period became rational, ethical, and tolerant, "not so much an act as a mood" (Veysey 1965:204). The shift was one of more substance, from theological study to the study of ethics. By the beginnings of the twentieth century, the educational concern for the "whole person" expressed in the writings of John Dewey and "organismic psychology," with its emphasis on holistic human interpretation, directed American higher education back to its beginnings — to its original concern for total individual development, the formation of character as well as intelligence (Brubacher and Rudy 1958:321).

It is Corwin's (1975) view that the early religious affiliation of our schools has had a tremendous impact upon the structure of education and the philosophy that guides it. Unlike the utterly rational German scientific training, American education has historically been concerned with such notions as morals, proper character, and the spirit. While the mission of our schools has been partly to prepare for the realities of vocation and social life, in a sense the role of American higher education has also been influenced by what some would say is the religious concern for extension of humankind beyond rational limits. While mundane realities and the limitations of the flesh guide us toward baser behavior, religion has sought to show us what we can be, how far the spirit may take us beyond what our worldly senses may tell us are our limits.

Others say that our schools have assumed the responsibility for character development out of necessity. Without a strong church, with the demise of the extended family and all of its support, some social institution must take upon itself responsibility for total training of the young. If indeed the mission of American higher education extends beyond vocational training, classical criticism, and scientific scrutiny into the realm of extending the sense of our capabilities and worth, then intercollegiate sport in at least its idealized form may very well live in harmony with this basic purpose of higher education.

According to Brubacher, the modern university indeed fulfills many of the functions of the church. In previous eras religious dogma was unquestioned, and people placed their faith in feudal and religious leaders for determining moral values. But the 1960s and 70s saw an era, critical of the sacred texts. Religious leaders themselves asked if God was dead. With this period only recently beyond us, we ask now where may we turn for "answers to the basic human questions concerning self-understanding, the nature of the universe and the 'right and wrong social relations.' The university serves as kind of a secularized church." *Alma mater* seems to be the American successor to mother church, *mater et magistra*" (Brubacher 1977:117).

According to Robert N. Bellah, Ford Professor of Sociology and Comparative Studies at the University of California at Berkeley, extreme individualism has given way to a search for roots and a high regard for tradition (Schumer 1984:90). With Hiroshima, Love Canal, Three Mile Island, and Bhopal have come the realization that the technological order of science does not have all the answers. Secularism, narcissism, and scientism are giving way to renewed spiritual and religious attention. Students of the 1980s are rebelling against the modern world view that, Douglas Sloan of Teacher's College observed, "left no room for dealing with purpose, meaning, value and [that] left out everything that's really important (Schumer 1984:93). Scientism and overrationalism cannot speak to larger questions about humankind, goodness, and the meaning of life.

In the secular American culture, one might ask, "What other social institution will lead this search for human meaning?" Certainly not the government or business, with their obviously conservative vested interests. Perhaps the space program? Yes — especially so before the Challenger disaster. We get glimpses of what we might be from heroes. Often these are ordinary citizens who when faced with circumstances beyond their control are forced to perform extraordinary feats, like anonymous citizens who knowingly forego rescue to save others, and who ultimately may die because of their unselfishness; like the passersby who braves icy waters to rescue victims of some disaster, the efforts of those few show us all what we can be. We are all indebted to them.

Heroism of this sort is, however, largely dependent upon accident:

The right person facing the right circumstances at the right time. Then there must be someone to record the event in order for society to hear of it. This seldom happens. We seem to need more heroes: and often they are manufactured through sport. With its rules and artificial obstacles, opportunities are created for the exhibition of heroic qualities. Exemplary models for imitation are created — symbols of the kind of people we should strive to be. Society benefits from such models.

Without a strong church to reinforce the spirit, to highlight the capabilities of humans beyond the limits of mundane realities and sensibilities, what other institutions are there to do this? Why not our educational institutions? With their historically open charter, they are able to accept such a mission. Furthermore, they represent a hope for the future through the youth that provides its basic stuff. Who better to symbolically portray the ideal model of humanity than the youth at the institutions designed to train them for the future?

Mrozek (1983) has suggested that Americans have a penchant for perfectionism, and not only the perfection of the divine kingdom; for Americans hold the peculiar belief that perfection is obtainable on this earth and through our own works. Through the mind and the body we may perfect the spirit. And what better place to seek this mission than in our universities? After all, these educate our children, who are our hope incarnate whose potential is to be turned into perfection by the teachings of the scholars of the physical universe in the "church" of higher learning. The relationship between masters of knowledge of the physical universe in the university and our youthful sport heroes speaks to the impulse for perfection which is central to American culture and which shapes its character. As part of the American dogma, our institutions must speak to this new faith in perfection — a state which, to uneasy, impatient Americans, must be demonstrated for all to see, not believed in with a blind faith.

While sport in the university may be a result of historical, economic, social, and political accident, in retrospect, the bond between the academy and athletics is far from unnatural. The university is America's secular response to the historical religious impulse for some form of perfection. In a culture based upon the principles of the Enlightenment and empiricism, in a world where nature is slave to civilization, in a country that believes in the melting pot and the Darwinian advancement of humanity, the university has come to embody America's belief in its perfectibility.

The sports hero serves as a "character myth" that encodes the value system of the society simply and efficiently. Such myths are an efficient means of presenting and transmitting that system. Such myths, because they are rooted in the society's past, create a sense of continuity, and contribute to the strengthening of group identity (Gordon and Ackerman 1984).

Figures such as Frank Merriwell had their historical ancestor in Davy Crockett. Substitute for the woods the playing field; replace the coonskin cap with the football helmet. Both myths portray the rugged individual capable of great achievement through the force of his will and determination. Character myths such as these stamp the spirit more deeply than is possible through literal pronouncements about what the American character ought to be. Sport provides some solution to the historical problem first faced by Rush, Webster, Franklin, and the other early Americans — that is, how to define the American character. Although this problem has been complicated by a diversity of peoples unknown in the colonial age, sport in its college form has provided a definition of the proper American character widely acceptable to a large body of the citizenry. They provide a means of understanding the world, directions for action and the comfort of group identity amid a pluralistic society.

Certainly, in the Israeli school system there are models of character whom students are to imitate in their values, attitudes, and behavior. In their research on the Israeli school, Gordon and Ackerman (1984) found that the *mechanech*, a sort of homeroom teacher who provides a model of character for the students, was essential for imparting desired character and values. These elements of social education stand outside the subject matter curriculum, yet are an integral aspect of the goals of the school. The critical function of character formation, a decidedly anti-intellectual activity, is able to coexist in the otherwise intellectual environment of the school through a partition of educational life. While intellectual components may be affected through the school's formal curriculum, "character" may be modeled through these *mechanech* exemplars of the values, attitudes, and behaviors thought important to that society.

While strict employment of an input-output model of educational effects would suggest that athletes directly gain qualities of character through their involvement in practice and competition, it seems that character inculcation, an apparently important goal of Israeli as well as English and American schools, may occur through a less formal modeling process. Athletics in America serves as an important component of the social education of the student. The nineteenth-century student, having rebelled against the strict intellectualism and puritanical piousness of college, found in sport a means of expression which also suited the character goal of the American school. Although sport has been corrupted in some cases by the giganticism of big-time programs, in a more moral form its particular suitability to the American need for character formation in the school remains.

A. Bartlett Giametti, former President of Yale, as a leader of American higher education, agrees in *The Idea of a University* with his nineteenth-century peer John Henry Cardinal Newman that the university is more than a place for instruction. Demonstrating the continuing high regard in which character formation has been held in American higher education, Giametti concurs with Newman that the university's province is larger than the mere training of mental nature. Character formation has been and continues to be a primary concern of American colleges and universities. As we have already seen, however, the college does not seem to directly alter student character through classes and assignments, just as sport does not seem to directly alter personality or values through participation. Yet college effects are documented; students graduating from college are somehow, for some reason, different from their noncollege peers. The process of student change, that is, their education, is less rational and far more dependent upon the entire milieu of the college and its environment than early input-output models would suggest. It appears as if its effects depend on the degree to which the institution intensely involves students in the entire college experience and gains their identification with the perceived traits of high character symbolically portrayed in the school by its agents.

That the American college might use sport as a vehicle for the modeling of positive character, for gaining student involvement and identity with the qualities of the institution, has been to some degree necessitated by the historical American reluctance to employ conventional religion for these ends. Faced with the many people, beliefs, and world views that might make up the university, there was understandable reluctance to employ the particular beliefs and personnel of only one faith.

The first Americans, profoundly affected by the European Enlightenment, placed reason above revelation. They set out to convince the citizenry that religion deserved a respect larger than their own sects. There were fundamental truths common to all religions, and these truths formed the basis of the American "public religion" — one that placed formation of a common social fabric above particular interests (Marty 1984:154–155). This was a view whose continuity was demonstrated by John Dewey in 1934 in *A Common Faith*, in which he made his argument for a broad secular faith based upon the common values found in the various churches.

With the development of the large nonsectarian university, there grew the need to find means of unifying the increasingly diverse population of these institutions. Whereas the smaller religiously affiliated institutions of the early nineteenth century, and the more homogeneous schools catering to the elite, might have begun their work of character formation from a common base, the new student population entering the land-grant universities had different interests. While the liberal arts may have attracted some, technology was more useful for others to study. The need to find some nonsectarian means of speaking to the historical character concerns of higher education, coupled with the resource requirements of the school and the avidity with which students, the media, and the public approached sport, and the freedom of the flexible charter of American higher education, encouraged educational leaders toward the formal incorporation of sport and its rationalization as character builder.

By the end of the nineteenth century, leisure and wealth had been extended with the nation's industrialization. New groups of students beyond the traditional classes of children from the "Standing Order" and those interested in the clergy began coming to the institutions. Colleges and universities needed a way to homogenize this heterogeneity of beliefs on campus. At the turn of the century, the American college was faced with a student body that brought with it a wide diversity of world views, goals, and religious affiliations. The university was faced with a science that challenged the traditional core of humanities in higher education and with a demand for technology and utility that was foreign to both the humanities and pure science.

Referring to revolutionary France, Geertz (1964:63) notes that in societies where "hallowed opinions and rules of life come into question, the search for systematic ideological formulations, either to reinforce them or to replace them flourishes." Where objectives, assumptions, values, and ways of doing things are all highly diverse, useable models are required to help the disoriented comprehend their rights and responsibilities. These models may take the form of "symbol systems," that is, extrinsic sources of information through which human life can be understood and patterned. They are "extrapersonal mechanisms for the perception, understanding, judgement and manipulation of the world"; these models for symbol systems provide "templates or blueprints for the organization of social and psychological processes" (Geertz 1964:62, 64).

American colleges and universities at the end of the nineteenth and beginning of the twentieth centuries found themselves on shifting intellectual and practical ground. They were faced with the need to coordinate emerging disciplines in the humanities, social sciences, sciences, and practical areas. The college had to contend with and not alienate the important philanthropic, government, and alumni groups in its environment. No longer wedded to the classics that had provided its historical substance and process, the university was uncertain as to its goals and methods. The open charter of American higher education, while it provided the flexibility to navigate through treacherous financial waters, still did not provide a firm blueprint for institutional behavior or a means of sifting through the endless proposals for the direction of the institution from its various constituencies. With the changeover to business-oriented governing boards, increased presidential attention to external affairs of the college, and the isolation of faculty in their own departments, a power vacuum resulted in the twentieth century that further exacerbated the loss of direction of American higher education.

As Geertz (1964:63) and others have remarked, it is precisely where institutional guides for behavior, thought, or feeling are weak or absent that cultural symbol systems are most firmly embraced and most crucially come into play as templates for social and psychological processes. Intercollegiate sport provided one such system of symbols through which a diverse population could interpret its environment. Faced with uncertainty and ambiguity concerning the purposes and goals of the university, the symbols of sport, its players and coaches, as symbolic representations of schools and their perceived qualities, were means of resolving confusion and gaining a sense of direction. In the first third of this century, the university with its diverse goals, and programs and its power vacuum, and American society disoriented by the mayhem of the First World War and its radically altered values and behavioral norms, found order in the heroes and antiheroes, ritual, and mythology of college sport.

According to Bolman and Deal (1984:151-159), symbols such as myth, metaphor, and scenarios are means of coping with confusion and uncertainty. They provide explanations for contradictions, make confusion comprehensible, and provide direction for action in ambiguous situations. While the mythology of Frank Merriwell may blind us to the realities of big-time sport, such symbolism also promotes solidarity among pluralistic peoples, stability among conflicting ideas, and the sense of certainty necessary for assertive action.

As the mythology of the All-American Athlete engendered a sense of solidarity, stability, and certainty, the rituals such as those in sport similarly reduce anxiety, and socialize, stabilize, and convey messages to external constituencies. Ritual that to Masland (1983:164) is like myth, but framed in behavior as opposed to words, is "stylized formalized behavior made in repetitive form which generates consistency between the expectations of the organization's member." Rituals such as those associated with athletics provide explanations for uncertainty. They symbolically portray the triumph of good over bad, of virtue over vice. Rituals, whether they accompany the formal review process of accreditation, behaviors in church at Christmas, or the events surrounding the Big Game, are means of reducing anxiety and uncertainty about the rightness of an institution and behaviors.

Higher education in the United States is still a social institution with unsatisfactory conscious rationalizations of obviously conflicting programs and goals. It is an academy facing the problems of competing disciplines, the push for money and the necessities of academic freedom. Universities are faced with external constituencies in conflict over their objectives for the institution and powerful in their resource capabilities. These are the realities of higher education in a world suddenly faced with the possibility of total destruction, where evil is no longer restricted to an abstract concept or war to some distant people. American institutions of higher education and the public that supported it found in college sport symbolic means of assuaging anxiety, promoting solidarity, and socializing others in the virtue of character manifest in the athlete.

That there is a strong similarity between the functions and process of religion and sport should come as no surprise. For eclectic philosopher Michael Novak, "sports are a form of religion." Sports are organized and dramatized in a religious manner, with rituals and vestments that speak to the deep human hunger for knowledge of one's place in the cosmos. Sports are religious in that they are organized

institutions with disciplines and liturgies that teach religious qualities
of heart, soul, and moral courage (Novak 1976:17–31). To Charles
Prebish, Associate Professor of Religious Studies at Pennsylvania State
University, while sport is not a religion to all people, for those who rely
on it to experience "the ultimate," sport fulfills the transformation
function of traditional theistic religion. He adds that "Sport is
America's newest and fastest growing religion, far outdistancing
whatever is in second place" (Vance May 16, 1984:25).

Geertz has described religion as

> a system of symbols which acts to establish powerful, pervasive, and
> long-lasting moods and motivations in men by formulating conceptions
> of a general order of existence and clothing these conceptions with such
> an aura of factuality that the moods and motivations seems uniquely
> realistic (1973:90).

College sport is replete with such symbolism. The combat of states, the
conflict between Trojans and Bruins, between good and evil. Symbolic
affiliation with institutions, and the strong emotions and contagious
excitement of the crowd create long-lasting moods and dispositions in
the fans consumed by intercollegiate sport. Somehow the action on the
field or court illustrate our belief systems — that hard work and talent
pay off; that the individual must cooperate; that if you win, you are
good. And through all the mimicry, contrived rules, and symbolisms,
sport seems terribly real — utterly important despite the fact that it has
little to do with the realities of daily existence.

Like religion, sport has its "sacred time." Cady's "Big Game" is
such an example. The fierce rivalries — Michigan versus Ohio State,
Texas versus Oklahoma, USC versus UCLA — are such examples of
sacred time. According to Novak:

> Sacred time is a block of time lifted out of everyday normal routines,
> a time that is different, in which different laws apply. . . . Sacred time
> is full of exhilaration, excitement, and peace, as though it were more
> real and more joyous than the activities of everyday life. (Novak
> 1976:30–31)

Sport in its intercollegiate as well as professional incarnations provides
this sacred time. It is a needed opportunity to transcend routine; a time
to see in bold relief human excellence, to see plainly the patterns and
symbols and myth that provide constancy over time; and a way to exhil-
arate the body and will.

According to this sense of sport as religion, it makes little if any difference that most of those involved are not active participants but merely spectators. After all, are not the rites and ceremonies of religion often performed by professional representatives? The sacred songs and rituals may be performed by surrogates for the good of all. Athletes through their ritualized actions may break through the surface of routine and [get] in touch with the ultimate realities of life" (Fromm 1965:131–132). Through the behavior of athletes, we may see ultimate reality devoid of the fog of everyday existence.

It is interesting that the radical critics of intercollegiate sport such as Jack Scott and Harry Edwards in the 1960s and 1970s saw big-time sport as dehumanizing. The authoritarian processes of college sport, where they were the norm and continue to be the norm, rob athletes of their individuality and strangle their search for self-realization. Whatever the happy or sad effect on the athlete, however, inter-collegiate sport may in its moral form serve the spectator as an aid toward self-realization. By modeling the heroic qualities of humans, athletes act as exemplars of character and behavior. Because "athletics teaches lessons valuable to the individual by stretching the human spirit in ways that nothing else can," President Giammetti (1981:82) believed that sport should be a part of the Yale education. If education is intended to show us not only how we have gotten here and what we now are but also what we can be, then intercollegiate sport — in some form — perhaps does belong as part of higher education in America.

While describing the type of institution that provides the best hope for higher education in America, Martin (1982:79) refers to the qualities of the "college of character." Such schools have

> the power to lift our spirits and focus our abilities, to exemplify true character so strongly that students will always have their experiences in the college as a point of reference, to unify a community and make it a model for society.

Extending Martin's vision, sport, as the most visible program of American higher education, may contribute to this image of the college of character. By demonstrating heroic moral behavior in the face of the contrived stress of symbolic competition, the young athletes with whom we identify may model for students and the community the highest qualities of the society.

To justify intercollegiate sport, to fully understand the peculiar function it fulfills in our institutions of higher education, we must go beyond the limits of empiricism. The university, for all of its factual knowledge and concern with the search for truth, must translate that learning. According to Brubacher, wisdom and learning must be translated into "human need and oriented to human hope" 1977:119). Through its sports teams, the anonymous face of higher education shows itself to the public as human. This is higher education that demonstrates concern for the human achievement — bound by social rules and infused with emotion — that is the concern of the public.

A part of American education has been traditionally concerned with the new human — with the formation of the ideal human unchanged by the restrictions of tradition. It is with the modeling of this ideal human form and with its empathetic diffusion among the throngs of spectators that intercollegiate sport is concerned. Unsatisfied with dull classicism, unwilling to subdue spirit to pure rationality, the American vision of humanity is one that will not face the logic of defeat, the deflation of heart. Secular America has found this vision of humanity in sport. Novak best describes the attraction of sport:

> I love the tests of human spirit. I love to see defeated teams refuse to die. I love to see impossible odds confronted. I love to see impossible dares accepted. I love to see the incredible grace lavished on simple plays — the simple flashing beauty of perfect form — but even more, I love to see the heart that refuses to give in, refuses to panic, seizes opportunity, slips through defenses, exerts itself far beyond capacity, forges momentarily with its bodily habitat an instrument of almost perfect will. . . . I love it when it would be reasonable to be reconciled to defeat, but one will not, cannot; I love it when a last set of calculated, reckless, free and impassioned efforts is crowned with success. When I see others play that way, I am full of admiration, of gratitude. That is the way I believe the human race should live (Novak 1976:150–151).

According to Becker, all humans desire self-esteem. The search for self-worth, for validation of one's value relative to others, is a "universal principle for human action akin to gravitation in the physical sciences"; after early childhood, "the rest of the person's entire life becomes animated by the artificial symbolism of self-worth" (Becker 1971:328, 67–68). To sociologist John Loy, sport spectatorship may act as an aid to individual self-construction, to personal and collective identity. Spectators, through comparison with heroic sport figures and by sharing the glory of their triumphs, may gain a sense of how they rank in the possession of society's valued attributes, while gaining some of the rewarded glory that accompanies those qualities. "The sports spectator may see the visible manifestations of heroic qualities — the goal line stand, the crucial free throw — and "bask in reflected glory" of the athlete's accomplishments" (Loy 1981:272).

The college athlete, unlike professional athletes, is at least on the surface less tainted by crass commercialism. We are better able to identify with Saturday's football hero then Sunday's, because the college kid is more like us. They are students like we all were, or small-town kids yet discovering their talents, more prone to foibles and failings endemic to humanity than the cosmopolitan professional who cashes in on proven abilities. Because collegians are younger and have less recorded history, the public is freer to paint its own impressions on the relatively blank canvas of youth. We make them into what we want to see — what we want to be. We identify with them because we have been relatively freer to create an image of those athletes acceptable to us. Furthermore, since their tenure at college is so short, there is a steady turnover of new would-be heroes. Hope springs eternal with every freshman fall.

We react differently to college sport because the players are like our own children, students like ourselves, or students from schools that we may attend or have attended. They embody the dreams of youth which were or are our own dreams. Through the eyes of these athletes we come closer to the realization of our own beliefs — or, at least, of our hopes. On the surface, at least, college sport is more innocent than admittedly professional sport. It is assumed that the kids are from our own hometown, and for the most part we assume that they stay through the course of college in one place without the chase for money which prostitutes the pros. They appear to play for love rather than for money, just as we play softball on Sunday because it is fun. Because there are so many more college athletes than professionals, there is a better chance of being able to say that we know them. "When I was playing high school ball we were in a tournament against — . . . . He was really somethin' then!" or "so and so is a cousin of a friend of mine" are much more common for the college athlete who competes for media space along with the select few pros in the world. The college athletes are the future. They are the promise of things to come, much more so than the pros who have already "peaked" or who "never reached their potential." There is something in America which values the future more than the present, the possibilities of unprecedented greatness over the established present.

The college game is so different from the professional game. In the infectious enthusiasm of college basketball, with the sweetheart innocence of cheerleaders, the human mistakes of youthful players, and the glory of achievement as it triumphs over immaturity, the average spectators can better identify and hence be better served in their fans' search for meaning. The professional game, with its ice-man performers, cheerleaders' cleavage, computerized and mechanized efficiency, symbolizes better the bureaucratization and impersonality of the times when any hope of the individual to make it the world is apparently beyond human control.

The American fascination with college sport is linked to self- and group evaluation and the almost religious concern with what we can be. In a diverse and fluid culture and a relatively mobile society, individuals feel less deeply stamped with a fatalistic sense of immutable social position and personal character. And while the formal curriculum aids in the process of learning who we are, the process may be incomplete without the emotional identifications with college athletes. It is somewhat odd that the religious influence on American higher education, which originally held physical activity in such low regard, should come to justify intercollegiate sport. Not only Notre Dame but also Fordham and St. John's, DePaul and Georgetown, rationalize athleticism. While some would argue that economic rationalizations for sports at colleges are primary, I suggest that this is insufficient. The primary value that big-time intercollegiate sport has is that it makes possible completion of the American mission of higher education — to show us not only what we were and what we are but also what we can be.

Through sport, especially the seemingly innocent intercollegiate variant, we see what we can be and what the American dream says we are capable of becoming. Within everyone there is the potential for greatness, for lifting spirit, for heart.

CHAPTER 6

Reflections on Diversity:
College and Sport

> Now that you have broken through the wall with your head, what will you do in the neighboring cell? S. J. Lec, *New Unkempt Thoughts*

In these pages I have taken a look at sport in American higher education. In so doing, I have invariably examined both sport itself and higher education. Each in their own way reflects the society in which it is embedded.

A number of factors combining at the end of the nineteenth and beginning of the twentieth century resulted in the peculiarly American institution of higher education we know today. The American college, though originally modeled from European institutions, was not blessed (or cursed) with singleness of purpose, consistent funding, or the student resources of its English and German counterparts. With freedom to multiply their programs, schools altered form and content to suit the American population — a population at the turn of the century feeling the material effects of industrialization, urbanization, and such technological advances as those leading to the development of the sports media. The public had more money to spend, and time to use that money. It was a public sometimes unfamiliar with its cities and neighbors. They were people living in an increasingly bureaucratized world, where the corporation was gaining at the expense of individual autonomy. Yet the United States was a nation looking for heroes to symbolize the dream upon which it was built and in which it still believed.

Strong presidential leadership and relatively weak faculty opposition (itself engendered by departmental specialization and isolation) allowed for rapid changes in order to gain the necessary share of resources required for institutional survival. Official governing boards, because of their part-time nonresidential nature, were highly dependent upon the president for information. The business orientation of these boards further encouraged the evaluation of institutional programs according to their productivity and contribution to the budget. Based upon a rational understanding of the charter of higher education that demanded natural logical verification of the college's purposes and programs, all structures incorporated into American higher education (including sport programs), had to be rationalized as aiding the pedagogical mission of the school through education, understood as the processing of raw material — individual participants — into the educated product.

At the turn of the twentieth century sport was used to gain institutional prestige and standing in the academic order. Justification of sport as an educational program, although consistent with the historical American concern for character training and coincidental with the invention of "the adolescent," was primarily for the consumption of the public, faculty, and educational concern groups whose support was still needed by college administration.

After an examination of the economic and character -building claims of intercollegiate sport rationalists, it can be concluded that there is no substantial empirical evidence to validate these claims. Sport in almost all cases loses money for the American college, and the process of sports participation does not itself alter values, attitudes, or personality directly through practices and contests. If there are positive benefits for sports participants — or, for that matter, all students attending a particular institution — these benefits may be the result of the degree to which programs such as sport encourage student commitment to the institution, as well as filtering and expectation effects, and a labelling process by outsiders, not the direct result of an interactive process whereby the athlete as raw material is transformed through sport's rigors. Instead, it has been proposed here that intercollegiate sport through its myth, ritual, and symbolism possesses value as a unifier of community and as a visible representation of heroic qualities. In a secular, federal America, with diverse sub-cultures, value systems, and norms for behavior, intercollegiate sport may unite the population under a common purpose and vision — a vision of what the American Dream tells us we can be. College sport for the spectator as well as the player may provide the spiritual vision of greatness that has been part of the American Dream in the past and which remains so today. The American education system, which has had thrust upon it the spiritual duties traditionally assigned to the church and the affiliative duties heretofore assigned to the family and the common culture, has incorporated sport within its charter in order to fulfill these new responsibilities.[1]

While intercollegiate sport may perform these very important functions for society and for the individual, however, this cannot serve as an apology for the present condition of intercollegiate sport. Far from it, abuses in recruiting and eligibility maintenance scandals visible in the common press and professional literature are terribly upsetting because such scandals demean the essential integrity of both sport and higher education.

While the American university fulfills many religious functions, it is also beset by many of the same problems as the church. Like churches, universities experience the tensions resulting "from embracing transcendent goals and ideals while having to exist and be of service in a practical, imperfect world" (Bok 1982:11). As the church lessened its distance from feudal society and lost much of its innocence, so has the university, shorn of the protecting walls of academe, become increasingly concerned with its own perpetuation. Overall standards of rationality and purpose which might provide guidelines for organizational behavior are not available (Brubacher 1977:118). In the search for the resources necessary for survival, too many schools have lost sight of their mission. The abuse of individual students for the supposed welfare of the institution is morally indefensible. But while we have seen racism, sexism, and unethical behavior in sport, we have also seen examples of indefensible behavior in the larger academic world as well. Sport as a program of the college reflects the beliefs and norms of the wider institution. Though the luminescent visibility of athletics naturally places it under close inspection, college sport is but a reflection of less apparent institutional behaviors and attitudes.

It has often been said that sport and education mirror society. Perhaps it is inevitable, then, that the diversity of American values should lead to conflicts in the goals and behaviors of higher education's programs. While one goal is the discovery of truth through objective techniques, from time to time we see evidence of scientists or humanists "fudging" data, plagiarizing a manuscript or a thought, just as we see football coaches seeking victory through their own versions of unethical behavior. While knowledge, free from social and material restriction, is valued, so is the government or corporate donation that keeps open the doors of the academy and funds the professor's lifestyles regardless of the implications of such donations and the inevitable strings attached to them. Many of the very same value and goal conflicts encountered in sport are those that confront other officers of the academic institution. The realities of tenure, the need to publish, to discover, to advance, fall on professional shoulders. For them, as for the coach, these are the purest means to advancement. As is so often the case, however, these pure means are usually time-consuming or seemingly ineffective. The demands to produce encourage all to modify processes to obtain sufficient scholarly output. But everyone can see the coach's work. Few see what goes on in the laboratory or library. It is easy to see the unethical play but most difficult to document biased administration or unethical research methods.

The very same conflict that confronted Jefferson, Webster, and Rush, the dichotomy between the "free-thinking American" and the "uniform American" is evident in critical attacks upon the sporting establishment. Sage (1980) and others have chided coaches for their overemphasis on the perpetuation of traditional values, business orientations, and bureaucratic mentalities. Autonomous individuals are not the product of our sporting system, say the critics. While this may be true, it may also be so for all of education, from the elementary to the highest levels. Reward systems reinforce quiet, cautious rule followers. A hidden as well as an overt curriculum prepare students for acceptance into the existing system far more than preparing students to question the system. If sport is illiberal, it reflects the very same characteristic in all of higher education. Our schools may indeed train far more than they educate. And while sport has been criticized because it is a filter more than it is a teacher of skills and characteristics, the very same may be said of schools that certify passage rather than educate. If our level of concern is the individual participant, then sport may indeed prepare the bureaucratic personality. But then is not this the accepted product of our colleges? If our schools produce graduates who are group-minded more than they are individuals, who accept the hierarchal structure of society as legitimate, who are product- as opposed to process-oriented, then perhaps intercollegiate sport is merely doing the job assigned to it by schools directed to produce the same.

Much of the controversy concerning intercollegiate sport stems from conflicting conceptions of the mission of higher education. While some contend that colleges and universities must educate the individual student, others see the institution as serving the interests of the community, the state and federal governments, or even big business. Those of us concerned with higher education differ in response to *cui bono* — who should be the primary beneficiaries?

What I suggest is that the particular mission of American higher education inevitably reflects the diverse, conflicting, and at times immoral culture that it serves and that sustains it. While traditional conceptions of the purpose of higher education may have centered about the cultivated individual and the quest for knowledge, secular and pluralistic America has altered the charter of its higher education institutions to include functions for spirit and community. The basic human need to know what one is and what one can be, and to know these things in the group, have been nourished by American colleges and universities through their sport programs. The intercollegiate athlete, while at times undeniably taken advantage of, serves the wider spectator population for the "greater good of the whole." The athlete sacrifices some personal freedom much as initiates into religious orders customarily do. A major difference between athletes and monks, however, is that the monk enters into the ascetic existence consciously, willingly, and upon much reflection, while the young athlete is made part of the system at too early an age to be able to make a studied decision to do so.

While the argument here should not serve as an apology for the abuses of intercollegiate sport, particularly the detrimental effects of product-oriented athletics upon the individual participant, I stand wholeheartedly for the notion that sport in some form now belongs in the American college and university. While some distinctive schools such as Chicago and MIT have been able successfully to deemphasize intercollegiate sport, these are special institutions with recognized purpose that draw a particularly homogenous population. While schools such as these may be accorded the public respect necessary to flourish, for the vast bulk of schools this would not be the case. Intercollegiate sport has become such an integral part of the public conception of our colleges and universities that it is difficult to conceive of campus life without it.

With the growth of community colleges there has also been a corresponding development of intercollegiate sport available at these two-year institutions. This growth may be a reflection of the possibility that campus sport has become part of the publicly acknowledged charter of American higher education. While sport may not make money nor build character in athletes, this mythology is not apparent to the public that for the most part cannot conceive of American schools like those in the Big 10, Big 8, Pac 10, SEC, and Ivies without their sports.

What is suggested here is that intercollegiate athletics may be part of the American charter for higher education. The peculiarity of this charter, expanding from the traditional meaning of cultural and scientific education, has come to include community and spiritual growth. While intercollegiate sport stands counter to the traditional (and perhaps outdated) conception of the purposes and processes appropriate for American higher education, campus sport may make a real contribution toward fulfilling the new objectives demanded of our colleges and universities by society.

What Is Needed?

While intercollegiate sports may do great service for society by drawing together the community and by providing a character myth which helps us see what we may be, the hypocrisy about sport is demeaning to the institutions that practice it. As resource availability continues to decrease in the next twenty years, there will be renewed public consciousness of the use of its dollars and human investments. For higher education to continue its toleration of corrupt hypocritical sport threatens to exacerbate the erosion of public confidence in the institutions of higher education (Carnegie Council 1981).

We have already seen that a number of factors impinge upon the reform of college athletics. The size of schools, the importance of external constituencies that value sport, the caution exercised by bureaucratically confined chief executive officers, the authority structure that sometimes places sport outside of the school leadership's immediate control, and the greater potential benefits to winning sport than the possible risks of abuse are some of the factors constraining change. There is another very important reason, however.

Grant has referred to the historical collegiate predicament that has produced the need for conscious ignorance in higher education:

> Simply put, presidents cannot acknowledge the problem. To do so
> would put them between the proverbial "rock and a hard place." On one

hand, they would risk antagonizing legislators, boards of regents, alumni, and the public who represent access to needed financial resources; on the other hand, they would have to confront the commercialism of athletics and coaches who comprise the institution's most salable product. (Grant 1979:413)

The need to appeal to so many different groups has led to a situation in which administrative leaders cannot easily deal with athletic practices that conflict with the proper purpose and process of higher education. Since no real response to athletic problems is seemingly possible, the historical response has been "the silence," that is, conscious ignorance of athletics. The response among administrators, often fearful for their jobs, has been to play the game. It is a response that has forced adults to pretend. In Laing's words:

> They are playing a game. They are playing at not playing a game. If I show them I see they are, I shall break the rules and they will punish me. I must play the game, of not seeing that I play the game. (Laing 1970:1)

According to Meyer and Rowan (1975), schools in America have a particular tendency toward isomorphism with the environment. Because of the many sources of pressure felt by the school, and the need to attract as many resources as possible, schools incorporate many programs and objectives to satisfy these groups. With so many programs and goals, some of which conflict, or which are contradictory and without clear-cut measures of goal attainment (that is, hard proof that the school is efficiently educating), schools are organized in terms of a "logic of confidence." "Parties bring to each other the taken-for-granted good-faith assumption that the other is in fact carrying out his defined authority" (Meyer and Rowan 1975:28). It is often assumed in the American school that programs are functioning efficiently and in accordance with school policy and overall objectives. Attempts to control more directly, to coordinate tightly, might otherwise cause internal conflict between program components and threaten support from the environment's many groups. The "logic of confidence" is another expression of inattention to program operation in the school. (Meyer and Rowan 1975)

George Hanford has said that "recent generations of college presidents have continued generally to ignore the responsibility for the ethical conduct of college sports which an earlier generation abdicated." It is his evaluation that "presidents are generally aware of

190   THE CHARACTER OF AMERICAN HIGHER

troubles on other campuses, often fearful that there may be problems
on their own, and usually reluctant to stir them up in the hope that they
will never surface" (Hanford 1974:28–29).[1] Presidential control over
athletics has typically taken the form of an assigned overseer or committee to monitor athletics — a monitoring that has permitted well-
rationalized presidential inattention to intercollegiate sport.

As cutting as this criticism is, however, Hanford recognizes that
the president does not bear full blame for inattention to problems in
intercollegiate sport. Trustees are not usually the agents of change
either. Neither do faculty escape blame, for according to Hanford
"most faculty members unless forced to do so do not think about intercollegiate athletics at all." Most do not feel these matters are worthy
of their attention (Hanford 1974:32). The same may be said of regional
agencies concerned with the legitimation of institutions through
accreditation. Warren B. Martin, former Vice-President of the
Danforth Foundation, has noted the conspicuous absence of those
agencies from involvement in matters of athletic impropriety. Apparently these agencies do not see the investigation of intercollegiate sport
abuses as within their domain. Sanctions are not applied to schools
which violate the integrity of higher education through sport abuses.
(Martin 1981)

At the big-time level of college sport, the coaches most directly
involved in the recruitment of athletes have few misconceptions concerning the importance of money. Intercollegiate sport at this level
often requires money to buy athletes. Weak sanctions imposed by the
NCAA are insufficient deterrents to future misbehavior.

To Don Canham and Bo Schembechler of the University of
Michigan, their purpose at the institution was business — winning and
bringing in money (Weiner 1973). To Ted Bredhoft of often-punished
Wichita State, big-time sport is an entertainment used to draw fans and
money (Middleton, March 3, 1982:6). And to much-revered "Bear"
Bryant of Alabama, the real priorities of big-time intercollegiate
athletics are clear:

> I used to go along with the idea that football players on scholarship were
> "student-athletes," which is what the NCAA calls them. Meaning a stu-
> dent first, an athlete second. We were kidding ourselves, trying to make
> it more palatable to the academicians. We don't have to say that and we
> shouldn't. At the level we play, the boy is really an athlete first and a
> student second. (Michener 1976:254)

While admitting the fiction of the student first, athlete second, Bryant also recognized the importance of rationalizing programs to concerned groups. For formal organizations to survive, especially in a restricted task environment with limited resources, they must always be sensitive toward maintaining support from resource-bearing groups. Although Bryant and other athletic personnel may denounce the student-athlete and other academic sport fictions, chief administrative personnel responsible for shaping and rationalizing overall organizational programs to date have not in any number espoused this reality. Instead, we encounter "the silence," the neglect, the inattention, however well-rationalized, to athletic program improprieties.

The silence — the conscious ignorance of college sport — runs deeper than surface level. Administrators, trustees, and faculty do not only know of abuses from public critiques of intercollegiate sport. The silence is deeper still. Given the existence and availability of empirical literature that evidences the improprieties themselves and the invalidity of the "Big Lie," it is difficult to believe that the problems of big-time sport and its alteration of values in higher education is not known to all who dare to read or listen,

According to Watzlawick et al. (1974), part of the socialization process in society involves teaching role aspirants what are thought to be skills, orientations and knowledge appropriate for those roles. But this is only half the story. Complementing this process is another set of learnings — what must *not* be seen, what must *not* be heard, what *not* to think, feel or say. These secrets are "open in the sense that everybody knows about them and are secrets in that nobody is supposed to know that everybody else knows" (Watzlawick, et al. 1974:42). In higher education, for example, an open secret might be the heavy weight given money matters in decision making. Although well known among college leadership, the fact that money considerations supercede other curricular considerations is not openly admitted. Instead, "educational criteria" - standards of academic quality and teaching performance — are claimed or intimated as primary. In the major university, another open secret concerns the quality of teaching itself. With few adequate means of empirically assessing good teaching, with research deemed important to draw necessary grant money and national recognition, with professional travel and outside consulting taking up much time away from campus, it is well known to college faculty that the quality of their teaching — in particular to the lower-level classes — suffers. Yet no one talks about this; it is not routinely discussed outside the circle of confidantes who are able to rationalize it. Similarly, we have the open secrets of big-time intercollegiate athletics. Although few college presidents and trustees will openly admit it, big-time sports is usually not itself educational; it is there to draw money, students, and high status. The student is second and the player is first. Furthermore, the athlete's welfare is secondary to the good of the institution. These are all elements of this "open secret."

As families may cohere in the face of deep potential conflicts, institutions with many different constituencies may continue to exist despite deep-seated disagreements. One reason for their continued existence is the power of open secrets to draw possibly fractious groups together by making visible common interests, needs, and aspirations, while hiding potential sources of disagreement. The ideology of "sport as education" engendered by the Big Lie permits maintenance of big-time sports within the historically intellectual institutions of higher education. Conflict between institutional market and resource needs of the college, on the one hand, and the traditional mission of the college and the harsh physical and economic realities of elite college sport, on the other hand, are permitted to coexist through public maintenance of the view of sport as educational. It is largely the power of the sport-and-education myth to render possible this difficult social situation that accounts for the intensity with which this view is held.

Myths concerning intercollegiate sport developed around the beginning of the twentieth century. As campus athletics took hold, and as what was to become the NCAA developed, supporters of campus sport searched for an image of college sport's purpose and process acceptable to important people and groups in the university/college environment, as well as to those directly involved in athletics. In a very real sense, the search for image is a negotiation. While rarely face to face, such negotiations are real in the sense that image is altered in response to pressures and criticisms. Unacceptable definitions and presentations of intercollegiate sport's image were deleted or refined. The product of these negotiations is the view of intercollegiate sport as money maker and character builder — a view that clashes with the realities of contemporary campus sport.

While this myth was originally negotiated by coaches, professors, administrators, and critics at the turn of the century as a means of justifying the presence of the heretofore foreign athletic program, time has changed the degree to which such assertions are plausible to the general public and critics alike. With the development of psychological and educational technology, it has become apparent that claims of character building through sport are unfounded. Similarly, decades of evidence has demonstrated that for the vast bulk of schools, college sport is an economic drain. Yet its money-making potential is still presented as a justification for intercollegiate sport. Believers in this system do not question the premises of the program's existence, despite the changes that have rendered this party line visibly invalid.

What is needed now? College administration must come to see what those directly involved in the college sport enterprise have already seen and admitted. They must question openly the assumptions of the Big Lie. Certainly, Bear Bryant understood and admitted, and Don Canham understands and admits, that college sport is a business. Steven Snyder, when he was a freshman at the University of North Dakota, was made to realize it well when his basketball scholarship and the scholarships of three teammates were cut because of their losing season (Vance, May 18, 1983). Even Walter Byers, Executive Director of the NCAA, has recently admitted that college sport is not the ideal haven for the student-athlete — that is, not a haven where scrupulous administrators run their athletic programs as models of high educational standards. After estimating that 30% of major sports institutions are engaged in serious violations of NCAA standards. Byers publicly mused whether the entire big-sport amateur system should be scrapped in favor of an admittedly semiprofessional system.

> I don't think the fabric of higher education as we believe in it and would like to see it function in this country can stand the strain of big-time intercollegiate athletics and maintain its integrity (Kirschenbaum 1984:11).

The NCAA Executive Director added that, while doubling the already recently enlarged enforcement staff would help to some degree, what is necessary is a renewed commitment from member institutions to police themselves. As higher education in this country presses for resources, lobbies Congress and state legislatures, cries about the soaring expenses which justify rocketing fees, the perception grows in the public that higher education is just another interest group. As science has reduced the aura of religion, and science itself has lost its air of invincibility, higher education in America risks tarnishing that most valuable of all assets — public confidence in its importance and necessity. Judith Rowan, Associate Chancellor for Public Affairs at the University of Illinois, Urbana-Champaign, declared, "For a long time higher education took it for granted that the public understood what it does and that it performs a function of value to society"; but she has seen a change in public perceptions: "The public is less willing to just accept what we do at face value" (Palmer, May 6, 1987:1). Every university impropriety stains the image of academe — made more apparent by the very visibility that is one of college sport's greatest assets. College leadership must reform college sport or risk the fate of Southern Methodist University — a diminished economic position and academic stature. The reputation that has taken generations of sacrifice to create may be destroyed through a few years of careless administration.

In the view of Robert Atwell, President of the American Council on Education, if colleges are to be accorded great respect, they must behave in a manner deserving of that respect (Palmer, January 7, 1987). Robert Rosenzweig, President of the Association of American Universities, agrees that higher education's support may erode if it is perceived as just another big-business with its own special interests. But the sport scandal does much to tarnish higher education's special image. Atwell has observed that "Athletics are probably the most visible aspect of a college and there's a perception that we haven't done enough to clean up the barnyard. . . . We look like we're in the entertainment business and it makes us look awfully shabby" (Palmer, January 7, 1987:28).

What is needed now? Chief executive officers need to admit that schools employ sport to gain leverage in the higher education market. At the big-time level, it must be recognized and openly admitted that athletes are admitted primarily for their sport talents and only secondly as students. It must be declared that sports in almost all cases lose money, as do almost all other programs in the college, and that sport participation, like class participation itself, probably does not build character, although it may engender a commitment to the institution — a commitment that facilitates student change. Primarily, college leadership must demonstrate the honesty that it expects from students, and the candor expected of the unbiased seeker of truth. The hypocrisy of maintaining the Big Lie demeans not only the university but the very strength of higher education's charter in America.

What is needed now? Barbara Uehling, former Chancellor of the University of Missouri, maintains:

> College leadership must *decide* about the best relationship between their institutions and big-time sport. Should athletics be divorced from academe and athletics recognized as professional or semi-professional or should the present system and rationale for sport be maintained? If athletics are to be maintained as part of the academic enterprise, should the university and the NCAA continue to make up more and more elaborate rules and penalties assuming that stricter enforcement will right sport's wrongs? Perhaps other options should be considered such as the accrediting or informal auditing of athletic programs, revenue sharing which might reduce some of the incentives to violate rules, the abolition of all rules, leading to a "free enterprise" sport system, or the replacement or detailed rules with general governing principles such as athletic budgets capped as a percentage of the academic budget. (Uehling 1983)

College leadership must decide. Although intercollegiate sport may be historically extracurricular, trustees, CEOs, and presidents must recognize that sport is central to the public image of higher education and, therefore, deserving of routine oversight by the central administration. Although curriculum and instruction may be at the heart of the academic enterprise, their relative invisibility makes sport all the more symbolic of the work in any institution. In a naturalistic society, one that distrusts the nonobservable, it is incumbent on college leadership to recognize that sport is at the very core of public perception of the work of higher education.

Only officers with academic oversight authority and expertise should be permitted to lead athletic programs. Athletic department structures separate from the authority of the CEO or president must not be tolerated. Clearly, at Michigan, Notre Dame, Pennsylvania State University, and Virginia, institutions with a successful marriage of sport and academics, it is the president who has been firmly in charge of athletics, responsible for academic and fiscal accounting of the intercollegiate program. As Gilley et al. (1986) have demonstrated, athletic impropriety is often related to unclear lines of authority, laissez-faire athletic leadership by the president, and semiautonomous or completely autonomous athletic departments. The college president must be responsible for and have the authority to govern the institution's sport program.

What is needed now is recognition that the NCAA's Presidents'

Commission has not and possibly will not alter the fundamental structure or purposes of big-time sport. A group housed within a larger organization, dependent for its own survival on semiprofessional football or basketball, will do little to encourage fundamental questioning of the play-for-pay brand of college sport we have today. Although the Presidents' Commission may readjust just the relationship between sport and studies through Rule 5-1-J, while it may exclude some external groups such as boosters from the recruiting process, the Commission's existence does little to ensure a comprehensive review of the concept of big-time sport. Should the university pay for athletic services? Should universities be in the entertainment business? Should our schools sanction behavior from coaches which should not be tolerated in the classroom? Should our institutions of higher learning provide special talent scholarships to athletes on any basis other than financial need?

The NCAA Presidents' Commission is in no position to question the power relationship that exists among trustees, presidents, and the faculty. As the Southern Methodist University case so aptly illustrates, an overzealous trustee can behave very much like a booster. So long as trustee groups have primary oversight responsibilities over athletics, the possibilities for abuse remain high. Can the Presidents' Commission speak to this point? One hopes that it can — that is, can strongly reassert the governing principle that control of campus programs belongs in the hands of academic officers.

Yet serious questions remain as to presidential ability and willingness to tangle with the athletic monster. As Maryland's Chancellor Slaughter has observed "but still, by and large, intercollegiate athletics is not directed by presidents and chancellors; they simply have not come to the fore as strongly as I hope they will" (Farrell, September 10, 1986:34).

Faculty must now reassert their governance authority and accept their responsibilities. Despite the isolation that results from specialization, despite the push to do one's own research, faculty must recognize that to concentrate on one's own publishing may mean that, brick by brick, the academic edifice may crumble. If nothing else, the academic ethic withers in the shadows of abuse. The faculty at Indiana University passed an athlete's "bill of rights" aimed at protecting them from verbal and physical abuse. Faculty at Southern Methodist University and the University of Maryland have begun to reassert themselves in the wake of the Mustang football and Len Bias revelations (Lederman, February 4, 1987). The assertion of governance authority must not, however, only follow on scandal or tragedy. A faculty concerned with the welfare of its institution must devote substantial energies to consistent oversight of sport programs, and not leave it to one academic-athletic liaison. If faculty shirk their responsibilities, they will get what they deserve.

The NCAA Presidents' group must not be accepted as a substitute for strong internal control of campus affairs. As Chancellor Slaughter's case at Maryland so strongly demonstrates, one may champion athletic reform nationally without having control of one's own institution. Time will tell if the Presidents' Commission becomes part of the governance myth that insulates the current form of big-time athletics, which makes the appearance of imminent reform so real that it deflects continued pressure for change — or if the Commission truly spurs a reassertion of the fundamental rights and responsibilities of presidential and faculty program governance. College leadership — that is, president's and their staffs, as well as faculty — must decide about sport on their own campuses.

What is needed now? The American college must accept its responsibility to blacks and women. If our institutions are to enroll them as "student-athletes" and have them play as symbolic representatives of the school, the American college must attempt to compensate for the lack of those cultural advantages that are typically associated with being male and white and from the middle class. As Harry Edwards (1984) has proposed, the realities of college sport should be offered to recruits concerning majors, graduation rates of athletes, and grades. Diagnostic testing should locate academic weaknesses, and tutors should be provided. Orientation programs should provide information concerning the temptations of drugs, and the fact that only 50 out of 15,000 college varsity basketball players and only 150 out of 41,000 college football players make the professional leagues. Colleges must adhere to their financial responsibilities to students who enroll under the assumption that they will be supported whatever their playing status. The termination of athletic scholarships because of less than "first-team" athletic performance, despite the concerted efforts of student-athletes, is a despicable maneuver to milk the highest athletic performance from adolescents. The entire matter of freshman eligibility also should be carefully considered. Most significant, coaches, boosters, and administration must be given the incentive to promote the education of their athletes. Availability of scholarships should be directly tied to the graduation rates of student athletes. This information should be made public so as to underline the importance of academic performance. Formal organizations so dependent upon the public's assumption of institutional legitimacy and efficiency must make a concerted effort to ensure academic propriety or risk losing its most important resource.

What is needed now? Although Rule 5-1-J establishing uniform eligibility standards for college scholarship athletes moves in the right direction, it is clearly at the wrong level. Regardless of the secondary school preparation of potential athletes, it is their real academic progress in the college which must be the primary concern of NCAA regulations. While Rule 5-1-J is a worthy effort to unify college leadership around the need for stricter academic standards, higher education must govern its own house[3] and ensure that athletes are making progress toward bona fide academic degrees while representing the institution — an oversight function properly performed by the general faculty of the institution. It is not sufficient to offer the utilitarian argument that college athletes must sometimes be sacrificed for the greatest good of the greater numbers on campus. What separates higher education from most other social institutions is that individuals themselves are important. Ultimately, the university must adhere to the Kantian notion that individuals themselves are the end — their full development as intellectual and social beings, not only the development of their biceps or rushing average. Without public confidence in the university, who will eventually trust their children to the school? Who will encourage their children to listen openly and respectfully, to trust the judgements of officers of the institution? — for it is these officers who are supposed to help youth mature in a manner proper for the individual.

College leadership must be willing to establish control over their own institutions. While the policy-making Presidents' Committee proposal of the American Council on Education was rejected by the NCAA delegates, such ACE action is needed to provide the emotional and professional support required for vigorous presidential action on athletic improprieties. Chief executives cannot afford to wait for the NCAA or any other organization to mandate national reform. Higher educational institutions must establish and uphold their own high standards as a demonstration of their integrity, and to earn the respect afforded to a self-governing profession.

What would be the result of denouncing the "Big Lie"? If proclaimed before a tradition-minded public, a public with English or German conceptions of the legitimate forms of higher education, it would not be well received. If stated before the modern American public, however, in an environment that continues to support campus athletics through all the travails of scandal and economic exigency, I believe that this statement would be received well by the vast majority.

So long as college and big-time sport leadership endorse and act upon the assumption that sport is an educational experience for the primary benefit of athletes, and that problems in the governance of athletics may be resolved within the existing system with minor tinkering, so long as these assumptions persist, then the history of college sport clearly shows that problems will persist. Instead, I offer that the very assumptions about what sport and education can and cannot do, should and should not do, must be actively questioned before meaningful reform in college sport may take place. Watzlawick et al. assert, "It is a fallacious assumption about the problem which precludes its solution" (1974:54).

Edward Shils (1981:183) has reflected upon the importance of respect for the traditions of higher education. Without a strict adherence to their core traditions in ethos, substance, and procedure, institutions of higher learning run the risk of losing public respect and, eventually, support. Because of the paucity of hard objective evidence that colleges do what they claim, that they efficiently educate toward agreed-upon goals, it is imperative that higher learning zealously defend the supporting population's fund of respect. Erosion of this respect and subsequent questioning of the legitimacy of higher education may directly parallel a loss of resources for those institutions. It may be too great an assumption to assume that the many publics of importance to colleges and universities in America will continue to stand for the hypocrisy of the "Big Lie."

In his discussion of the ethical crisis in American higher education, Martin (1982) considers the seriousness of the situation:

> Again, why is the ethical crisis the most serious and important? Without moral principles, the institutions of higher education and the teaching profession lose moral authority. Moral authority, not technical services

or professional skills, is a college's most prized possession. Despite a tradition of detachment and claims to value neutrality, the institution of higher education, along with the church and synagogue, is expected by the people to be an instrumentality of idealism. Without ideals that direct and correct behavior, institutions of higher learning are like a perfectly outfitted ship without a rudder. (Martin 1982:24–25)

With moral principles, higher education in America may model the character so strongly prized for our students. Character which is "disciplined, evident, enduring commitment to principle" requires "fidelity to duty under pressure, dignity amid controversy, courage in the presence of adversity" (Martin 1982:19). Can an institution really expect more of its students than it is willing to exhibit itself? By forthrightly admitting and remedying the problems of college sport, American higher education may utilize the visibility of sport to model the high standards that give the social institution its special standing.

The Crisis in College Leadership

The contemporary American college and university is in the midst of a leadership crisis. Whereas the college presidents of the nineteenth and early twentieth century may have exercised firm control over their small, single-purpose institutions, increased school size, functions, and resource requirements have markedly weakened the presidency and rendered it more of a management position than one of strong leadership. Presidents find themselves buffeted from government agencies, trustees, foundations, accrediting agencies, faculty, staff, and students. Although the trustees are nominal governors of the institution through historical precedent, the inner workings of the institution remain relatively untouched. The faculty, so departmentally isolated and concerned with their own academic territories, are unable to oversee the programs of the college, which span disciplinary boundaries of programs, such as sport, which are important to the environment outside the institution. Presidents have become increasingly involved with this environment through necessity. They have become concerned with money and students, with defending and defining the interests of their schools. Faculty isolation, historical and practical limits on trustee controls, and the growing outer-directedness of the president has created a power vacuum within the institution. Also — perhaps partly the result of the stress of the presidency, the rapid turnover of leadership, and the too-great respect given the diversity of opinion — institutional leadership has been reluctant to evaluate the appropriateness of programs. They have been reluctant to risk their position by standing up to coaches, boosters, and wealthy alumni whose behavior is detrimental to the students and the integrity of the institution.

This is most unfortunate. The college that does not root out obvious vileness within it presents an image that decays all higher education. As Lasch (1984:60) has so clearly recognized, the contemporary milieu is one where the "images of things have become more vivid than things themselves." Regardless of the great goodness remaining in the academic world, the image of the immorality within the institution does violence to it. Zingg (1983:12) agrees with Ewald Nyquist that the central issue about intercollegiate athletics does not shortsightedly end at violations of NCAA regulations. The issue instead goes to the moral core of the social institution of higher education in America. The moral institution must face the timeless challenge of trying to do what is right.

Referring to the behavior of the wider university, Bok (1982:299) outlines its basic obligations — obligations required of every participant in a civilized society:

> They must fulfill their contractual commitments. They must refrain from acts of deception. They must abide by the requirements of the law. More broadly still, they should endeavor not to inflict unjustified harm on others.

By so doing, the university will constantly address moral issues and ethical responsibilities in its relations with the outside world.

We can safely extend this common sense to college sport. Colleges must make every effort to educate and graduate all they enroll, taking into account and compensating for student characteristics accepted upon admission. They must plainly present factual information about the sort of education students are likely to receive, and about athletic opportunities available at the university when academic eligibility is maintained. Schools must abide by the spirit as well as the letter of the law concerning participation and leadership opportunities, and concerning the athletic regulations they have voted for. And, most broadly, the university must refrain from harming its students or competitors. All this only makes sense for a moral institution.

But it is important, however, that observance of the obligations required of every citizen in a civilized society must not be left to others to enforce. Robert Atwell, President of the American Council on Education, has urged trustees to be "part of the solution." Those not part of the solution are part of the problem. Trustees must not be blinded by athletic fanaticism or feel a lack of responsibility because of their historic exclusion from the programmatic decision-making process of the institution. Atwell urges that the trustees must "realize the degree of courage it takes for a chief executive officer to take on some of these problems in athletics and [they] should support him" (Winkler, April 11, 1984:33, 34).

Realistically, though, while trustees can give their support it must be the chief executive officer of the institution who takes the lead in athletic reform. In the report on higher education commissioned by the National Institute of Education, professors who cheat on their research data, student athlete exploitation, and the hypocrisy of the colleges' public claims of the primacy of academic values are cited as examples of major problems. There is a call for presidential leadership: presidential behavior must "evidence the ideals of honesty, justice, freedom, equality, generosity and respect for others — the necessary values of community" (Scully 1984:44–45). These are simple truths, but all too often overlooked in the day-to-day grind. They are values too often ignored and sidestepped by being referred to the safety of committee study or tabled for future consideration. Presidents who do not see athletics as a primary issue sitting atop the concerns in the decision makers' "garbage can" are part of the problem.

Garvin (1980) has argued that image and prestige are crucially important in today's college market. The perception of unethical behavior damages institutional prestige and corrodes carefully cultivated reputations for excellence. The president who does not act on so publicly visible improprieties as those in sport risks much damage to the resources available to prestigious schools, the valuation placed on that school's education by employers, and the status of students of that institution. The media, which has so readily fostered the perception of institutional status through its glossy depictions of athletic success, can just as quickly tear down the public facade of institutional quality and integrity. Reform of athletics is necessary to reinforce and establish an image of the rationality, efficiency, and responsiveness of the school. As Popkewitz (1982) notes, reform activity is a "dramaturgy" which is necessary for both control within the institution and its very stability. Such evidence of reform is especially necessary for organizations with conflicting objectives and unclear technologies. Without such dramaturgy, organizational members and constituents are left with little direction as to the appropriateness of behaviors and programs.

While we cannot expect college presidents to shirk all other responsibilities to tackle the athletic problem, presidents must be convinced that the visibility of athletic abuses labels it a problem of immediate importance. Presidents who do not act risk both their school's public reputations and their own personal image.

Upon consideration, it may be that the more stringent measures recently adopted at NCAA conventions will encourage adherence to NCAA regulations. Certainly, coaches who heretofore had been able to escape sanctions imposed on their athletic programs by moving to some other school will think twice before engaging in some major violation of rules. Presidents' attention to athletic abuses, and their support of these new regulations, seems to suggest a new era in college sport. It may be that chief executives will no longer tolerate athletic fiefdoms controlled by powerful coaches, athletic directors, and boosters. Sports in which abuses are uncovered, and the staff responsible, may now be severely penalized.

Efforts to reform athletics will certainly be easier with trustee support. Presidents cannot be expected to effectively clean their houses without the full backing of their legal overseers. Trustees and administrative leadership must come to some agreement concerning the responsibility for intercollegiate athletics — is it to be seen as an internal program to be effectively governed by central administration or as an external appendage primarily outside of institutional officers' oversight? And the anxieties of reform will be exacerbated by the number of presidents at other institutions similarly engaged in reform. Too often, however, chief executive officers have looked to external agencies for help with their problems. They have looked to the safety of company. But as Millard (1983:32, 34–36) points out in response to calls for a more active involvement of accrediting agencies in the determination of institutional quality, the primary guardian of educational quality must be the institution itself.

In a view offered by the Carnegie Foundation for the Advancement of Teaching (Boyer 1986) it is apparent that, given failure to adhere to the moral and contractual obligations of all society's citizens, and given the lack of any national policing educational agency, it becomes incumbent on accreditation agencies to include consideration of athletics in their institutional evaluations. While accreditation agencies may more comfortably consider traditional measures of institutional quality, such as number of volumes in the library, teacher-student ratios, and the proportion of terminal degree holders among the faculty, such measures pale in importance compared to the moral bankruptcy evidenced by a school's failure to educate its student-athletes. Can even a 1-to-10 teacher-student ratio compensate for school leadership that condones racist or sexist treatment of student-athletes? While accrediting boards cannot reasonably expect all school personnel to behave ethically, it is to be expected that school leadership will condone neither sexual advances to students by professors nor illegal recruiting practices on the part of coaches without concerted effort to intervene. Institutions that will not deal with these abuses should be censured or lose their accreditation. Accrediting agencies that provide the only regional oversight of higher education risk losing their own credibility if they do not act.

Critics of recent NCAA reform efforts have one of their most salient points here, for supporters of these reforms have not addressed the core problems. While the 1985 regulations signal greater NCAA determination to oversee athletic propriety, as demonstrated by the resistance to the reforms proposed before the summer 1987 NCAA special convention, such efforts still do not reach to the heart of problems in the sport system. Any attempts to significantly alter the pattern of consistent abuses historically demonstrated by big-time sport must address at least three major problems — the first, technical, having to do with the capabilities of the NCAA; the second, unclear goals for athletics; and the third, unstable resources.

First, can the NCAA with its limited staff and resources police its approximately 800 colleges and universities that engage in anywhere up to twenty to twenty five sports for men's and women's teams ranging in size up to forty to sixty students per team? Can the NCAA effectively police coaches and boosters who have historically shown such cleverness and stealth in recruiting and maintaining athletic eligibility? Clearly, policing such a population will be difficult if not impossible. While the New Orleans reforms are laudable, they still place the ethical burden on the wrong shoulders. If at all possible, external agencies should not be asked to police the profession. Professions must police themselves — especially those professions that guard their autonomy so zealously. The university must set its own high standards and live by them.

Second, the American college must address the core problem of unclear goals facing athletics and, for that matter, facing higher education more generally in this pluralistic country. First and foremost is the need to consider the importance of winning. The old dilemma between the means and the ends remains an ever-vexing problem — one which will not go away with lip service given to the importance of excellence. If winning is of paramount importance, then a certain sort of behavior is appropriate. The same sort of institutionally sanctioned behavior is inappropriate if education is more important. Are these young men and women playing on the teams athletes first and students only if possible? This must be addressed and clearly stated. Reform efforts that strengthen the sanctions against rule violators does more to thicken the already voluminous NCAA rule book than to make American colleges and universities face up to this core question.

Third, the 1985 reforms do not touch the core problem of institutional control. Problems of institutional control stem partly from improper administrative structure and partly from the school's pressing need for funds. While the former may be remedied relatively rapidly, the latter problem requires a longer-term solution. In no institution at any level of competition should intercollegiate athletics — a formal program of the educational organization — be administered by nonacademic officers. The athletic director must answer to an officer of the university whose primary responsibilities require academic oversight of programs and/or personnel. But can the university govern itself when external power groups have already gained such importance in institutional decision making? While recent NCAA efforts prohibiting booster participation in athletic recruitment have addressed the problems of booster overzealousness, they have not been able to speak to the problem of trustees and other influential individuals who care more for sport success than the right principles of the university. This may continue to be a problem so long as money remains an important factor in the selection of trustees and in the decision making of central administration. With the search for resources continuing today to be so important, the influence of money-bearing trustees and other external groups will remain great. Regardless of the president's personal wishes, chief executive officers and others in central administration will be greatly influenced by those exerting control over the resources essential for school survival and growth.

As the special NCAA convention of summer 1987 has shown, unified action remedying the abuses of college sport are far more difficult than may have been expected by the CEOs leading the reform movement. The diversity of opinion among sporting powers, the inconsistent support of college presidents for changes in the sport system, and lack of conviction that the current sport system is seriously flawed all but guarantee that the status quo will continue at least in the near future. Major changes in the existing college sport structures, values, expectations, and norms of behavior are probably not possible within the NCAA organization. Presidential leadership is clearly required.

Louis Benezet, previously president of Alleghany College, Colorado College, Claremont University Center, and the State University of New York at Albany, has spoken to the function and importance of presidential leadership. In the article "Do Presidents Make A Difference" (1982:13), he quotes the president of one of the largest campuses in the United States:

> There are fifty thousand full-time students down there and I could walk up the street and be recognized perhaps by a couple of dozen of them. But what I think I must do is to come down now and then on an issue of principle where the president can do something that publicly holds up the standards of this place.

The president and trustees of one major university have chosen to confront the abuses of athletics head on. Despite a rich tradition of intercollegiate basketball, the leadership of the University of San Francisco chose to terminate its fifty-eight-year-old program in the face of seemingly uncontrollable misconduct on the part of alumni boosters and players. The problem was difficult, but the decision was clear. Announcing the decision, the Rev. John LoSchiavo remarked that,

> the price the university has had to pay for those problems has been much greater than the heavy financial price. There is no way of measuring the damage that has been done to the university's most priceless asset, its integrity and its reputation. (*Chronicle of Higher Education*, August 11, 1982:1)

In a strictly rational sense, the course of action chosen is easily justified. If, indeed, institutional prestige is a precious possession required for the acquisition of students and funds sufficient for survival, then colleges and universities must jealously guard against any undermining of public perception of high institutional status. While arguably it may be justified to promote athletics as a means of constructing institutional prestige and making that prestige highly visible, it is unquestionably in the best interests of a college or university to forcefully deal with the athletics that destroys its prestige.

The athletic programs that run counter to the educational purposes of our schools must be made more consistent with the spirit and broad objectives of American higher learning. In no way is under-the-table money or phantom course credit consistent with educational purpose. Attitudes of this sort must not be reserved for romantics who cling to an Old World conception of higher learning. Instead, thinking of this sort is totally appropriate for hard-headed rationalists who tally costs and benefits on decision sheets. The intercollegiate sport that has gained tremendous visibility for schools is as easily capable of losing institutional prestige. Hard-won legitimacy and status must be protected, for they provide the life's blood for institutional survival and make it possible to achieve institutional purposes. Winning athletics cannot come at any price. It must fit within the broad umbrella of publicly acceptable programs. The activities whose purpose and/or process fall outside of this must be altered or terminated.

Leaders with boldness are required — leaders with enough vision of the problem not to allow themselves to be constrained by apparently reasonable but invariably damaging caution. In the case of athletics, too much caution will lead to slow suffocation. Leadership must admit that big-time intercollegiate sport has its racial and gender problems; that athletes at the big-time level are not primarily at the school for their own educational benefit; that players are paid to symbolically represent the school and community; and that while they may serve in this professional capacity, they may also serve as models of valued characteristics for all who identify with the school. The real functions of college sport are significant enough so that hypocritical rationalization and the Big Lie are unnecessary justifications.

Leadership is required that can recognize the change that time has brought. Sport brings satisfactions worthy enough to warrant sports inclusion in some ethical form in the American college. Sport need no longer be justified as the shaper of personality, as of fiscal benefit to the university, or as the absolute meritocracy it was touted to be in the early twentieth century. College sport promotes community. The Big Game produces character myths which provide heroic models for the student and the public. Intercollegiate sports aid institutional prestige and help establish the school among its educational peers. College sport encourages a commitment of the individual to the institution and the qualities perceived in the organization as central to its identity. Athletics can create respect for the graduate of the institution.

College sport is not primarily of direct material benefit to the institution. Instead, athletics are of abstract worth — as abstract and meaningful as the spirit itself. In this book we have looked at the combination of factors which permitted and encouraged incorporation of sport within the formal responsibilities of American higher education. Although this connection is peculiar when placed in cross-cultural perspective, it is most reasonable considering the spiritual responsibilities of the American educational institution.

College leaders must now recognize just how immediately important is attention to athletic abuses that stain the image of higher education. Reform is necessary now to end unethical behavior and the hypocrisy of the Big Lie.

I for one have faith in the ability of the public to accept these realities. By admitting them, college leadership will be ultimately protecting the respectability and prestige of the institution of higher education.

Notes

Intercollegiate Sport: An Overview

1. Division I itself is broken up into Division IA for the largest football powers and Division IAA for those with a less ambitious program. At the time of writing, there has been pressure brought to bear by the biggest schools in Division IA to exclude smaller athletic programs from a proposed super league composed of the largest IA members. Many of those big-time schools are represented in football by the College Football Association.

The Development of American Higher Education and Intercollegiate Sport

1. The cloth with no discernible pattern is a fabric that today allows university status at one and the same time to the multiversities of Ohio and Michigan, with their tens of thousands of students, and to Dropsie University in Philadelphia, a graduate school specializing in Judaic studies, with an enrollment of 47 (*Chronicle of Higher Education*, July 7, 1982:19).

2. See Kneller (1955:59) on how the English government has given the universities "gentle guidance," yet has left them relatively free to pursue academic matters. Knowledge belongs to humankind of all through the ages and must not be tampered with by nonacademics. The faculty are the guardians of this knowledge.

3. German institutions of higher education (except for the theological and pedagogical schools) are public corporations which in 1964 were 82% funded by local and federal government sources (Burn et al. 1971:181). In addition to appropriations, colleges and universities in 1984–1985 received 10.7% of their incomes from federal grants and contracts (*Chronicle of Higher Education*, April 1, 1987:2).

4. College tuition costs have increased more rapidly than inflation during the last six years. The percentage of median income needed to pay for college by families with 18- to 19-year-old children in four-year colleges has risen from 18.6% in 1976–1977 to 21.8% in 1983–1984 and from 33.8% to 41.8% for families with children in selective universities (Evangelauf 1986).

5. In fact, the English system has been criticized as being unresponsive to the needs of society — pursuing classical study and the humanities in an increasingly technological era.

6. See Lowell (1934) on the regularity of support enjoyed by continental universities.

7. Of course, for some analysts the diversity of funding sources for American higher education has had a positive effect. To John Burgess, such diversity has limited the degree to which any one interest group can dominate the direction of higher education. If these institutions were to become dependent upon state appropriations, Burgess feared the conflicting philosophies of transient state legislators (Hofstadter and Smith 1961:659). For Burgess, it was much better for the institution's own governing board to retain primary authority over the affairs of the college.

8. More recently, Embry-Riddle Aeronautical University placed an ad in the *Wall Street Journal* soliciting donations. In return for a contribution of $1 million, that school would not only provide a nice tax deduction but would also consider that benefactor as a trustee. When Chancellor Jeffrey H. Ledewitz was asked about the bluntness of the ad, he commented, "The university does not view what we're doing as any different philosophically than institutions that name buildings after people or give honorary doctorates to donors. Higher education in reality is a business. I don't think there's anything wrong with being very direct." (*Chronicle of Higher Education*, June 9, 1982:3). More recently, Drexel University ran this ad in the *Wall Street Journal*: "We're looking for a special type of entrepreneur — one who will support American business by supporting the resource it most depends on — American education" (*Chronicle of Higher Education*, November 3, 1986:29).

9. The percentage of estimated income for various occupations consumed by average tuition and fees for college between 1840 and 1880 declined as follows: for the urban male teacher, from 15% to 3%; for the rural male teacher, from 34% to 8%; for a mason, from 13% to 6%; and for the common laborer, from 25% to 7% (Burke 1982:217).

10. For other accounts of the rise of intercollegiate sport, see Lucas and Smith 1978; Spears and Swanson 1978; Sage 1975; Scott 1975; Betts 1974; Hackensmith 1966; Rudolph 1968; Slosson 1910. For chronicles of excesses in American educational institutions for the purpose of athletic victory, see Crase 1974; Hanford 1974; Scott 1971; Shaw 1972; Boyle 1963; Savage 1929. For histories of American higher education, see Cremin 1970, 1980; Henry 1975; Rudolph 1968; Veysey 1965; and Hofstadter and Smith 1961.

11. See Struna (1977) for exception to this rule.

12. The importance of negotiating for support will increase with the drastic cuts in resources available to American higher education projected for the next twenty years (Carnegie Council 1981).

13. See Gamson and Horowitz (1983) for an account of definitions of goals and methods and the loose coupling of formal structure with actual practice in the Israeli higher educational system.

14. It should be noted that this functionalist interpretation of law differs markedly from the conflictist view of law as that imposed upon the masses by the ruling class.

15. Hoch (1972) contends that the fiction of the well-rounded college man developed at precisely the same time that the demands of specialization required a narrowing of mental development.

16. See Rugg, Warren, and Carpenter (1981) for empirical verification of different values held by faculty in various disciplines at a major public university.

17. Before consumers could fund the institution, they must be aware of that school's existence. Visibility is as important a concern today as it was at the beginning of the century. To that end, colleges and universities have hired Nobel laureates, supported prize-winning programs, held highly publicized conferences, and at Florida State University, hired a former football coach to stage a circus. According to the University president at the time, Doak Campbell, that circus was almost as significant a factor in the establishment of Florida State's image as the rest of the university's activities combined (*Chronicle of Higher Education*, July 28, 1982:5-6).

Intercollegiate Sport: The Search for Rationalization

1. In addition, the National Education Association has accepted the notion that sports promoted educational, moral, cooperative, and individual values (Betts 1974:213). However, while most people believed in the positive values available through sport, the excesses in play, recruiting, and spectatorship, and the diversion of attention and resources from the real purposes of higher education worried others. See Betts 1974:211-218.

2. But then again, this view of the function of the university is not new. See Veysey (1965:440) concerning the American university of the early twentieth century: "The university . . . had become largely an agency for social control. . . . The custodianship of popular views comprised the primary responsibility of the American university." See also Hall (1982:1) on the role of private corporations in the evolution of American nationality. According to Hall, private corporations took over from the state, family, and locality "the

tasks of coordinating production and distribution, formulating and implementing social policy, and shaping the ideological framework and intellectual
instruments through which reality was defined and acted on."

3. The labelling of individuals which occurs may or may not be
associated with actual differences in mental, physical, or spiritual
characteristics between individuals. As work by Rosenthal and Jacobson
(1968), Brophy and Good (1974), and others has demonstrated, individuals
labelled as successful may not vary significantly from those labelled unsuccessful in task-related personal characteristics. The labelling of an individual
through success or failure in sports may trigger a self-fulfilling prophecy that
leads to differential behavior and response.

4. Another example of the reorientation of college programs in response
to economic realities is the transformation of the university press during the
last ten years, from a publisher primarily concerned with the production of
specialized works of crucial importance for the academic process to a press
which searches for the "blockbuster" book that will contribute to the funding
of the institution (*Chronicle of Higher Education*, December 2, 1981:17).
While the traditional purpose of the university press is the dissemination of
significant knowledge to the academic community, the rising costs of operation have forced the university press into a more pragmatic alteration of this
traditional purpose.

5. Total incomes at the big-time football level are gained from the
following sources: ticket sales, 43%; guarantees and options, 10%; special
events, 10%; student fees and assessments, 8%; alumni contributions, 11%;
government support, 6%; other revenues, 12%. Total expenses at the big-time
level come from the following sources: salaries, 30%; scholarships, 16%;
travel, 13%; guarantees and options, 11%; other expenses, 25% (Raiborn
1982:52).

6. It is interesting to note, however, that athletic matters were more
significant to the alumni leadership than the expansion of academic programs,
and special programs for the disadvantaged, minorities, recreation, or the
arts.

The Condition of Higher Education and Athletics
in America

1. See Boutilier and SanGiovanni (1983) for more detailed accounts of
the historical time periods of women's sport. According to these authors, the
period 1880–1917 was one of sport limited to the upper class and rationalized
as "conspicuous consumption" and for health reasons; 1917–1936 saw the

extension of sport to women in other classes, as the entrance of women into the labor force during World War I justified their new roles as workers, citizens, and athletes; 1936–1960 saw a retrogression of sport to the less competitive, strictly "feminine" physical activities; 1960–present saw the reextension of competitive strenuous sport to many more women and feminist insistence that there is nothing inherently alien to females, including sports.

2. Also in this regard, see Veysey 1965:440.

3. For the still peripheral status of sport at Oxford and Cambridge, see Walker 1985:35, 38. Far from being a central part of university life, "sport has become an adjunct, something useful to have in the margin of a resume" (38). In no way is interinstitutional athletics as well supported by central English university administrations as it is in the large American universities.

4. The NCAA has recently passed legislation making booster assistance in the recruitment of athletes illegal. Schools are now liable for the violations of their boosters (Vance, August 3, 1983:15).

5. As of March 1987, 24 schools were under NCAA sanctions: Alabama A & M, Baylor, Bradley, East Carolina, East Tennessee State, Idaho State, University of Iowa, Iowa State, Louisiana State, Loyola of Maryland, Memphis State, University of Mississippi, Mississippi State, University of Nebraska, University of South Florida, University of Southern California, Southern Illinois at Carbondale, Southern Methodist, University of South Carolina, University of Tennessee, University of Texas at El Paso, Texas Christian, Texas Tech, and University of Wisconsin at Madison. Football programs were cited in eleven cases and basketball in ten cases. Also included as programs in which abuses were detected were men's soccer, swimming, track and field, and cross-country. Women's programs were not immune from sanctions either, with some women's golf, tennis, softball, track and field, and cross-country sports programs found in violation of NCAA regulations (*Chronicle of Higher Education*, March 18, 1987:49).

6. An example of this is the lack of real enforcement against violators such as Jerry Tarkanian, with a record of 122–20 from the years 1968–1973, left his coaching position at Long Beach State University after the school was placed on NCAA probation, but later signed a lucrative contract with the University of Nevada — Las Vegas (Rader 1983:280).

7. The immediate effect of college sport deregulation has been that schools have made about the same television money, but have had to appear on television more often to do so. Apparently, the freedom to regulate television contracts has led to an "unhealthy glut" of college television. There may indeed be some NCAA-coordinated television plan for college sports in the near future.

8. The relationship of private business to colleges and universities has lost any semblance of informality with the growing sponsorship of football's prime showcases — its bowl games. In 1986, Sunkist increased its support of the Fiesta Bowl to $2.4 million in order to sweeten the offers made to first-place Miami and second-place Penn State. United States Fidelity and Guaranty Corporation supports the Sugar Bowl with its $2.55 million, while Mazda Motors pays $1 million to affix its title to the Gator Bowl. According to John R. Davis, then NCAA President, "Anything that can help college athletics survive, we're all for that, and corporate sponsorship can do just that" (Lederman, December 3, 1986:34–36).

Sport and the Mission of American Higher Education

1. See Randall Collins, "Functional and Conflict Theories of Educational Stratification," *American Sociological Review*, December 1971, 36:1002–1019.

2. The alteration of characteristics may occur not only during college but before and after actual school attendance.

3. Clearly, general student recruitment data of this sort will not escape the notice of college leadership, which has increased budgets for recruitment by 63% in four-year schools — a rate more than twice the rate of inflation (*Chronicle of Higher Education*, October 8, 1986:43).

Reflections on Diversity: College and Sport

1. The extent to which sport has become part and parcel of higher education in American students' eyes is reflected in the vote by students of Southern Illinois University. When faced with the prospect of terminating the varsity football program, given approval of a proposed reduction of the athletic fee from $30 to $20, students at that institution voted down the proposal by a margin of 2 to 1 (*Chronicle of Higher Education*, October 28, 1981). Of 287 undergraduates in a survey of a college with little athletic history, 83% agreed with the statement (with 15% neutral and 2% disagreeing) that "intercollegiate athletics have been a part of the American tradition and should remain so" (Jensen et al. 1980). Another survey of undergraduates at a predominantly women's college with no athletic tradition and a fledgling intercollegiate program found that more than two-thirds indicated that they would not have attended a college or university that had no intercollegiate athletics (Chu 1984).

2. Also see Hanford (1976) in this regard.

3. Research by Ervin et al. (1985) indicates that the 700 SAT criteria does provide a usable measure of student ability to perform college-level

work. Students scoring below this level seem to require more remediation than those scoring above that level. In addition, an NCAA study demonstrates the effects of Rule 5-1-J: Of the 88% responding of all institutions at the Division I level, 168 of the 250 reporting schools indicated their enrolling "partial qualifiers" — students who had 2.0 or better secondary school GPAs but who did not enter with satisfactory core curriculum GPA or test scores. Another 38 schools indicated the enrollment of "non-qualifiers" — that is, students who did not meet a 2.0 GPA and without a core curriculum GPA of at least 2.0 or standardized test score requirements. Of the 599 "partial qualifiers," 372 received some sort of athletically related financial aid, with the bulk of athletes (260) who received such aid being designated to play football or basketball (*NCAA News*, April 29, 1987).

Bibliography

Academe. "Higher education revenue sources." 67(6), December 1981:12.

Academe. "Bottoming out?" 70(3), July-August 1984:14.

Acosta, R. Vivian, and Linda Jean Carpenter. "Women in sport." In Donald Chu, Jeffrey Segrave, and Beverly Becker (eds.), *Sport and American Higher Education.* Champaign, Ill.: Human Kinetics, 1985.

Adler, Peter, and Patricia Adler. "From idealism to pragmatic detachment: the academic performance of college athletes." *Sociology of Education* 58 (October 1985):241–250.

Alfano, Peter. "NCAA head asks assault on rampant abuse of rules." *New York Times,* October 13, 1984:1, 48.

Altbach, Phillip G., and Robert O. Berdahl (eds.). *Higher Education in American Society.* Buffalo, N.Y.: Prometheus Books, 1981.

Alwin, Duane F. "Socioeconomic background, colleges and post-collegiate achievements." In William H. Sewell, Robert M. Hauser, and David L. Featherman (eds.), *Schooling and Achievement in American Society.* New York: Academic Press, 1976.

American Association of University Professors Bulletin 13(6) October 1927; 12(4) April 1926:228; 17(4) April 1931.

American Institute for Research. "Studies of Intercollegiate Athletics." Report sponsored by the Presidents' Commission of the NCAA, 1987–1988.

Anderson, Charles J. *Factbook for Academic Administrators: 1981–1982.* Washington, D.C.: American Council on Education, 1981.

Anderson, Dave. "Majoring in probation." *Sunday New York Times.* February 7, 1982:S3).

Arnove, Robert. "Values education: sociological perspective." In *Education and American Culture.* New York: Macmillan, 1980.

Ashby, Sir Eric. "The case for ivory towers." Paper delivered at the International Conference on Higher Education in Tomorrow's World. University of Michigan, Ann Arbor, April 26–29, 1967.

Asher, Mark. "Abuses in college athletics." *The Washington Post*, June 16, 1985:D1, D4; June 17, 1985:C1, C4; June 18, 1985:B1, B4.

Astin, Alexander. "Undergraduate achievement and instructional 'excellence.' *Science* 161(1968):661–668.

Astin, Helen, and Alan E. Bayer. "Sex discrimination in academe." *Educational Record* 53(2) Spring 1972:101–118.

Astin, Alexander. *Achieving Educational Excellence*. San Francisco: Jossey-Bass, 1985.

Astin, Alexander. *Four Critical Years*. San Francisco: Jossey-Bass, 1987.

Atwell, Robert. "Some reflections on collegiate athletics." *Educational Record* 60(4) Fall 1979:367–373.

Atwell, Robert H., Bruce Grimes, and Donna Lopiano. *The Money Game*. Washington, D.C.: American Council on Education, 1980.

Bach, Rebecca, and Carolyn Perucci. "Organizational influence on the sex composition of college and university faculty: a research note." *Sociology of Education* 57 (July 1984):193–198.

Barney, R.F. "Physical education and sport in North America." In Earle Ziegler (ed.), *History of Physical Education and Sport*. Englewood Cliffs, N.J.: Prentice-Hall, 1979:171–227.

Beck, H.P. *Men Who Control Our Universities*. New York: King's Crown Press, 1947.

Becker, Debbie, and Steve Weiberg. "New academic rule for athletes felt across USA." *USA Today*. August 18, 1986:7C.

Becker, Ernest. *The Birth and Death of Meaning*. New York: Free Press, 1971.

Beezly, William H. "The 1961 scandal at North Carolina State and the end of the Dixie Classic." *Arena* 7(3) November 1983:33–52.

Benagh, Jim. *Making It to Number 1*. New York: Dodd, Mead, 1976.

Bend, E. *The Impact of Athletic Participation on Academic and Career Aspirations and Achievement*. New Brunswick, N.J.: National Football Foundation and Hall of Fame, 1968.

Benezet, Louis. "Do presidents make a difference?" *Educational Record* 63(4) Fall 1982:11–13.

Bennett, Bruce L., Maxwell L. Howell, and Uriel Simri. *Comparative Physical Education and Sport*. Philadelphia: Lea and Febiger, 1975.

Berg, Ivar. *Education and Jobs: The Great Training Robbery.* New York: Praeger, 1970.

Berkow, Ira. "Why Lefty got fired." *New York Times*, November 5, 1986:D23.

Bernard, Jessie. *Academic Women.* Pennsylvania State University Press, State College: 1964.

Betts, John R. *America's Sporting Heritage: 1850-1950.* Reading, Mass.: Addison-Wesley, 1974.

Blann, F. Wayne. "Intercollegiate athletic competition and students' educational and career plans." *Journal of College Student Personnel* March 1985:115-118.

Blau, Peter M., and O.D. Duncan. *The American Occupational Structure. New York: John Wiley, 1967.*

Blau, Peter, and W.R. Scott. Formal Organizations. San Francisco: Chandler, 1962.

Bok, Derek. *Beyond the Ivory Tower.* Cambridge, Mass.: Harvard University Press, 1982.

Bok, Derek. "Presidents need power within the NCAA to preserve American standards and institutional integrity." *Chronicle of Higher Education* 27(16), December 14, 1983:33.

Bolman, Lee G., and Terrence E. Deal. *Modern Approaches to Understanding and Managing Organizations.* San Francisco: Jossey-Bass, 1984.

Boorstin, D. *The Exploring Spirit.* New York: Random House, 1977.

Boutilier, Mary, and Lucinda SanGiovanni. *The Sporting Woman.* Champaign, Ill.: Human Kinetics Press, 1983.

Bowles, Samuel, and Herbert Gintis. *Schooling in Capitalist America: Educational Reform and the Contradictions of Economic Life.* New York: Basic Books, 1976.

Boyer, Ernest L. "Higher educational systems: myth and reality." In James Perkins and Barbara Burns (eds.), *Access Systems, Youth and Employment.* Papers presented at the 1976 Aspen Seminar. New York: International Council for Educational Development, 1977:69-72.

Boyer, Ernest L. *College: The Undergraduate Experience in America.* New York: Carnegie Foundation for the Advancement of Teaching, 1986.

Boyle, R.H. *Sport: Mirror of American Life.* Boston: Little, Brown, 1963.

Brinkerhoff, Merlin B., and Phillip R. Kunz. *Complex Organizations and Their Environments*. Dubuque, Iowa: William C. Brown, 1972.

Brooker, G., and T.D. Klastorin. "To the victors belong the spoils? College athletics and alumni giving." *Social Science Quarterly* 62(4), December 1981:744–750.

Brophy, Jere, and Thomas Good. *Teacher-Student Relationships*. New York: Holt, Rinehart and Winston, 1974.

Brubacher, John S. *On the Philosophy of Higher Education*. San Francisco: Jossey-Bass, 1977.

Brubacher, John S., and Willis Rudy. *Higher Education in Transition*. New York: Harper, 1958.

Bryce, James. *The American Commonwealth*. London: Macmillan, 1889.

Budig, J. "The relationship among intercollegiate athletics, enrollment and voluntary support for higher education." Unpublished doctoral dissertation, Illinois State University, 197.

Buhrman, H. "Scholarship and athletics in junior high school." *International Review of Sport Sociology* 7(1972):119–131.

Burke, Colin B. *American Collegiate Populations: A Test of the Traditional View*. New York: New York University Press, 1982.

Burn, Barbara B., P. Altbach, C. Kerr, and J. Perkins. *Higher Education in Nine Countries*. New York: McGraw-Hill, 1971.

Cady, Edwin H. *The Big Game*. Knoxville: University of Tennessee Press, 1978.

Carnegie Bulletin no. 23, 1929.

Carnegie Council on Policy Studies in Higher Education. *The Thousand Futures: The Next Twenty Years in Higher Education*. San Francisco: Jossey-Bass, 1981.

Carnegie Foundation for the Advancement of Teaching. *Current Developments in American College Sport*. New York: 1931.

Carnegie Foundation for the Advancement of Teaching. *The Control of the Campus*. Washington, D.C.: 1982.

Carpenter, Linda Jean, and R. Vivian Acosta. "The status of women in inter-collegiate athletics — a five year national study." In Donald Chu, Jeffrey Segrave, and Beverly Becker (eds.), *Sport and American Higher Education*. Champaign, Ill.: Human Kinetics, 1985.

Chronicle of Higher Education. July 10, 1981.

Chronicle of Higher Education. "Students vote against cut in athletic fee." 23(9) October 28, 1981:2.

Chronicle of Higher Education. "Former player is convicted in college basketball fix." 23(14) December 2, 1981:10.

Chronicle of Higher Education. "University presses take a page from big business' book." 23(14) December 2, 1981:17.

Chronicle of Higher Education. "US provided a sixth of private institutions' income in fiscal 1980." 23(18) January 13, 1982:13.

Chronicle of Higher Education. "Large expenses for sports programs lead more colleges to seek funds from donors." 24(1) March 3, 1982:5.

Chronicle of Higher Education. "Officials see state funds for colleges lagging over the next 3 years." 24(3) March 17, 1982:7.

Chronicle of Higher Education. "Forty six percent of athletes get degrees within 5 years, a study finds." 24(9) April 28, 1982:9.

Chronicle of Higher Education. "Top 20 college football coaches all earn more than $100,000." 24(14) June 2, 1982:13.

Chronicle of Higher Education. "Position available: university trustee; price: $1 million." 24(15) June 9, 1982:3.

Chronicle of Higher Education. "Two universities challenge NCAA's TV–Football Rule." 24(16) June 16, 1982:10.

Chronicle of Higher Education. "Court orders worker compensation for injured athletes." 24(18) June 30, 1982:3.

Chronicle of Higher Education. "Footnotes." 24(19) July 7, 1982:19.

Chronicle of Higher Education. "An all-student circus is still flying high at Florida State University." 24(22) July 28, 1982:5-6.

Chronicle of Higher Education. "Applications for fall admissions decline at private and public colleges." 24(22) July 28, 1982:8.

Chronicle of Higher Education. "A big basketball power drops the sport, blaming abuses by alumni 'boosters'." 24(24) August 11, 1982:1, 11.

Chronicle of Higher Education. "Sidelines." 28(7) April 11, 1984.

Chronicle of Higher Education. "Big bucks of televised football." 28(19) July 5, 1984:23.

Chronicle of Higher Education. "Factfile." 29(18) January 16, 1985:15.

Chronicle of Higher Education. "In brief." 30(19) July 10, 1985.

Chronicle of Higher Education. "Sidelines." 31(17) January 8, 1986:29.

Chronicle of Higher Education. "Sidelines." 32(4) March 26, 1986:34.

Chronicle of Higher Education. "Sidelines." 32(13) May 28, 1986:26.

Chronicle of Higher Education. "Sidelines." 32(18) July 2, 1986:17.

Chronicle of Higher Education. "Factfile: racial and ethnic makeup of college and university enrollments." 32(21) July 23, 1986:25.

Chronicle of Higher Education. "Football powers get $71 million in TV pact with CBS and ESPN." 33(5) October 1, 1986:40.

Chronicle of Higher Education. "Colleges' recent enrollment growth credited to recruiting efforts." 33(6) October 8, 1986:43.

Chronicle of Higher Education. "Black enrollment found down in 18 or 19 states under federal orders to desegregate colleges." 33(6) October 8, 1986:43.

Chronicle of Higher Education. "Give and Take." 33(10) November 3, 1986:29.

Chronicle of Higher Education. "Sidelines." 33(17) January 7, 1987:34.

Chronicle of Higher Education. 33(17) January 7, 1987:28.

Chronicle of Higher Education. "Sidelines." 33(22) February 11, 1987:35.

Chronicle of Higher Education. "In brief: Go-ahead to upgrade sports given to State University of New York–Buffalo." 33(22) February 11, 1987:36.

Chronicle of Higher Education. "Twenty-four institutions under NCAA sanctions." March 18, 1987.

Chronicle of Higher Education. "Revenues and expenditures of colleges and universities, 1984–1985." 33(29) April 1, 1987:2.

Chronicle of Higher Education. "In box." 33(31) April 15, 1987:15.

Chu, Donald. "Origins of the connection of physical education and athletics at the American university: and organizational interpretation." *Journal of Sport and Social Issues* 3(1) 1979:22–31.

Chu, Donald. "Sport and the charter of American higher education: a case study." *Proceedings of the Annual Meeting of the National Association for Physical Education in Higher Education, 1984.* Champaign, Ill.: Human Kinetics Publishers, 128–137.

Chu, Donald, and Jeffrey O. Segrave. "Leadership recruitment and ethnic stratification in basketball." *Journal of Sport and Social Issues* 5(1) Spring-Summer 1980:13–22.

Chu, Donald. Jeffrey O. Segrave, and Beverly J. Becker (eds.). *Sport and American Higher Education*. Champaign, Ill.: Human Kinetics Publishers, 1985.

Chu, Donald, and Sheldon Solomon. "The relationship between sport performance and college application rates: pilot study." Paper presented at the North American Society for the Sociology of Sport annual meeting, Las Vegas, October 30–November 1, 1986.

Clark, Burton R. *The Distinctive College: Antioch, Reed and Swarthmore*. Chicago: Aldine, 1970.

Claxton, P.P. "The American college in the life of the American people." In W.H. Crawford (ed.), *The American College*. New York: Henry Holt, 1915.

Coakley, J. *Sport in Society: Issues and Controversies*. St. Louis, Mo.: C.V. Mosby, 1978.

Cohen, M.D., and J.C. March. *Leadership and Ambiguity: The American College President*. New York: McGraw-Hill, 1984.

Collins, Randall. "Functional and conflict theories of educational stratification." *American Sociological Review* 36 (December 1971):1002–10019.

Conable, Charlotte Williams. *Women at Cornell: The Myth of Equal Education*. Ithaca: Cornell University Press, 1977.

Cooper, Clayton S. "The American undergraduate — first paper: general characteristics." *The Century Magazine*, January 1912.

Cooper, L. "Athletics, activity and personality: a review of literature." *Research Quarterly* 22 (March), 1969.

Corson, John J. *Governance of Colleges and Universities*. New York: McGraw-Hill, 1960.

Corwin, Ronald G. "Out of the past: sociological perspectives on the history of education." In Holger Stub (ed.), *The Sociology of Education*. Homewood, Ill.: Dorsey Press, 1975:6–31.

Couglin, Ellen K. "Fieldwork takes anthropologist to the Los Angeles Olympics." *Chronicle of Higher Education* (17) June 20, 1984:5–6.

Craft, Stuart. "The unfortunate decline of higher education." *Stanford Daily*, August 3, 1984:4.

Crase, Darryl. "Athletics in trouble." In George H. Sage (ed.), *Sport and American Society.* Reading, Mass.: Addison-Wesley, 1974:402–408.

Cremin, L.A. *American Education: The Colonial Experience: 1607–1783.* New York: Harper & Row, 1970.

Cremin, L.A. *American Education: The National Experience: 1783–1876.* New York: Harper & Row, 1980.

Curtis, M.H. *Oxford and Cambridge in Transition, 1558–1642.* Oxford: Clarendon Press, 1959.

Davis, E., and J. Cooper. "Athletic ability and scholarship." *Research Quarterly* December 5, 1934:68–78.

Desruisseaux, Paul. "Big universities must run harder to stay even, Stanford University chief says of $1.1 billion campaign." *Chronicle of Higher Education* 33(23) February 18, 1987:23.

Desruisseaux, Paul. "Survey finds record totals in giving 71 colleges in 1984–1985." *Chronicle of Higher Education* 33(5) October 1, 1986:35.

Dewey, John. *A Common Faith.* New Haven: Yale University Press, 1934.

Doyle, Denis P. "Education and values: a consideration." *The College Board Review* 118 (Winter 1980–1981):15–17.

Dreeben, Robert. "The contribution of schooling to the learning of norms." *Harvard Educational Review* 37(2) 1967:211–237.

Dressel, Paul L., and William H. Faricy. *Return to Responsibility.* San Francisco: Jossey-Bass, 1972.

Dressel, Paul L., F.C. Johnson, and P.M. Marcus. *The Confidence Crisis.* San Francisco: Jossey-Bass, 1970.

Dubois, Paul E. "Participation in sports and occupational attainment: a comparative study." *Research Quarterly* 49(1) 1978:28–37.

Dubois, Paul E. "The occupational attainment of former college athletes: a comparative study." *International Review of Sport Sociology* 1(15) 1980:107–126.

Duncan, O.D., D.L., Featherman, and B. Duncan. *Sociological Background and Achievements.* New York: Seminar Press, 1972.

Dziech, Billie Wright, and Linda Weiner. *The Lecherous Professor.* Boston: Beacon, 1984.

Edwards, Harry. "Race in contemporary American sports." *National Forum* 62 (Winter 1982):19–22.

Edwards, Harry. "The black dumb jock: an American sports tragedy." *The College Board Review* 131 (Spring 1984):9–13.

Eidsmore, R.M. "The academic performance of athletes." *School Activities* 32 (December 1961):105–107.

Eidsmore, R.M. "High school athletes are brighter." *School Activities* 35 November 1963):75–77.

Eliot, C.W. "Inaugural address as president of Harvard." In C.W. Eliot (ed.), *Educational Reform: Essays and Addresses*. New York, 1869. Also in S.E. Morison (ed.), *The Development of Harvard University Since the Inauguration of President Eliot, 1869–1929*. Cambridge, Mass.: Harvard University Press, 1930:lxvii–lxix.

El-Khawas, E. "Self-regulation and collegiate athletics." *Educational Record* 60(4) 1979:510–517.

Ely, Richard T. *The Ground Under Our Feet*. New York: Macmillan, 1938.

Emery, Lynne. "The first intercollegiate contest for women." *North American Society for Sport History Proceedings*, 1979.

Enarson, Harold L. "Collegiate athletics: views from the front office." *Educational Record* 61(4) Fall 1980:22–31.

Enarson, Harold L. "The ethical imperatives of the college presidency." *Educational Record* 65(2) Spring 1984:24–26.

Ervin, Leroy, Sue Saunders, H. Lee Gillis, and Mark Hogrebe. "Academic performance of student-athletes in revenue producing sports." *Journal of College Student Personnel* March 1985:119–124.

Evangelauf, Jean. "Presidents say they're spending more time away from campuses." *Chronicle of Higher Education* 29(13) November 21, 1986:1.

Farrell, Charles S. "Supreme court strikes down NCAA control of football on television; colleges free to negotiate own contracts." *Chronicle of Higher Education* 28(19) July 5, 1984:1, 22.

Farrell, Charles S. "NCAA votes tougher rules, penalties; 198 presidents at special convention." *Chronicle of Higher Education* 30(18) July 3, 1985:1, 19.

Farrell, Charles S. "NCAA admits difficulty in catching violators of recruiting and financial aid regulations." *Chronicle of Higher Education* 29(2) September 2, 1984:29, 33.

Farrell, Charles S. "Sport rule will bar able blacks, NCAA study says." *Chronicle of Higher Education* 29(2) September 5, 1984:1, 31.

Farrell, Charles S. "Proposition 48: presidents who backed academic rules for athletes seem ready to compromise." *Chronicle of Higher Education* 29(7) October 10, 1984:1, 31.

Farrell, Charles S. "Big TV revenues now tougher to get, most college football powers discover." *Chronicle of Higher Education* 29(17) January 9, 1985:37–38.

Farrell, Charles S. "Colleges eye limits on time players give to sport, toughen tests for drug abuse." *Chronicle of Higher Education* 32(19) July 9, 1986:19, 23.

Farrell, Charles S. "A long summer for Maryland's chancellor." *Chronicle of Higher Education* 33(2) September 10, 1986:33.

Farrell, Charles S. "About 400 freshman athletes in big-time sports are eligible to compete under new rules." *Chronicle of Higher Education* 33(2) September 10, 1986:1, 34.

Farrell, Charles. "NCAA presidents commission to weigh new proposals for college sport reform." *Chronicle of Higher Education* 33(5) October 1, 1986:39–40.

Farrell, Charles. "SMU campus is stunned by charge board knew of payment to player." *Chronicle of Higher Education* 33(26) March 11, 1987:1, 38.

Feldman, K.A., and T.M. Newcomb. *The Impact of College on Students: an Analysis of Four Decades of Research.* San Francisco: Jossey-Bass, 1969.

Feldman, Saul D. *Escape from the Doll's House.* New York: McGraw-Hill, 1974.

Ferreira, Antonio J. "Family myth and homeostasis." *Archives of General Psychiatry.* 9(5) November 1963:457¢463.

Fields, Cheryl M. *"College found to have little impact on students' social, political views."* Chronicle of Higher Education 28(11) May 9, 1984:1, 14.

Fields, Cheryl M. "Title IX at X." *Chronicle of Higher Education* (June 23, 1982):1, 12.

Figler, Stephen K. *Sport and Play in American Life.* Philadelphia: Saunders, 1981.

Finkelstein, Barbara. "Pedagogy as intrusion: teaching values in popular primary schools in nineteenth-century America." In *History Education and Public Policy.* Berkeley, Calif.: McCutchan Publication, 1978:239–270.

Fiske, Edward B. "Colleges seek status gains by rubbing shoulders with 'right' schools." *New York Times,* February 16, 1983:A14.

Fletcher, Robert S. *History of Oberlin College to the Civil War*. Oberlin, Ohio, 1943.

Flexner, Eleanor. *Century of Struggle*. New York: Atheneum, 1972.

Footnotes. "Jan Kemp speaks out." 5(1) Spring 1987:10.

Forester, Norman. *The American State University*. Chapel Hill: University of North Carolina Press, 1937.

Fox, Mary Frank. "Sex, salary and achievement: reward dualism in academia." *Sociology of Education* 54 (April) 1981:71–84.

Frey, James H. "The place of athletics in the educational priorities of university alumni." *Review of Sport and Leisure* 6(1) Summer 1981:48–64.

Frey, James, (ed.). *The Governance of Intercollegiate Athletics*. West Point, New York: Leisure Press, 1982.

Fromm, Eric. *The Sane Society*. New York: Fawcett World Library, 1965.

Froomkin, Joseph. "Sports and the post-secondary sector." In George Hanford, *An Inquiry into the Need for and Feasibility of a National Study of Intercollegiate Athletics*. Washington, D.C.: American Council on Education, 1974:Appendix F.

Fulton, Oliver. "Needs, expectations and responses: new pressures on higher education." *Higher Education* 13(2) April 1984:193–224.

Gamson, Zelda F., and Tamar Horowitz. "Symbolism and survival in developing organizations: regional colleges in Israel." *Higher Education* 12 April 1983:171–190.

Gardiner, John F. "Education is always religious." In Sheldon Staff and Herbert Schwartzberg (editors), *The Human Encounter*. New York: Harper and Row, 1969:249–254.

Garvin, David A. *The Economics of University Behavior*. New York: Academic Press, 1980.

Gaski, John F., and Michael J. Etzel. "Collegiate athletic success and alumni generosity: dispelling the myth." In Andrew Yiannakis, Thomas D. McIntyre, Merrill Melnick, and Dale Hart (eds.), *Sport Sociology: Contemporary Themes*. Dubuque, Iowa: Kendall Hunt, 1987.

Geertz, Clifford. "Ideology as a cultural system." In David E. Apter (ed.), *Ideology and Discontent*. New York: Free Press, 1964:47–76.

Geertz, Clifford. *The Interpretation of Cultures*. New York: Basic Books, 1973.

Gerber, Ellen. "The controlled development of collegiate sport for women, 1923-1936." *Journal of Sport History* 2(1) Spring 1975:1-28.

Gerber, Ellen W. "The legal basis for the regulation of intercollegiate sport." *Educational Record* 60(4) 1979:468-481.

Giammatti, A. Bartlett. *The University and the Public Interest.* New York: Atheneum, 1981.

Gideonse, Harry D. *The Higher Learning in Democracy.* New York: Holt, Rinehart and Winston, 1937.

Gilley, J. Wade, A. Hickey, M. Barnsback, E. Gerber, and K. Sears. *Administration of University Athletic Programs: Internal Control and Excellence.* Washington, D.C.: American Council on Education, August 1986.

Glazer, Walter S. "Participation and power: voluntary associations and the functional organization in Cincinnati in 1840." *Historical Methods Newsletter* 5 (September 1972):153.

Goode, William J. *The Celebration of Heroes.* Berkeley: University of California Press, 1978.

Gordon, David, and Walter Ackerman. "The mechanech: role function and myth in Israeli secondary school." *Comparative Education Review* 28(1) February 1984:105-115.

Grant, Christine H. "Institutional autonomy and intercollegiate athletics." *Educational Record* 60(4) Fall 1979:409-419.

Greenhouse, Linda. "High court ends NCAA control of TV football." *New York Times*, June 28, 1984:1, 8.

Grundman, Adoph H. "The image of intercollegiate sports and the civil rights movement: an historian's view." In Don Chu, Jeffrey Segrave, and Beverly Becker (eds.), *Sport and American Higher Education.* Champaign, Ill.: Human Kinetics, 1985.

Guttman, Allen. "The tiger devours the literary magazine or intercollegiate athletics in America." In James Frey (editor). *The Governance of Intercollegiate Athletics.* West Point, New York: Leisure Press, 1982.

Hackensmith, C.W. *History of Physical Education.* New York: Harper, 1966.

Hadley, Arthur Twining. "Wealth and democracy in American colleges." *Harper's Monthly* 113 (August 1906):452.

Hall, Peter Dobkin. *The Organization of American Culture: Private Institutions, Elites and the Origins of American Nationality.* New York: New York University Press, 1982.

Handlin, O., and M.F. Handlin. *The American College and American Culture*. New York: McGraw-Hill, 1970.

Hanford, George H. *An Inquiry into the Need for and Feasibility of a National Study of Intercollegiate Athletics*. Washington, D.C.: American Council on Education, 1974.

Hanford, George. "Intercollegiate athletics today and tomorrow: the president's challenge." *Educational Record* 57(4) 1976:232–235.

Hanford, George H. "Controversies in college sport." *Educational Record* 60(4) Fall 1979:351–366.

Hanks, M.P., and B.K. Eckland. "Athletics and social participation in the educational attainment process." *Sociology of Education* 49 (October 1976):271–294.

Harris, Seymour E. *A Statistical Portrait of Higher Education*. New York: McGraw-Hill, 1972.

Hartnett, Rodney T. "College and university trustees: their backgrounds, roles and educational attitudes." In Elizabeth Useem and Michael Useem (eds.), *The Educational Establishment*. Englewood Cliffs, N.J.: Prentice-Hall, 1974.

Hartwell, E.M. "Report of the chairman on section on history and bibliography in physical education." *Physical Educator* 2(8) October 1893:127–130.

Heller, Scott. "Number of black faculty members has dropped slightly since 1975." *Chronicle of Higher Education* 33(17) June 26, 1985:20.

Heller, Scott. "One of 6 female graduate students in psychology reports having sexual contact with a professor." *Chronicle of Higher Education* 31(22) February 12, 1986:23.

Henry, David. *Challenges Past, Challenges Present*. San Francisco: Jossey-Bass, 1975.

Henschen, Keith P., and David Fry. "An archival study of the relationship of intercollegiate athletic participation and graduation." *Sociology of Sport Journal* 1(1984):52–56.

Hoberman, John M. *Sport and Political Ideology*. Austin: University of Texas Press, 1984.

Hoch, Paul. *Rip-off the Big Game*. New York: Doubleday/Anchor, 1972.

Hochberg, Phillip R. "The four horsemen ride again: cable communications and collegiate athletics." *Journal of College and University Law* 5(1) Fall 1977:43–54.

Hoffman, James. "The role of accreditation in preserving educational integrity." *Educational Record* 63(3) Summer 1982:41–44.

Hofstadter, Richard, and Wilson Smith (eds.). *American Higher Education.* Chicago: University of Chicago Press, 1961.

Husband, R.W. "What do college grades predict?" *Fortune* 56(1957):157–158.

Hyde, William DeWitt. *The College Man and the College Woman.* Boston, 1906. Cited in Joseph Kett, *Rites of Passage.* New York: Basic Books, 1977.

Hyman, Mervin D., and Gordon S. White, Jr. *Big-Ten Football.* New York: MacMillan, 1977.

Ingham, Alan. "Occupational subcultures in the workworld of sport." In Donald W. Ball and John W. Loy (eds.),* *Sport and Social Order: Contributions to the Sociology of Sport.* Reading, Massachusetts: Addison-Wesley, 1975:333–390.

Iowa State Agricultural College, Fourth Biennial Report of the Board of Trustees, 1871. Des Moines: G.W. Edwards, 1872.
Jable, Thomas. "Pennsylvania's early blue laws: a Quaker experiment in the suppression of sport and amusements, 1682–1740." *Journal of Sport History* 1(2) November 1974:103–121.

Jacobson, Robert E. "Typical college trustee, survey finds, is a middle-aged white businessman." *Chronicle of Higher Education* 31(22) February 12, 1986:23.

Jacobson, Robert L. "Sunshine laws harming public colleges' decision making report says." *Chronicle of Higher Education* 29(6) October 3, 1984:11.

Jacobson, Robert L. "Strains of the job limit president's role, panel says." *Chronicle of Higher Education* 29(6) September 26, 1984:1, 26.

Jarausch, Konrad H. (ed.). *The Transformation of Higher Learning, 1860–1930: Expansion, Diversification, Social Opening and Professionalization in England, Germany, Russia and the United States.* Chicago: University of Chicago Press, 1983.

Jencks, Christopher, and David Riesman. *The Academic Revolution.* Garden City, New York: Doubleday, 1968.

Jensen, Ted M., W.M. Leonard II, Robert D. Liverman. "College students' attitudes toward intercollegiate athletics." Paper presented at the first annual conference of the North American Society of Sport Sociology. Denver, Colorado, October 16–19, 1980.

Kadzielski, Mark. "Legal approaches to sex discrimination in amateur athletics: the first decade." In Ronald Waicukauski (ed.), *Law and Amateur Sports*. Bloomington, Indiana: Indiana University Press, 1982:95–113.

Kallen, Horace M. *The Education of Free Men*. New York: Farrar, Straus and Company, 1949.

Kamens, David H. "Legitimizing myths and educational organizations: the relationship between organizational ideology and formal structure." *American Sociological Review* 42(1977):208–219.

Katz, J. "Benefits for personal development from going to college." Paper presented at the annual meeting of the Association for the Study of Higher Education, Chicago, March 6–7, 1976.

Keller, George. *Academic Strategy: The Management Revolution in American Higher Education*. Baltimore: Johns Hopkins University Press, 1983.

Kett, Joseph F. *Rites of Passage*. New York: Basic Books, 1977.

Kirschenbaum, Jerry. "Scoreboard: Why is this man saying the things he's saying?" *Sports Illustrated* 61(14) September 17, 1984:11.

Kirschenbaum, Jerry. "As bad as anything that's ever come along." *Sports Illustrated* 53 (February 25, 1980):11.

Kneller, G.F. *Higher Learning in Britain*. Berkeley: University of California Press, 1955.

Knoles, T.C. "American education — whence and wither." in P.A. Schlipp (ed.) *Higher Education Faces the Future*. New York: Horace Liveright, 1930.

Koch, James, and W.H. Leonard II. "The NCAA: a socioeconomic analysis: the development of the college sports cartel from social movement to formal organization." American Journal of Ecnomics and Sociology 37 1978:225–239.

Koppett, Leonard. "Editor can't read." Stanford Observer. January 1984:8.

Kotschnig, Walter M. (ed.) *The University M a Changing World*. Oxford University Press, 1932.

Kretchmer, R. Scott. "At the heart of athletics." Joper 53(1) January 1982:35–36.

Laing, Ronald D. "Mystification, confusion and conflict.;; in Ivan Boszormenyi-Nagy and James L. Framo (eds.) *Intensive Family Therapy*. New York: Harper and Row, 1965:343–364.

Laing, Ronald D. *Knots*. New York:Pantheon, 1970.

Lapin, J. "Law without order: trouble with Title IX "Women's Sports January 1979;43–45.

Lasch, Christopher. "1984:Are we there?" Sal Amagundi 65 Fall 1984:51–67.

Lawson, Hal A., and Alan G. Ingham. "Conflicting ideologies concerning the university and intercollegiate athletics: Harper and Hutchins at Chicago, 1892–1940." Journal of Sport History 7(3) 1980:37–67.

Lebar, J. "An analysis of achievement of selected groups of Duke University graduates." Proceedings of the 76th Annual Meeting of the National Council of Physical Education and Athletics for Men, 1973:32–38.

Lederman, Douglas. "On the trail of 'visibility' added income, University of Akron's moving up to big-time sports." Chronicle of Higher Education 33(7) October 15, 1986:45.

Lederman, Douglas. "Football bowl games leading the way as large corporations begin to underwrite college sports events; Sunkist raises ante to get top game." Chronicle of Higher Education 33(14) December 3, 1986:34–36.

Lederman, Douglas. "Football troubles at Southern Methodist boil down to: who runs the university." Chronicle of Higher Education 33(17) January 7, 1987:34–37.

Lederman, Douglas. "Many faculty members seek greater role in athletic decision making on campus." Chronicle of Higher Education (February 4, 1987):29–30.

Lederman, Douglas. "NCAA bars football at Southern Methodist for year; penalties are the toughest ever." Chronicle of Higher Education 33(25) March 4, 1987:1, 36.

Lederman, Douglas. "Documents suggest football players at Houston were paid; governor apologizes for role in Southern Methodist payoffs." Chronicle of Higher Education 33(27) March 18, 1987:47–49.

Lederman, Douglas. "In wake of football scandal, Southern Methodist confronts tough questions about its reputation." Chronicle of Higher Education 33(34) May 6, 1987:41.

Lederman, Douglas. "Players spend more time on sports than on studies, an NCAA survey of major-college athletes finds." Chronicle of Higher Education 25(15) December 7, 1988: A33–A38.

Leighton, J.A. "Report of Committee T on place and function of faculties in university government and administration." Bulletin of the American Association of University Professors (6) 1920.

Leonard, Wilbert M. II. *A Sociological Perspective of Sport*. Minneapolis: Burgess, 1984.

Looney, Douglas S. "Jackie hits the jackpot." *Sports Illustrated* 56(4) February 1, 1982:26–29.

Lopiano, Donna A. "A political analysis of the possibility of impact alternatives for the accomplishment of feminist objectives within American intercollegiate sport." In Richard Lapchick (ed.), *Fractured Focus*. Lexington, Massachusetts: D.C. Heath, 1986:163–176.

Lopiano, Donna A. "Solving the financial crisis in intercollegiate athletics." *Educational Record* 60(4) Fall 1979:394–408.

Lowell, A. Lawrence. *At War with Academic Traditions in America*. Cambridge, Mass.: Harvard University Press, 1934.

Loy, John W. "The study of sport and social mobility." In Gerald S. Kenyon (ed.), *Aspects of Contemporary Sport Sociology*. Chicago: The Athletic Institute, 1969:101–133.

Loy, John W. "An emerging theory of sport spectatorship: implications for the Olympic Games." In Jeffrey Segrave and Don Chu (eds.), *Olympism*. Champaign, Ill.: Human Kinetics, 1981:262–300.

Lucas, John A., and Ronald A. Smith. *Saga of American Sport*. Philadelphia: Lea and Febiger, 1978.

MacArthur, Douglas. *Saturday Review*. October 16, 1971:75.

Magarello, Jack. "US says number of private colleges is increasing." *Chronicle of Higher Education* 23(19) January 1982:3.

Mangan, J.A. *Athleticism in the Victorian and Edwardian Public School*. New York: Cambridge University Press, 1981.

Mantel, R.C., and Lee VanderVelden. "The relationship between the professionalization of attitude toward play in preadolescent boys and participation in organized sport." Paper presented at the Third Annual Symposium on the Sociology of Sport, Waterloo, Ontario, Canada 1981.

Martin, Warren Bryan. "Why don't accreditors investigate the abuse in college athletics?" *Chronicle of Higher Education* 21(20) January 26, 1981:64.

Martin, Warren Bryan. *A College of Character*. San Francisco: Jossey-Bass, 1982.

Marts, Arnaud C. "College football and college endowment." *School and Society* 40 July 7, 1934):14–15.

Marty, Martin E. *Pilgrims in Their Own Land*. Boston: Little, Brown and Company, 1984.

Masland, Andrew T. "Simulators, myth and ritual in higher education." *Research in Higher Education* 18(2) 1983:161–178.

McClellan, B.E. "Equal educational opportunity: historical perspective." In Elizabeth Steiner, Robert Arnove, and B.E. McClellan (eds.), *Education and American Culture*. New York: Macmillan, 1980:123–124.

McCormick, Robert E., and Maurice Tinsley. "Athletics versus academics." Working Paper Series No. 19, Center for Policy Studies, College of Commerce and Industry, Clemson University, August 1986.

McKelvie, D., and E. Huband. "Locus of control and anxiety in college athletes and non-athletes." *Perceptual and Motor Skills* 50(3) 1980:819–822.

Mengen, Bernard. *Play and Playthings: A Reference Guide*. Westport, Connecticut: Greenwood Press, 1982.

Menges, Robert J., and William M. Exum. "Barriers to the progress of women and minority faculty." *Journal of Higher Education* 54(2) March/April 1983:123–144.

Messner, Steven F., and Daniel Groisser. "Participation in intercollegiate athletics and academic achievement: a study of an Ivy League college." Paper presented at the Second Annual Meeting of the North American Society for the Sociology of Sport, Ft. Worth, Texas, November 1981.

Meyer, John. "The charter: conditions of diffuse socialization in schools." In W.R. Scott (ed.), *Social Processes and Social Structure*. New York: Holt, 1970:564–578.

Meyer, John W., and Brian Rowan. "Notes on the structure of educational organizations: revised version." Paper presented at the American Sociological Association annual meeting, San Francisco, August 1975.

Meyer, John W., and Brian Rowan. "Institutionalized organizations: formal structure as myth and ceremony." Unpublished paper, Sociology Department, Stanford University, 1977.

Meyer, John W., and W. Richard Scott. *Organizational Environments*. Beverly Hills, Calif.: Sage Publications, 1983.

Meyer, Marshall. "Organizational domains." *American Sociological Review* 40(5), 1975:599–615.

Michener, James A. *Sports in America*. New York: Random House, 1976.

Middleton, Lorenzo. "Excessive boosterism plagues sports programs at Wichita State." *Chronicle of Higher Education* 23(20) January 27, 1982:5.

Middleton, Lorenzo. "Large expenses for sports programs lead more colleges to seek funds from donors." *Chronicle of Higher Education* 24(1) March 3, 1982:5-6.

Middleton, Lorenzo. "How one institution tries to ensure that its athletes make academic progress." *Chronicle of Higher Education* 24(15) June 9, 1982:1, 14.

Millard, Richard M. "The accrediting association: ensuring the quality of programs and institutions." *Change* 15(4) May/June 1983:32, 34-36.

Millet, John D. *Financing Higher Education in the United States*. New York: Columbia University Press, 1952.

Miracle, Andrew W. Jr. "School sport as a ritual by-product: views from applied anthropology." In Helen B. Schwartzman (ed.), *Play and Culture*. West Point, N.Y.: Leisure Press, 1980:98-103.

Monaghan, Peter. "University of Georgia president and state regents avoid confrontation but remain at odds." *Chronicle of Higher Education* 32(7) April 16, 1986:38-40.

Monaghan, Peter. "New troubles in tiger country: this time, Clemson University's president becomes the victim." *Chronicle of Higher Education* 30(2) March 13, 1985:27-28.

Mulkeen, Thomas A. "Higher education in the coming age of limits: an historical perspective." *Journal of Higher Education* 52(3) May/June 1981:310-316.

Mooney, Carolyn J. "Bad news for public colleges: economies slump in many states." *Chronicle of Higher Education* 33(23) February 18, 1987:1, 20.

Mrozek, Donald J. *Sport and American Mentality, 1880-1910*. Knoxville: University of Tennessee Press, 1983.

Murray, Thomas H. "Drug tests: just one more instance of treating college athletes like children." *Chronicle of Higher Education* 33(27) February 11, 1987:42-43.

National Collegiate Athletic Association Enforcement Program, Part 2, Attachment "I." Committee on Interstate and Foreign Commerce, House of Representatives, 95th Congress, Serial #95-160 Washington, D.C. 1977:1512.

National Collegiate Athletic Association News. 34(3) January 14, 1987:2.

National Collegiate Athletic Association News. "Eighty-eight percent of Division I schools participate in survey of 5-1-(J)." 24(18) April 29, 1987:1, 7.

Nearing, S. "Who's who among college trustees." *School and Society,* 6, 1917.

Nevins, Allen. *The State University and Democracy.* Urbana: University of Illinois Press, 1962.

New York Times. August 12, 1951:Sec. 5; August 5, 1951:1; March 21, 1951:1.

New York Times. "NCAA telecast rights on football struck down." September 16, 1982:B19, 24.

Newman, John Henry Cardinal. *The Idea of a University.* New York: Holt, Rinehart and Winston, 1968.

Novak, Michael. *The Joy of Sports.* New York: Basic Books, 1976.

Nyquist, Ewald B. "The immorality of big-power intercollegiate athletics." In Donald Chu, Jeffrey Segrave, and Beverly Becker (editors), *Sport and Higher Education.* Champaign, Ill.: Human Kinetics Publishers, 1984.

Nyquist, Ewald B. "Win, women and money: collegiate athletics today and tomorrow." *Educational Record 60(4) Fall 1979:374-393.*

Odenkirk, James E. "Intercollegiate athletics: big business or sport." *Academe* 67(2) April 1981.

Ogilvie, B.C., and T.A. Tutko. "Sport: If you want to build character, try something else." *Psychology Today* 5 1971:61-63.

Ogilvie, B.C., and T.A. Tutko. *Problem Athletes and How to Handle Them.* London: Pelham, 1966.

Ogilvie, B.C., and T.A. Tutko. "Self-perception as compared with measured personality of selected male physical educators." In G.S. Kenyon (ed.), *Contemporary Psychology of Sport.* Chicago: Athletic Institute, 1970.

Otto, L.B., and D. Alwin. "High school athletes are brighter." *School Activities* 32(50) December 1977:102-113.

Pace, C. Robert. *Measuring Outcomes of College: Fifty Years of Findings and Recommendations for the Future.* San Francisco: Jossey-Bass, 1979.

Palmer, Stacy E. "Higher education losing credibility in Congress, council chief warns." *Chronicle of Higher Education* 33(17) January 7, 1987:1, 28.

Palmer, Stacy E. "Fearing loss of public confidence, some colleges change ways they deal with their constituencies." *Chronicle of Higher Education* 33(34) May 6, 1987:1, 24.

Paul, Angus. "Growing deficits force colleges to eliminate some varsity sports." *Chronicle of Higher Education* 21(4) September 15, 1980:1, 10.

Paulhus, D., J. Molin, and R. Schuchts. "Control profiles of football players, tennis players and non-athletes." *Journal of Social Psychology* 1979 (108):199–205.

Paulsen, Friedrich. *The German Universities and University Study.* New York: Charles Scribner's Sons, 1906.

Perkins, James A. (editor). *The University as an Organization.* New York: McGraw-Hill, 1973.

Perrucci, C.C. "Minority status and the pursuit of professional careers: women in science." *Social Forces* 49 (1970):245–249.

Popekwitz, Thomas S. "Educational reform as the organization of ritual: stability as change." *Journal of Education* 164(1) Winter 1982:5–29.

Prebish, Charles S. "Heavenly father, divine goalie: sport and religion." *Antioch Review* 42(3) Summer 1984:306–362.

Pritchett, Henry S. "Shall the universities become a corporation?" *Atlantic Monthly* 96 (September 1905):295–299.

Rader, Benjamin G. "The quest for subcommunities and the rise of American sport." *American Quarterly,* September 1978:355–369.

Rader, Benjamin G. *American Sports.* Englewood Cliffs, N.J.: Prentice-Hall, 1983.

Raiborn, Mitchell H. *Revenues and Expenses of Intercollegiate Athletic Programs: Analysis of the Trends Plus Relationships.* Shawnee Mission, Kan.: National Collegiate Athletic Association, 1982, 1986.

Richardson, D.E. "Ethical conduct in sport situations." National College of Physical Education Association for Men, Proceedings 66, 1962:218–220.

Rogovia, V.Z. "The discussions on problems of daily life and culture in Soviet Russia during the 1920s." *Soviet Sociology* 14(2) Summer 1976:30–31.

Rosenthal, Robert and Lenore Jacobson. *Pygmalion in the Classroom.* New York: Holt, 1968.

Ross, Earle D. *A History of the Iowa State College of Agriculture and Mechanical Arts.* Ames, Iowa: 1942.

Ross, Murray G. *The University: The Anatomy of Academe*. New York: McGraw-Hill, 1976.

Rudolph, F. *The American College and University*. New York: Alfred A. Knopf, 1968.

Rugg, Edwin A., T.L. Warren, and E.L. Carpenter. "Faculty orientations toward institutional goals: a broken front with implications for planned change." *Research in Higher Education* 15(2) 1981:161–173.

Rushall, Brent. "Three studies relating personality variables to football performance." *International Journal of Sport Psychology* (3) 1972:12–24.

Sack, Allen L., and Robert Thiel. "College football and social mobility: a case study of Notre Dame football players." *Sociology of Education* 52(1) January 1979:60–66.

Sack, Allen L., and C. Watkins. "Winning and giving: another look." Paper presented at the annual meeting of the North American Society for the Sociology of Sport, Denver 1980.

Sage, George H. "An occupational analysis of the college coach." In Donald Ball and John Loy (eds.), *Sport and the Social Order: Contributions to the Sociology of Sport*. Reading, Mass.: Addison-Wesley, 1975.

Sage, George H. "American values and sport: formation of a bureaucratic personality." *Journal of Physical Education and Recreation*, 49(8) October 1978:42–44.

Sage, George H. "Humanism and sport." In George H. Sage (ed.), *Sport and American Society*, 3rd edition. Don Mills, Ontario: Addison-Wesley, 1980:353–368.

Sage, George. "The intercollegiate sport cartel and its consequences for athletics." In Richard E. Lapchick (editor), *Fractured Focus*. New York: Lexington, 1986:45–51.

Savage, Howard J., Harold W. Bentley, John T. McGovern, and Dean F. Smiley. *American College Athletics*. New York: The Carnegie Foundation for the Advancement of Teaching, 1929.

Savage, Howard J. *Economy in Higher Education*. New York: Carnegie Foundation for the Advancement of Teaching, 1933.

Schafer, W.E., and J.M. Armer. "Athletes are not inferior students." *Transaction* (November 1968):21–26, 61–62.

Schendel, Jack. "Psychological differences between athletes and non-participants in athletics at three educational levels." *Research Quarterly* 36 (March 1965):52–67.

Schonemann, Friederich. "A German looks at American higher education." In P.A. Schlipp (ed.), *Higher Education Faces the Future*. New York: Horace Liveright, 1930.

Schupp, M.H. "The differential effects of the development of athletic ability of a high order." *Research Quarterly* 24(1952):218–222.

Schumer, Fran. "A return to religion." *Sunday New York Times Magazine*, April 15, 1984:90–94, 98.

Scott, Harry A. "New directions in intercollegiate athletics." In James Frey (editor) *The Governance of Intercollegiate Athletics*. West Point, New York: Leisure Press, 1982:29–39.

Scott, Jack. *The Athletic Revolution*. New York: Free Press, 1971.

Scott, Peter. *Strategies for Post-Secondary Education*. New York: Wiley, 1975.

Scully, Malcolm G. "Prediction for the 80s: rich colleges will get richer." *Chronicle of Higher Education* 23(18) January 13, 1982:14.

Scully, Malcolm. "4000 faculty members laid off in 5 years by 4 year institutions, survey shows." *Chronicle of Higher Education* 27(9) October 26, 1983:21.

Scully, Malcolm. "US colleges not realizing their full potential panel says; urges a national debate on quality." *Chronicle of Higher Education* 29(9) October 24, 1984:1, 34.

Selznick, P. "Cooptation." In Merlin B. Brinkerhoff and Phillip Kunz (eds.), *Complex Organizations and Their Environments*. Dubuque, Iowa: William C. Brown, 1972:141–151.

Senn, David J. "Views of sport: what is at stake when an athlete scandal hits." *New York Times*, March 10, 1985:25.

Sewell, William H., and Robert M. Hauser (eds.). *Education, Occupation and Earnings*, New York: Academic Press, 1975.

Sewell, William H., and Robert Hauser. "Causes and consequences of higher education: models of the status attainment process." In William H. Sewell, Robert M. Hauser, and David L. Featherman (eds.), *Schooling and Achievement in American Society*. New York: Academic Press, 1976.

Shapiro, Beth J. "Intercollegiate athletic participation and academic achievement: a case study of Michigan State University student-athletes, 1950–1980." *Sociology of Sport Journal* 1984 (1):46–51.

Shaw, Gary. *Meat on the Hoof: The Hidden World of Texas Football*. New York: St. Martin's: 1972.

Shifers, M.F. "What happened to seventy-four former country town athletes and what did they think of their high school experience." Unpublished Ph.D. dissertation. Brigham Young University, Provo, Utah, 1956.

Shils, Edward. *Tradition*. Chicago: University of Chicago Press, 1981.

Sigelman, Lee, and Robert Carter. "Win one for the giver? Alumni giving and big-time college sports." *Social Science Quarterly* 60(2) September 1979:284–294.

Slosson, E.E. *Great American Universities*. New York: Macmillan, 1910.

Smith, David N. *Who Rules the Universities*. New York: Monthly Review Press, 1974.

Smith, Huston. "Beyond the modern Western mind set." *Teachers College Record* 82(3) Spring 1981:434–457.

Smith, Ronald. "Reaction to the historical roots of the collegiate dilemma." Proceedings of the National College Physical Education Association for Men. Hot Springs, Arkansas: January 8–11, 1976:154–162.

Snyder, E. "High school athletics and their coaches: educational plans and advice." *Sociology of Education* 45 (Summer 1972):313–325.

Snyder, E., and E. Spreitzer. *Social Aspects of Sport*. Englewood Cliffs, N.J.: Prentice-Hall, 1978.

Solomon, Lewis C., and Nancy Ochsner. *New Findings on the Effects of College*. Washington, D.C.: American Association for Higher Education, 1978.

Spears, Betty, and R. Swanson. *History of Sport and Physical Activity in the United States*. Dubuque, Iowa: William C. Brown, 1978.

Sports Illustrated. "Diggers non-bombshell." 56(14) April 5, 1982:10, 12.

Standish, Burt L. (Pseudonym Gilber Patten). *Frank Merriwell's Loyalty*. New York: Street and Smith, 1904.

Steiner, Elizabeth, Robert Arnove, and B. Edward McClellan (editors). *Education and American Culture*. New York: Macmillan, 1980.

Stern, Robert N. "The development of an interorganizational control network: the case of intercollegiate athletics." *Administrative Science Quarterly* 24(2) 1979:242–266.

Stevenson, Christopher L. "Socialization effects of participation in sport: a critical review of the research." *Research Quarterly* 46(3) October 1975:287–301.

Struna, Nancy. "Puritans and sport: the irretrievable tide of change." *Journal of Sport History* 4(1) Spring 1977:1–21.

Stuart, Debra L. "Academic preparation and subsequent performance of intercollegiate football players." *Journal of College Student Personnel* March 1985:124–129.

Sutton-Smith, Brian. *A History of Children's Play: The New Zealand Playground, 1840–1950.* University of Pennsylvania Press, 1981.

Synnot, Marcia G. *The Half-Opened Door: Discrimination and Admissions at Harvard, Yale and Princeton, 1900–1970.* Westport, Conn.: Greenwood Press, 1979.

Swindler, Ann. *Organization Without Authority.* Cambridge, Massachusetts: Harvard University Press, 1979.

Thompson, J.D. *Organizations in Action.* New York: McGraw-Hill, 1967.

Torgerson, Stan. "How high is up?" *The National Collegiate Athletic Association News* 24(3) January 14, 1987:2.

Tugend, Alina. "Sociologist ties poor student performance to lack of self-discipline." *Education Week* 4(3) September 19, 1984:10–15.

Turner, Ralph H. "Sponsored and contest mobility and the school system." In R.R. Bell and H.R. Stub (eds.), *The Sociology of Education.* Homewood, Illinois: Dorsey, 1968:219–235.

Turner, R. Stever. "University reformers and professorial scholarship in Germany 1760–1806." In Lawrence Stone (editor), *The University in Society* (volume II). Princeton University Press, 1974:495–532.

Tyack, David. "Forming the national character." *Harvard Educational Review* Winter 1966:29–41.

Uehling, Barbara S. "Athletics and academe: creative divorce or reconciliation?" *Educational Record* 64(3) Summer 1983:13–15.

Uhlir, Ann. "The wolf is our shepherd: shall we not fear?" *Phi Delta Kappan* 64 (November 1982):172–176.

Underwood, John. "The writing's on the wall." *Sports Illustrated* May 19, 1980:36–73.

U.S. Commission on Civil Rights, 1980. "More hurdles to clear: women and girls in competitive athletics." Clearinghouse publication #63. United States Government Printing Office, Washington, D.C.

U.S. Department of Education. "Digest of educational statistics, 1982." National Center for Educational Statistics.

U.S. House of Representatives. National Collegiate Athletic Association Enforcement Program, Part 2, Attachment "J" (Committee on Interstate and Foreign Commerce, House of Representatives, 95th Congress, Serial #95-160), United States Government Printing Office, Washington, D.C.: 1978:1513.

Vance, N. Scott, and Cheryl Fields. "Supreme Court rules anti-sex bias covers only college programs that get direct US aid." *Chronicle of Higher Education* 28(2) March 7, 1984:1, 26.

Vance, N. Scott. "Colleges must offer women and men same minimum number of teams." *Chronicle of Higher Education* 27(19) January 4, 1983:98.

Vance, N. Scott. " 'I guess I understand it' says player who lost aid." *Chronicle of Higher Education* 26(12) May 18, 1983:1, 24.

Vance, N. Scott. "NCAA to begin investigations and enforcement of rules in women's sports programs." *Chronicle of Higher Education* 26(23) August 3, 1983:15.

Vance, N. Scott. "Panel to review proposed NCAA rules and weigh impact on women's sports." *Chronicle of Higher Education* 27(5) September 28, 1983:24.

Vance, N. Scott. "Competing plans to give greater role to presidents highlight NCAA agenda." *Chronicle of Higher Education* 27(14) November 30, 1983:21.

Vance, N. Scott. "Bigger and better or smaller and saner: Rice University's debate over big-time football." *Chronicle of Higher Education* 27(10) November 2, 1983:21–22.

Vance, N. Scott. "CBS to pay $96 million to televise 3 NCAA basketball championships." *Chronicle of Higher Education* 27(14) November 30, 1983:21.

Vance, N. Scott. "US investigating pro-football's ban on hiring college undergraduates." *Chronicle of Higher Education* 27(16) December 14, 1983:1, 30.

Vance, N. Scott. "NCAA weighs plan to divey up money from a TV-rich basketball tournament." *Chronicle of Higher Education* 28(1) February 29, 1984:23.

Vance, N. Scott. "Networks veto plan to permit colleges to make own deals for saturday night football on TV." *Chronicle of Higher Education* 28(3) March 14, 1984:31.

Vance, N. Scott. "Sport is a religion in America, controversial professor argues." *Chronicle of Higher Education* 27(12) May 16, 1984:25, 28.

Veblen, Thorstein. *The Higher Learning in America*. New York: B.W. Huebsch, 1918.

Vecsey, George. "Who's watching the store?" *New York Times*, January 11, 1984:B7.

Veysey, Lawrence R. *The Emergence of the American University*. Chicago: University of Chicago Press, 1965.

Waicukauski, Ronald J. "The regulation of academic standards in intercollegiate athletics." In Ronald J. Waicukauski (editor), *Law and Amateur Sports*. Bloomington: Indiana University Press, 1982:161–190.

Walker, David. "British universities 'have fallen from athletic grace.' " *Chronicle of Higher Education* 30(11) May 15, 1985:35, 38.

Wallenfeldt, E.C. *American Higher Education*. Westport, Conn.: Greenwood Press, 1983.

Warfield, E.D. "The expansion of our great universities." *Munsey Magazine*, August 1901. Also in James C. Stone and Donald P. Denevi *Portraits of the American University, 1890–1910*. (editors), San Francisco: Jossey-Bass, 1971:24–38.

Watkins, Beverly. "Number of woman college presidents has doubled in decade, study finds." *Chronicle of Higher Education* 31(3) September 18, 1985:1, 33.

Watkins, Beverly. "State support for colleges up 12 percent in 2 years." *Chronicle of Higher Education* 27(9) October 26, 1983:13.

Watzlawick, Paul, John H. Weakland, and Ronald Fisch. *Change: Principles of Problem Formation and Problem Resolution*. New York: W.W. Norton, 1974.

Wayland, F. *Thoughts on the Present Collegiate System in the United States*. Boston: Gould, Kendall and Lincoln, 1842. Reprinted New York: Arno Press, 1969.

Wayland, F. *Report to the Corporation of Brown University on Changes in the System of Collegiate Education*. Providence, R.I.: George H. Whitney, 1850.

Webb, Harry. "Success patterns of college athletics." Paper presented at the annual convention of the American Alliance for Health, Physical Education, Recreation and Dance, St. Louis, 1968.

Webb, Harry. "Professionalization of attitudes toward play among adolescents." In Geral S. Kenyon (editor), *Aspects of Contemporary Sport Sociology*. Chicago: Athletic Institute, 1969:161–188.

Wehrwein, Austin C. "Court orders University of Minnesota to admit athlete to degree program." *Chronicle of Higher Education* 13(18) January 13, 1982:5.

Weiberg, Steve. "Sherrill deal no longer in class by itself." *USA Today*, September 24, 1986:1C, 2C.

Weiner, J. "The high cost of big-time football." *College and University Business* 55(3), 1973:35–42.

Welch, A.S. "Iowa State Agricultural College, Fourth Biennial Report to the Board of Trustees." Des Moines, Iowa: G.W. Edwards, 1871.

Werner, Alfred, and Edward Gotheil. "Personality development and participation in college athletics." *Research Quarterly* 37(1966):126–131.

White, Gordon S. "College presidents' bid for powers rejected." *New York Times*, January 11, 1984:B5, 7.

Whitney, Casper. *A Sporting Pilgrimage*. New York: Harper and Brothers, 1895.

Wilder, Steve. "Diggers bombshell!" *New York Times*, March 26, 1982:120.

Will, George. "Our schools for scandal." *Newsweek*, September 15, 1986:84.

Williams, George H. (ed.). *The Harvard Divinity School*. Cambridge, Mass.: Harvard University Press, 1954.

Williams, R.L., and Z.I. Youssef. "Consistency of football coaches in stereotyping the personality of each player's position." *International Journal of Sport Psychology* 3(1) 1972:3–11.

Williams, R.L., and Z.I. Youssef. "Division of labor in college football along racial lines." *International Journal of Sport Psychology* 6(1) 1975:3–13.

Wilson, Thomas A. "Delegates act swiftly to ban booster, cut costs." *National Collegiate Athletic Association News* 24(3) January 14, 1987.

Winkler, Karen J. "Presidents or faculties: who should make the key decisions about the curriculum?" *Chronicle of Higher Education* 27 January 25, 1984:21–22.

Winkler, Karen J. "Trustees urged to join fight against abuses in college sports, avoid athletic fanaticism." *Chronicle of Higher Education* 28(7) April 11, 1984:33, 34.

Wood, Miriam M. "Crosscurrents and undercurrents in the trustee-president relationship." *Educational Record* 65(1) Winter 1984:38–42.

Zingg, Paul J. "No single solution: Proposition 48 and the possibilities of reform." *Educational Record* 64(3) Summer 1983:6–12.

Index

coaches
  leadership styles, 69
  playing positions of, 94
  power of, 150–51
  racial proportions of, 94
  sanctioning poor academic
    performance, 96
College Football Association, 7, 151
colleges
  as cultivator, 77–78
  as miner, 77–78
  as prime beneficiary of athletics,
    79–90
Commission on Intercollegiate Athletics
  for Women, 99
community
  need for, 158–60
cooptation of faculty, 130–31
Coubertin, Baron Pierre de, 66
cult of athleticism, 52

Dartmouth College case, 22, 152
Darwinism, 172
dehumanizing sport, 179
Dewey, John, 52, 170, 175
diffuse socialization, 164, 168
doctrine of good works, 87–88
domain consensus, 64
diversification
  athletics as, 43–44
diversity
  pluralistic society, 173
  in United States, 11

economics of college sport
  categories of expenses, 84–85
  deficits, 81
  funding as related to image, 112
  men's sport, 82–83, 87
  profit orientation of, 80–90
  uniqueness to United States, 80–90
  women's sport, 86–87
education
  social institution's transformation in
    United States, 11–12
effort–optimism, 163
Eliot, Charles, 170
English public schools, 52

Enlightenment
  effect on American higher education,
    14, 50, 61, 172, 174
epistemology
  American, 113
  naturalistic, 195
equalizer
  education as, 163

faculty, 64, 200
  cooptation of, 130–31
  departmentalization, 148
  lack of power in United States, 27
  need for in college governance, 196
  perception of intercollegiate sport,
    34–35
  power relative to administration, 131
  power relative to president, 144
Faust, Gerry, 8
filtering model, 77–78, 93
football, 1
formal organization, 191
  higher education as, 29
  loose coupling, 139
  and task environment, 29–36, 62–64,
    114, 144
formal structure as myth and ceremony,
  141
Fromm, Eric, 10

garbage can model of decision making,
  45, 47–49, 202
Garvin, David, 168
Geertz, Clifford, 175–76
  need for order, 175–76
Georgia, University of, 109–10
Grove City case, 104

Hall, G. Stanley
  interpretation of adolescence, 51
Hanford, George, 8
Harper, William R., 25–26
Harris, Billy, 96
heart, 180, 182
heroes
  need for, 171–72, 183–84
  sport as, 173–74